STARTING OVER ✲
YOU
IN THE
NEW WORKPLACE

BY JO DANNA, Ph D.

Palomino Press

86-07 144 Street ✲ Briarwood, N.Y. 11435 ✲ (718) 297-5053

Copyright© 1990 by Jo Danna

Published by:

Palomino Press
86-07 144th Street
Briarwood, NY 11435-3119
(718) 297-5053

Book cover by Sue Danna
Artwork by:
    Dover, Mineola, NY
    Dynamic Graphics, Peoria, IL
    Volk Corp., Pleasantville, NJ

Printed and bound in the United States of America.

Library of Congress Catalog Card Number: 90-061119

Includes Endnotes, Appendix, Index.
1. Occupational & Educ. Information. 2. Personal & Practical Guides. 3.
Reference Books. 4. Self-help/Psychology.
I. Title
ISBN 0-9610036-3-4

Contents

1. CHANGES   2

Changes in the job market 5; Changes in the workplace 6; Changes in hiring criteria 10

2. CHOICES   13

How to overcome fear of change 15; Poor excuses for quitting your job 18, good reasons for quitting 20, what to do before you quit 22; If you are now unemployed 24

3. ARE YOU READY FOR A CHANGE?   27

Stress: causes 27, symptoms 29, harmful consequences 29; Anxiety: symptoms 30, consequences of untreated chronic anxiety 30; Depression: when it's normal 31, when it's time to get help 31, consequences of untreated chronic depression 32; How to get rid of harmful stress 34; Are you a depressive person? Test yourself 38; How to get rid of self-defeating thoughts 39; Mental alertness 41; Courses, workshops, self-help books and tape recordings 42; When it's time for professional help 42, cognitive behavior therapy 43, rational-emotive therapy 44, interpersonal and family therapy 44; Who is qualified to administer therapy? 44, cost 44, where to find reputable help 45

4. HOW WELL DO YOU KNOW YOURSELF?   47

How a self assessment helps 47; How to do a self assessment 49; Homemaker skills used in paying jobs 58, job skills developed in volunteer work 59, where to find help 62; How to identify compatible occupations 62, aptitudes 63, personality 65, aptitude tests and interest inventories 68, health and physical limitations 71; Skills and knowledge to update/learn 71; Career counseling services 73

5. FACTS YOU WILL NEED   79

About occupations: changes in an occupation and its requirements 79, conditions likely to affect its future 79, current need for workers 80, opportunities for advancement 80, work conditions 80, buzz words 81; About companies and industries 81: products/services 82, culture 82, reputation 85, key persons 86, future developments 86, opportunities/barriers to advancement 88, company size 89, family-run companies 91, companies with policies favorable to older workers 92; Before you accept a job offer 93; How to find the facts you need 94

6. HOW TO FIND A GOOD JOB   105

How long will it take? 105; Best times for job hunting 106; Contact the person who makes the hiring decision 107; Mass market yourself 107; Barriers job hunters create for themselves 108; Other paths 109; Networking 111, networking by computer 113; Contact employers directly 114, create your own job and convince an employer to hire you 115; Employment agencies 117, computerized placement services 120; Recruitment firms 121; Non-profit employment services 121, community organizations, public libraries 121, schools 122, Job Service 123, state and municipal services 124, civil service jobs 124, Private Industry Councils 125, Forty Plus Club 126, senior employment services 127, employment services for women 130; where rural residents can get help 134; Newspapers 134: Job fairs 137; Industry publications 138, Professional and trade associations 139; How to deal with rejection 139

7. FIND A JOB THROUGH VOLUNTEER WORK   141

8. SO LONG 9-TO-5!   147

Part-time and temporary jobs 147: advantages 148, disadvantages 150, high-skill and professional jobs 151, where to find them 152; Job sharing 154; Flextime work 155: advantages/disadvantages 156, where to find jobs 156; Telecommuting jobs 15: in rural communities 157, professionals and high-level 157, advantages/disadvantages 158, how to find a work-at-home job 160, jobs suitable for working at home 160, companies that have telecommuting programs 161, work-at-home schemes 161

9. *WHY NOT BE YOUR OWN BOSS?*   163
Personal qualities needed for success 167; How to get a good business idea 170; Recipe for success 175; Market research 179; Sole proprietorship, partnership 182; Selecting the site 184: home based business 184, small business incubators 185; Estimating costs 189; Raising money without a loan 189; Getting a loan 190: Small Business administration 190, Small Business Investment Companies 191, Small Business Innovation Research 191, Job Training Partnership 191, community organizations 192, foundations 192, credit union loans 192, bank loans 192, commercial credit companies 193; Legal necessities 194; Problems that might occur 196; Promotion and advertising 198, direct mail 200; Franchising: the easy way 201

ENDNOTES   207

APPENDIX   221
Psychological readiness 221; Career assessment 222; Jobs, occupations, salary and benefits 224; How to protect your job rights 226; Job training and education 227; Job market 230: occupations with the best hiring outlook 230; How to get information on companies 231; A sample of family-run companies 232; Companies with policies favorable to older workers 232; How to find the facts you need 233; Resources to help you find a job 238; Flexible work styles 244; Starting a small business 245; Resources for women 252

Preface

Most guidebooks on job or career changing ignore the reader's mental and emotional preparedness for this very unsettling and major event. As long as the rate of technological and social change is slow enough for us to adapt without too much stress and confusion, it doesn't matter. But America is now engulfed by a tidal wave of revolutionary changes. The first two chapters prepare readers for these changes. The first gives an overview of what to expect in the new workplace. It's especially important for homemakers who are returning to the job market and older workers who are changing jobs or careers after many years. The second and third chapters deal with the reader's psychological readiness for the task ahead and how to reduce the stress and anxiety involved in making such a big change. Readers who feel they don't need this information can skip ahead to chapter four.

ABOUT THE AUTHOR

Jo Danna is the author of five books to this date, all of them
dealing in one way or another with culture change. The last three
books — *It's Never Too Late To Start Over, Winning The Job
Interview Game,* and *Starting Over: You In The New Workplace*
— are practical guidebooks. She has been listed in several Who's
Who directories — *Who's Who in American Women, Community
Leaders of America, World's Who's Who of Women,* etc. She has
degrees in psychology, anthropology and education. Her Ph.D. and
M.A. were earned at Columbia University in New York City and
her B.A. was granted by Hunter College of the City University of
New York. She is also a graduate of the Career Opportunities
Institute, University of Virginia in Charlottesville.

Changes

If it's been years since you looked for a job or changed careers you might think you've entered a Flash Gordon future. The pre-high technology workplace — which was managed according to assembly line guidelines — is disappearing. A more humane one is emerging in which workers are no longer treated like mindless robots. They work in self-management teams, solving problems and creating new products and services.

"As someone once said, 'A lot of things have happened in the 20th century and most of them plug into the wall.' Every time you plug something into the wall, you plug it into yourself. We aren't the same persons we were before we decided to sit down and watch television. You have to accept a different reality." — Alan Kay[1]

Major technological innovations — such as the wheel, automobile and assembly line — start chain reactions which radically alter the way we live, work and relate with one another. The current high-tech revolution will have even more profound consequences. Nations and people around the world can now be linked by satellites and computer networks. An engineer in El Paso who has a design problem can turn on his computer modem; instantaneously, advice comes in from engineers living anywhere on the globe.

As you cross the boundaries of time into the new workplace you'll know what it feels like to be an immigrant in a foreign land. Your coworkers will be different. Your equipment will be unlike any you've ever seen. Your relationships with superiors and colleagues will be radically changed. Traditional male-female roles will be blurred. Even the language used in the new workplace will sound "foreign." Your job responsibilities will surely have changed, also.

It's no use resisting the changes that are about to engulf you. Better to learn about them *before* you change jobs or careers than suffer repeated rejection and frustration. Knowing in advance what lies ahead will help you make a smoother, more successful transition.

"You have to keep up with the times to be successful," said Carl Gray of Petersburg, IN. He was a country lawyer who was born in the horse-and-buggy days. At the age of 88, he used computers in his office and attended seminars on the future of the legal profession.[2]

Unfortunately, today's mature workers face false negative employer stereotypes which influence their hiring, training and promotion opportunities. Many employers view them as unprepared and ill-equipped, even dangerous, for the high-tech workplace.[3] The nuclear accidents at Three Mile Island and Chernobyl were caused by poorly trained workers.

There are ways to counter such stereotypes, to convince an employer that you combine the best of both worlds: the old-fashioned work ethic, reliability, and loyalty plus updated skills and knowledge of the new workplace and its demands.

Despite all the media coverage on the current revolution in the workplace, some people still don't understand, or don't want to acknowledge, the extent of what's happening. When the Pennsylvania steel mills shut down in the early '80s, programs were set up to retrain dismissed workers for new jobs. Many failed to take advantage of the opportunity. They were waiting for the good old times to return. Similar situations have occurred recently.

Workers whose skills are obsolete or need updating, who have spent their working lives in declining industries, will adapt to the changes whether they like it or not. They may have to face a temporary period of insecurity in order to find a good job. Those who take the easy way will have to settle for a low-paying, low-skill job like janitor, dishwasher or hamburger slinger.

CHANGES IN THE JOB MARKET

"The old days when you learned a skill and could count on it for the rest of your life — or at least for several decades — are gone," said a manager at Control Data Institute.[4] Even occupations that take years of training are vulnerable. A 25-year-old engineer may need retraining eight times within a 40-year career, reports the American Society of Engineering Education.

Occupations are changing

Many jobs are becoming more challenging and interesting. When an automation equipment operator in a General Electric plant had a problem recently, he phoned a manufacturing engineer in another office and ordered $40,000 worth of new parts. He didn't report it to a supervisor as in the old days. He also serves on a committee that hires new workers to operate the machine.

Some secretaries must learn to work with desktop publishing or spreadsheet software, let alone word processing. Bank tellers — finally freed from boring, routine transactions by computerized teller machines — analyze cash flow and sell mortgages. The old fashioned insurance office had five workers to record the application information, enter it into a computer, retrieve data from files, assess the applicant's risk, and write the policy. Today, one service representative processes the entire application.[5]

New occupations are emerging

Many combine the skills and expertise of two or more traditional occupations. Example: People who have a master's degree in business administration and an undergraduate degree in biology or engineering are in demand.

Occupations are disappearing

As many as two million jobs may be vanishing each year in the U.S. Up to 75% of all factory jobs may be replaced by robots by the end of this decade.[6] Many clerical workers will lose their jobs because of computerization.

Job/career changing is increasing

To keep up with all the changes, Americans are switching jobs and careers at an exceptional rate. Four or more career changes may soon become the norm. Many dismissed managers, for example, have become consultants. Others have gone back

to school to prepare for new careers as stockbrokers, real estate brokers or insurance agents.

CHANGES IN THE WORKPLACE

The following is a brief description of major trends in the new workplace.

New and better ways to work

► *Employers now appreciate their workers' intelligence.*

The assembly line symbolizes a dying era in which workers were mindless appendages to the machine and the organization. The computer symbolizes a new era in which workers are the masters of these "smart" machines. Instead of doing one mind-numbing, repetitive, simple task one worker handles an entire process. Instead of working in isolation, teams of workers from different departments — production, engineering, design, marketing, etc. — pool their expertise to manage an entire project from start to finish.

In the old-style workplace, managers did the thinking and workers did the doing. In the new workplace everyone thinks and everyone does. *"We're tapping the brain power of the entire organization,"* said an officer of the newly restructured Kodak Corporation. There, each team operates as a sub-company with responsibility for an entire production process. They do the problem solving, equipment maintenance, quality control, budgeting, salary and benefits administration, material planning, receiving and distribution.[7] As you can see, the new workplace needs workers with broader skills. It needs managers who advise and coach, not bark orders.

► *So long 9-to-5, hello flexible work styles*

The days of battling rush hours are disappearing, thanks to computer networks, satellites and FAX machines. There will be plenty of jobs closer to home as more companies open branches in, or relocate to, suburban and rural communities.[8] You may even find a job that allows you to work from home. There will also be more challenging part-time and temporary full-time jobs.

Your co-workers will be different

In your next job they will look, talk and act different from the mostly male, youngish European type you're used to working with. By the year 2000 more than 80% of new workers will be women, non-European, and immigrants. White males of European origin will represent only about 15%. More retirement age workers and handicapped persons will be hired as the shortage of skilled workers continues into the next century.

Your next manager or employer may no longer represent the old power elite — the predominantly older (55+), Anglo-Saxon, white male. A younger, more culturally diverse group of managers and executives are taking over — aging baby boomers, women, and "foreign" types. Already they are bringing fresh ideas on how to organize and manage a company.

▶ *More women coworkers, managers, employers*

Their influence as workers, employers and managers is growing. Women will comprise two thirds of the 15 million new workers through 1995, predicts the Bureau of Labor Statistics. Many others are starting their own business.

Sex discrimination in hiring, firing and promotion will be more vigorously opposed. As more women enter formerly "male" occupations, male bosses and coworkers will change their traditional beliefs about a woman's proper role.

Women employers are more willing to offer flexible hours and work-at-home jobs. They understand the need for elder care and new promotion systems that make it easier for working mothers to get promotions. Their management style typically reflects the new, more democratic style described below.[9] Older, male subordinates who patronize them, resist taking orders from them, or do not adapt to their style of leadership are in for a rough time.

▶ *Less age segregation, more young bosses*

From kindergarten through high school and in all walks of life America has been a rigidly age-segregated society. We tend to think this is natural, but it is unnatural. In most other societies people of all ages mix more easily. Americans will now have to learn to do the same. The workforce is aging. By the year 2000 there will be fewer 18-24 year olds. Workers over 55 will be the fastest-growing group.

Like it or not, younger employers and managers must overcome their negative stereotypes about older workers' capabilities. They will have to get rid of childhood hangups that make them uncomfortable working with or supervising older employees.

Older workers need to be careful about talking and behaving in a way that seems patronizing to younger colleagues or managers. They must face the reality that a young manager is probably more up-to-date and more compatible with the new workplace.[10]

As a result, age discrimination in hiring, promotion, training, and firing will be more vigorously opposed. In order to lure and keep older workers, employers will use job performance guidelines instead of chronological age in deciding whom to hire, promote or dismiss.

The international workplace

Satellites, telecomputer networks and international trade bring all nations into immediate contact. Soon we will all be neighbors in a global village. More American companies are opening branches and plants overseas. More foreign companies are buying into American firms and opening branches here. In 1989 Japanese companies owned over 600 factories in the U.S. employing over 200,000 American workers. American companies are also teaming up with foreign owned companies. Your next employer may be English, Japanese, Indian, Chinese or Latin-American.

More people from different cultures will be working together and doing business with one another. Your next employer may ask you to serve in a foreign country for a while. If you are an executive or manager you'll probably be responsible for workers whose customs and beliefs differ considerably from yours.

The clash of new ideas, values, customs and management styles will ultimately lead to a stronger hybrid culture. It will, of necessity, diminish narrowness and xenophobia. A broader world view will bring more understanding between peoples and lessen the prospects of another world war.

However, the initial clash of cultures in the workplace will cause misunderstandings and problems. American workers at every level must learn to understand and get along with coworkers of different cultural backgrounds. Managers, executives, salespersons, marketing experts and other high-level workers must learn more about the foreign countries in which they will serve or do business. An executive for Boeing's Asian operations recalls his first contact with a Chinese executive. "*Mr. Fong, time is money,*" he said. "*Mr. Van der Kuylen, time is eternity,*" Mr. Fong replied.[11] How do such different worldviews translate into greater cultural sensitivity? In negotiating with Asians, for example, Americans must avoid pressuring them to reach quick decisions.

A mere tourist's guidebook won't help an American executive select the right country in which to build a factory. It won't provide answers to problems such as how to adapt a product or service to a different culture. Nor will it provide solutions to new problems. Productivity at a General Electric plant in Singapore dropped sharply because some of the factory workers believed the devil was living there. After the traditional American solutions failed, GE officials found the answer. They brought in an exorcist.[12] Americans cannot afford to make the ridiculous mistakes they made in the past like trying to sell blond, blue-eyed dolls in Kenya. In order to capture and keep foreign markets we need skilled global managers not just skilled American managers.[13]

The new work culture

The bureaucratic organization — in which orders from above come military-style to an army of obedient workers at the bottom — is dying. This style may still be necessary in organizations where tight precision and the immediate execution of orders is essential; e.g., armed forces, hospitals, police force. In fast-changing times it is counterproductive, especially as practiced by private industry, public school systems, and government agencies.

Workers who are comfortable with this type of work culture generally dislike change and prefer to carry out other people's orders. If you're in this category, look for a job in a slowly-changing organization which has this type of culture. According to William F. Whyte, the *Organization Man* is still very much alive and running things in America.[14] But not for long.

This is the new trend in American industry: workers at all levels making decisions together, teamwork, informality, direct communication between upper and lower levels, broader work skills. This new work culture has a more flexible, creative and democratic workplace.[15] It will spread as surely as the sun comes up in the morning because:

▸ Companies adopting this work culture report increased productivity and profits.

▸ Workers will report to the new generation of managers and executives who value this style of doing things.

▸ Computers and foreign competition force this work culture on American employers. High technology enables all levels of workers to share in the flow of information. To get their money's worth out of this expensive equipment, employers must give workers more freedom to participate in decisions that affect their job responsibilities and production goals. General Motors learned this lesson the hard way. It spent billions on robots, computers, telecommunications equipment and software so as to compete more efficiently with Japanese auto makers. However, its former bureaucratic-style organization remained and profits continued to plummet. This style is incompatible with the electronic democracy imposed by the new technology.

▸ The new work culture is necessary in fast-changing times; new problems require creative solutions. Information sharing, creativity and risk-taking must be encouraged among all workers.

It also requires a new type of manager. Managers who still see their main responsibility as controlling employees, making all the key decisions and giving orders feel threatened by all these changes, but there is little choice.[16]

CHANGES IN HIRING CRITERIA

Employers can no longer afford to hire the person with the classiest credentials, the most persuasive manner or the best looks. They now ask, *"Are your skills up-to-date?" "Will you fit in?" "Are you flexible enough to change as we change our products and methods of doing things?" "Are you willing to learn new skills?" "Can you work well with others?"*

Willing to upgrade old skills and learn new ones

Even the simplest jobs are becoming more complex. Most jobs now require higher levels of reading, writing, mathematics and other skills.[17] Job descriptions must continually be revised to include the changes brought about by technological and scientific discoveries. While employers complain about an engineering shortage, they turn away engineers who fail to keep up with changes in their field. Recently Olin Chemicals fired 50 scientists and hired 32 more with training in new materials and electronics research. IBM's products are changing so rapidly that old jobs are constantly phased out and new ones created. The company must continually educate, retrain and redeploy workers. Changing jobs has become such a way of life that workers joke that IBM stands for "I've Been Moved."[18]

The ability and willingness to learn are now more important than job experience and impressive resumes, as you can see from the following incidents.[19]

▸ Fascinated by data coming from a new monitoring system, a blue-collar worker in a power plant began to study the theory of combustion. The new knowledge helped him find an error in plant procedure.

▸ When Motorola executives decided to change the work culture, the first step was to teach new values and skills to every employee, including those at the top. They also had to change their hiring criteria.

▸ Quad/Graphics company even has its own education department. A staff of eighteen teach courses ranging from remedial reading and mathematics to computer programming. Every Friday morning employees attend classes. Founder and CEO Harry Quadracci tells each new person hired, *"Welcome to boot camp. For the next three years we're going to give you the proper equipment, and it's your responsibility to learn how to use it."*[20]

Broad skills/knowledge

"You can't be an expert in one field anymore," says a training supervisor at Caterpillar Company.[21] In the new work culture, where employees share responsibility for an entire project, they need a variety of skills in order to move from one task to another. At the General Motors assembly plant in Van Nuys, CA, for example, workers are trained to do as many as 10 different jobs.

Management-level employees also need broader skills and knowledge. Chief executive officers want managers *"who can look beyond their own fiefdoms and consider the capabilities and needs of the company as a whole."*[22]

Employers are revising job descriptions to include multiple skills. Pay increases now reflect the number and level of skills learned, not seniority. General Electric workers can increase their pay by as much as 40 percent by completing college courses that are job-related. The credits earned also qualify them for better jobs.

Creativity

The way a society defines "intelligence" depends on whether it is past, present or future oriented. Future-oriented societies value progress and innovation. Intelligence is defined as creativity and the ability to solve new problems. The U.S. is a dynamic, future-oriented society. High on its list of national heroes are entrepreneurs, inventors and scientists — people like Henry Ford, Thomas Edison, Robert Fulton, Jonas Salk and others — whose creativity improves our lives. In slowly changing societies people with a prodigious memory of the past are viewed as intelligent. Those who dare to analyze and critique outdated customs and beliefs are condemned.

"The most important strength a company can have in this era is the ability to change and the capacity to manage it fruitfully . . . to find ways to encourage and channel the creative instincts of people. That's why companies have many get-togethers, conferences, and interdepartmental visiting. It's what you need to get creativity and innovation," writes Rosabeth M. Kanter, author of *The Change Masters: Innovation and Entrepreneurship in the American Corporation.*[23]

"We're a knowledge company, a R&D (research and development) company. We're also a people company, because where else are the ideas going to come from," says Quad/Graphics' Harry Quadracci.[24]

"Innovating — creating new products, new services and new ways of producing them cheaply — has become the most urgent concern of (American) corporations," reports *FORTUNE.*[25]

Many employers now include these abilities in their hiring and job performance criteria. They need workers who can help them create new products and better marketing strategies and office procedures. During the planning phase of the Ford Taurus sedan, managers asked assembly-line workers for advice, and they were inundated with ideas. One of the suggestions has reduced the time needed to install doors on the assembly line. Worker involvement in problem solving played a key role in boosting Ford's profits 40% in 1987.[26]

Basic computer skills

Computer literacy is now necessary for all levels of employees. Sales clerks must know how to enter sales and returns figures into a computer. Secretaries must know word processing. Accountants must know how to work with spreadsheets. Managers and top level officers must understand spreadsheets so they can make more accurate projections. Production managers must learn about robotics and flexible manufacturing systems.

Adaptability, flexibility

"In almost every department of our printing operation, there is virtually no similarity to the way things were done six months ago," says Quad/Graphics' Quadracci.[27] *"I like change because it wakes you up,"* says the chief executive of a large corporation.[28] His workers had better like it too if they value their jobs. A Digital Equipment plant had to transfer old-line supervisors who refused to relinquish their former authority as required by its new emphasis on teamwork. The manager's guide of Federal Express has a chapter titled *Change*. The chief executive of Proctor & Gamble Corporation made a videotape in which he warns that people who can't change could end up like dinosaurs.

Employers in a fast-changing global economy cannot afford to hire and keep people who can't or won't adapt. More employers see them as an obstacle to needed change. Because of this new emphasis, some employers are wary about hiring older job applicants. Stereotypes about their unwillingness or inability to adapt persist.[29] *"Older workers don't learn new tricks unless forced to by crisis,"* said an economist.[30] In this book you will read about ways to calm such fears.

Ability to work in teams

Teamwork is necessary in the modern organization. Employees with different skills and from different departments must be able to work together on an entire project and agree on decisions which influence its outcome. General Electric's factory worker teams decide even when to work overtime. They make their own production and scheduling decisions. They also recommend hiring people who they think will fit in.

Compatible with the work culture

Employers prefer to hire and promote people whose values and personality are compatible with the way things are done in the organization. Many workers lose their jobs because of their inability or refusal to conform to these unspoken rules of behavior.

An international outlook

As the international economy grows many jobs, especially mid- and upper-level jobs, require the ability to speak one or more foreign languages and deal with representatives of different cultures. Recently a major accounting firm became aware that more of its clients are operating in the international economy. Now it seeks to hire accountants who have a good knowledge of other cultures.

Yet many American corporate leaders still lack an international outlook, writes Claudia H. Deutsch. To compound the problem, they even fail to acknowledge international experience in the people they hire.[31] *"We'll see the greatest increase in executive turnover in history over the next 10 years, because American businessmen do not know how to run global businesses in the 21st century,"* predicts the head of an outplacement firm.[32] *"Today any business person who doesn't have a global perspective is either dead or dumb,"* said a corporate chief executive.[33]

Works well with people of different cultures

As employers hire more immigrants from Asia, Latin American and the Middle East, they want to avoid conflicts which arise from negative stereotypes based on ignorance. They will require managers and other employees to be more understanding and appreciative of other systems of beliefs and customs.

Choices

Americans are the most mobile people in the world. We think nothing of changing course in mid-life, of packing up and leaving old friends and comfortable places for better opportunities elsewhere. We're willing to put up with the initial loneliness and discomfort of adapting to a new job or career. We'll even move to a new community, because we know the payoff will be worth it.

But many people live as though they were leaves blowing in the wind. They allow their lives to be directed by outer forces rather than their inner strength and will. When a technological change wipes out a career, when a company merger leads to a dismissal, they react passively instead of seizing the opportunity to find more satisfying work. They blame their lot on "bad luck" or the government, or they point a finger at family members. They never blame themselves for failing to take the steps necessary to make a better life choice.

Look at the people around you whose lives are filled with unhappiness, failure, even tragedy. You'll find that before each sad event occurred many of them had made a wrong choice. Discounting poor health and accidents most of the sorrowful things that happen to people begin with a wrong choice. Almost always the wrong choice is to allow "fate" to decide for them. Or, tunnel vision determines their choice: *"I probably won't get a better offer." "It's a job, just like any other." "Salary-wise, I don't think I can do much better."*

Successful, happy people view life as a series of choices to be made, in which their decisions can profoundly influence what happens to them. Instead of surrendering passively to events, they take an active, positive stance. They look at the long term rather than the short term consequences of each decision. They ask themselves the right questions, *"What information do I need to change careers?" "How can I transfer my sales and marketing experience to a new industry?"* They learn all the options that are available. After deciding which ones to follow through, they map out the steps needed to reach their goal.

HOW MUCH CHANGE CAN YOU TAKE?

Change is exciting, but it's also stressful. Before you make a decision regarding your next career move, consider how it will influence your health and lifestyle and that of your family. Your answers to the following questions will help you determine the extent of changes you can take now.

- Am I adaptable? Do I like to try new ways of doing things?
- When faced with something unfamiliar am I curious or do I become nervous and uncomfortable?
- When planning a vacation do I choose new, exotic places or places that are as similar as possible to my own way of life?
- Do I like to try new recipes or do I prefer to rely on the dependable ones?
- Am I comfortable with, do I find it stimulating to be with, persons of a different nationality, race or religion?
- Do I make friends easily?
- Do I have friends of various ages or are they mostly in my age category?
- Is my health up to making a big change now?

Are you self-confident?

Some people become immobilized by fear when it's time to make a job or career change. They fear rejection, failure and the unknown. They view a job loss as evidence that they'll never succeed again whereas others see it as an opportunity for growth. No matter how talented and skilled they are, they become trapped in a web of false beliefs about limited options that accompany growing older. Many other people change careers after they are forty or fifty and become successful.

It's not in the American national character to give up in the face of obstacles or failure. *It is* in the American national character to face challenge and try harder after failure. Henry Ford didn't give up after his first two companies failed. Lee Iaccocca had his greatest success after Ford Motor Company fired him. Many other successful people have used loss or failure as springboards to a better future.

How to overcome your fear of change

"Necessity and fear in short spurts are great motivators," says Barbara Grogan. She started her own business, Western Industrial Contractors, in 1982 to support herself and two children after a divorce. By 1987 her Denver company was earning $5 million.[34]

► **List the ways a job or career change can improve your life.**

Here are some ideas to get you started.

- I always felt like a square peg in that bureaucratic hole. My next job will be in a company whose culture suits me better.
- I never enjoyed my work. Finally, I have an opportunity to prepare for the career I've always wanted.
- I hate the 9-to-5 grind. Now I can look for a job that has flexible hours.
- I can afford to live on a reduced income. I'll do temporary or part-time work whenever and wherever I want.
- It's always been a worry leaving the kids home. Now I'll look for a job which allows me to work from home.
- I always wanted to manage my own business.
- I have nowhere to go but up.

► **Plan, prepare and get the information you need.**

► **Get your family involved.**

Consider how they might feel about your job or career change, especially if it requires moving to another community or living on less income for a while. Allay their fears by discussing your plans with them and asking them to express their feelings. Also ask for suggestions on how to make the change so that everyone, or at least the majority, will be happy about it. Prepare a list of all the benefits they will receive from the change beforehand. Learn about the schools, clubs and other social activities in the new community.

Discover at least one irresistible lure about it. This will help them to see your point of view.

▶ *Make sure you can pay the bills.*

The time it takes to find another job depends on your job level, how much competition you'll have, and economic conditions. The old rule of thumb that it takes x number of months for every x number of dollars in salary does not apply in rapidly changing times.[35] What the surveys do show is that the higher the job and salary level, the longer it takes to find another comparable job.

Make a new budget to see if you'll have enough to live on until the next paycheck. You'll know if you have to work part-time while looking for another job or stay in your present job until you can afford to quit. That's much safer than taking out a second mortgage, using up your retirement benefits, selling investments or withdrawing from your IRA account. (Many unemployed managers exhaust their severance pay before finding a new job.)

First estimate how much you'll need for necessities — food, rent, courses you must take to upgrade your skills, and job hunting expenses. You may be tempted to cancel your health insurance. Don't take any chances. Get coverage under a family member's plan or look into group health insurance from a professional or trade association or a credit union. Ask your current employer to allow you to continue group coverage at your expense after you leave. A recent law enables fired and dismissed workers to maintain this protection for up to 18 months. Also ask creditors to reduce your debt payments or give you a grace period until you find another job.

▶ *Upgrade your skills/learn new skills*

In 1988 when many farmers were losing their farms, local colleges offered tuition-free courses to help them prepare for a new career. One farmer, 48-year-old Marvin H., lost a 650 acre farm with a net worth of nearly $2 million. Instead of wallowing in self-pity, he enrolled for a degree in international development. He had decided to prepare for a new career as agri-

cultural consultant overseas. To pay the bills, he worked part-time for a farm equipment company and his wife got a job as a legal secretary.[36] Mr. H. and his family asked themselves a lot of questions and planned carefully to make sure the investment in more education would pay off.

- *"Must I change occupations if I don't want to? Maybe all I need to find a better job in my present occupation is a course to upgrade my skills and knowledge."*

- *"What level of education and training does the new career I'm considering require? How long will it take?"*

- *"Do I need a degree or a certificate?"*

- *"If I must go back to school how much will it cost? Will I have to quit my job and enroll full-time? If I can't afford to do that what other alternatives are there?"*

Today many colleges and universities have weekend, evening and home study programs for working adults. A 54-year old farmer's wife earned a bachelor's degree from Idaho State University, some 120 miles away from her home. She also taught part-time at the local high school. She attended some courses at the university, some at a nearby community college, and the others through a home study program. After graduating she began a new career as school librarian.

If you want to study for a higher degree, make sure there will be enough jobs when you graduate. You can't afford to spend all that time and money and then discover jobs are scarce or too many graduates are applying for the same type of work. Less than ten years ago people were rushing to get degrees in computer programming. The field was hot then. Now it's glutted with computer graduates. Worse yet, new technology may eliminate the need for human programmers. You can get this information from publications issued by the U.S. Department of Labor which you'll find in the library. See Appendix B.

If you're not ready for a major change

If you can't afford to make a radical change or if it involves more stress than you can take now, you may be better off if you:

► Choose a job or career that is as similar as possible to your present or last one.

▸ Transfer to a similar job in the same company or industry. If you're a typist, for example, learn word processing. If you're a bookkeeper, you will probably enjoy computer programming or working on spreadsheets.

▸ Stay in the town where you now live no matter how gloomy its present job prospects. Prepare yourself, however, for a longer period of unemployment. Try part-time or temporary full-time work while you wait for a better job.

▸ The Almighty helps those who help themselves. Find out what others in a similar situation are doing in your community. Get together and form your own job club (See Forty Plus) or find an already existing group which helps the unemployed.

TO QUIT OR NOT TO QUIT

Quitting your job is a drastic step to take without analyzing all the reasons you want to do it and what the consequences may be. The real reason may have nothing to do with the job itself. The following exercise can help you sort things out.

● List the reasons for wanting to quit your job. Next to each write down things you can do to make it more enjoyable.

● Next, list the negative consequences of quitting now. Do this even if you have a good reason for quitting.

● Finally, list the improvements a job or a career change might make in your life.

Poor excuses for quitting a job

▸ Are you subconsciously transferring a family or personal problem to the job? Is an underlying depression at the root of your dissatisfaction? If so, changing your job or career won't help.

▸ Is the work environment depressing? Think of ways to brighten it or transfer to another office.

▸ Do you feel tired, depressed and miserable most of the time? Is an emotional conflict draining your energy and optimism? Are you run-down? A medical checkup might reveal a health problem.

▸ Has your job become boring? What can you do to make it more interesting? Is it because you're burned out? Will getting away for a while help?

► Has the work load become too heavy? Do other workers feel the same way? Is it a temporary matter while the company undergoes a change? Or is an overly ambitious new manager making unrealistic demands? If so, tell him/her the pressure is causing some workers to think about transferring or resigning.

► Is it because you didn't get the promotion or pay raise you think you deserve? Find out why. Maybe your job performance isn't up to par or your skills need updating. Maybe the company is going through a temporary rough period.

► Is it because you dislike your boss or coworkers?

Even if you have reason to quit, consider the following

► **You may have to start over.**

A worker is at greatest risk when starting over in a new company, with a new boss.[37] You must prove yourself before you can be considered for salary increases, training programs and other benefits. Finding a job comparable to the one you now have may not be easy if your skills need updating. You may have to settle for a lower-level job or a lower starting salary. You may have to move to another community.

► **Quitting may/may not look good on your resume.**

A survey by *Industry Week* found that almost 2 out of 3 respondents believed that periodically changing employers advances business careers only during the *early* phase of one's career. It suggests an ambitious person seeking experience. But changes later in one's career may be viewed as a sign of job performance or capability problems.[38] It depends on how often you've job-hopped. If often, you need to convince a prospective employer that you are reliable and not a quitter when things get rough. If you're at the management level frequent job-hopping may not pay. Another survey found that managers who had worked for 1 to 3 employers had higher pay than those who had 4 to 10 employers.[39] Most employers prefer workers who stay with a company a minimum of three years.

► **There may be a better job in your company.**

Transfer to a more interesting job or another department instead of starting over in another company. If your present job is on a direct line to a better position try to endure it for a while longer.

It may still provide valuable training. Many people take a lower--level job, a lower salary, or poor working conditions if it opens doors to something better. Make yourself more valuable by taking on added responsibilities. And make sure your superiors know about it.

Find out whether the company pays tuition for job-related courses at a local college. If your employer agrees to invest in more training it's a sign that you will be given higher responsibilities later.

► **Moonlighting can help you make a better decision.**
A second job in the evenings or on weekends has its advantages and disadvantages. If you're thinking about a career change, you'll be able to observe the conditions of the new occupation first-hand. You can acquire skills and experience needed to qualify for a better paying job in your field. If you're an office clerk, secretary, or bookkeeper you can get free training in word processing, spreadsheet software or desktop publishing at a temporary placement agency. Then ask for weekend or evening assignments. Get a physician's opinion on whether your health permits the extra hours of work. The increased workload may also take a toll on your family life. It may seriously affect your performance in your regular job.

Good reasons for quitting

► **Your occupation is becoming obsolete.**
Read chapter five for ways to find out whether your particular job or industry is in jeopardy.

► **The company or industry is failing.**
If your company is the target for a hostile takeover or merger, expect a massive staff reduction. Just before the pink slips appear people start whispering in corridors, managers tell everyone not to worry, and upper level employees start leaving. These are some of the warning signs.

Many dismissed workers waste valuable time thinking it can't happen to them. If there is no doubt that your company will be merged or taken over, first find out which company will be involved. Not all employees will lose their jobs. Generally management- and upper-level employees are the ones to go. The new officers need some old hands to maintain continuity.

▶ *You want to expand your skills and responsibilities.*

► Your job has reached a dead-end. You are not given added responsibilities or training even though you're at a top salary level. If the company won't allow you to grow, it suggests they are waiting for you to resign or retire.

► You are given a prestigious job title which merely increases your workload. You don't have any new responsibilities that will look good on your resume.

▶ *You're in the wrong occupation.*

► The job may have been right for you many years ago but your interests and abilities have matured. Maybe they've taken a completely different turn.

► You're not cut out for that kind of work. This often happens to people who did not plan their careers. They took the first well-paying job offer and were stuck there because they had to support a family.

► You invested time and money training for a better job and now that you've got it you are miserable. This happens when people prepare for a new career because it pays well, or it seems glamorous, or their friends are in it.

▶ *The job-related stress is killing you.*

▶ *You're not getting fair pay.*

If you can't live on your salary and there is no chance that your employer will loosen the purse strings, it's time to look for a better job. After you learn, from labor market reports, that your employer is short-changing you, it's time to quit.

▶ *Your chances of getting a promotion are poor.*

► The company has discriminatory practices that keep women, older workers, and others out of good jobs.

► Too many employees are aiming for the position you want. Or, the person who has it is still young and you don't want to wait forever.

► Your manager thinks you're too valuable to lose. He/she needs your skills or gets good job performance ratings from your excellent work.

▶ *Is a rotten boss reason enough?*

If you are hopelessly incompatible you'll be overlooked when new opportunities arise. You won't get promotions. Ask for a transfer. If your request is refused, quit.

▶ *Your personality and values are incompatible with the work culture.*

You will eventually explode from the pressure of putting on a false front.

▶ *You get warning signals.*

It's better to quit of your own accord than be fired.

- Your boss or manager avoids you, treats you like an outsider.

- Someone else gets the promotion you were expecting.

- You are the only one at your level of work who gets a stingy bonus or no bonus at all.

- You do not get a pay raise.

- Information needed to do your work stops coming. You're not told about important meetings. Messages that others receive do not reach you.

- Your last three or more job performance ratings were poor.

- There are mysterious delays in supplies and equipment you need, or they fail to arrive.

- Some of your responsibilities are delegated to another person.

- Finally, you ask for a meeting to discuss your future with the company and you get an evasive answer or they ignore your request.

What to do before you resign

▶ Research the job market. Learn about other companies, industries and occupations where your skills can be transferred. You wouldn't want to go through what happened to Tom, a dismissed manager. He received two new job offers. He accepted the one which paid a higher salary. Several weeks into the new job he learned the company was to be sold. A year later he was still jobless. Had he done some research before joining the company, he would have known which way the wind was blowing.

▶ Upgrade your skills or learn new skills.

▶ Start networking. Join your trade or professional association. Ask your outside contacts to let you know about vacancies they hear about.

▶ Start contacting employers.

▶ Register with employment agencies.

▶ **_Do it the right way._**

Leave on good terms so you'll get a good reference or at least a better one than you would have gotten otherwise. The higher the job level, the more important a good reference becomes. In your letter of resignation say you'll try to complete unfinished business and help the person who will replace you. Stay in contact with your former coworkers. Send greeting cards. Phone your former boss occasionally to say hello and let him/her know what you are doing.

Make them sorry to lose you. Give your boss a report on your achievements and contributions to the company while you were there. Include letters of recognition from clients, courses you've taken to upgrade your skills and other evidence of growth. Mention that some day you hope to return in a more challenging position.

The company might even call you back later when there is a better vacancy. Abraham Bernstein resigned from Aamco because someone else had the position of general manager he wanted at the time. For six years he worked as general manager at another company. One day he received a call from his former boss at Aamco saying the job he had wanted was now open. If he had quit on poor terms, if he had not maintained contact with his former colleagues, he would not have become president and chief executive officer of Aamco Transmissions Inc., in Bala-Cynwyd, Pennsylvania.[40]

—⊶⊷⊶—

IF YOU ARE UNEMPLOYED

Opportunity knocks in strange, unpredictable ways. Losing your job may be the kick-in-the-pants you need to find a better way to earn a living, to do the kind of work you've always wanted. Many people made a successful change after forty. So can you! Some have turned a lifelong hobby or interest into a profitable business. Several have even become millionaires. Wayman Presley had only $1,000 when he retired as a rural postman in Illinois. During the years of delivering mail he spent weekends touring local scenic spots with groups of children. Retirement gave him the time to transform a pastime into a tour business which eventually grossed millions of dollars yearly.

Should you change employers, transfer to another industry, or change careers?

This decision ranks in importance with the decision to marry. The consequences can influence the rest of your life. It also influences how you view yourself: as a success or as a failure.

► *Find out what to expect in the current job market.*
These are some of the questions you need to find answers to before you start looking for another job.

► Which occupations and industries have the best job. opportunities?

► Which towns, cities and regions of the country offer the best opportunities for the type of job you want?

► What changes, if any, have occurred in your occupation?

► What changes will confront you in the new company? (For example, technological, management style, new criteria for evaluating job performance)

► Which companies have a good record of hiring and promoting older workers? Which industries and companies are oriented toward young people and more difficult to get into? (Important if you are near the traditional retirement age.)

► *Assess whether your interests, values and goals have changed.*
What do you want at this stage in life? Do you want to stay in your present occupation and simply change employers or in-

dustries? Do you want a new career? Ask yourself, *"What are my strengths? What do I need to build on?"* Don't make a career decision without knowing what you're good at doing and what you most enjoy doing. You may have changed a lot since starting on your present career years ago. If the results of a reassessment suggest that a career change is in order, it can show which of your current skills and abilities can be transferred. Chapter four will show you how to do it and where to go if you need help from a career counselor.

► Some changes are more difficult to make

One expert says *"It's more difficult to jump the gulf from the public (government) to the private (for-profit business) sector."* No study has been done which shows this holds true across all occupations. Furthermore, recent reports show that more private industry employers are hiring people who've worked for the government or in a different industry if they have the skills needed to do the job.[41]

"Dismissed managers shouldn't go into business for themselves. The risks are too great. People who have spent many years working in a bureaucratic company are ill-equipped to become instant entrepreneurs," says another expert. He's talking about those who failed. How many succeeded and did not come to his attention? How many closet entrepreneurs have stifled their creative, risk-taking impulses for years because they couldn't afford to quit their job?

"Returning homemakers should not expect to resume a career that was interrupted years ago at the same level as where they left off." *"A college degree earned ten or twenty years earlier is as good as no college degree these days."* Unfortunately, this is true for almost everyone. Yet responsible, mature women who take evening courses to upgrade their skills can start over in a rewarding career with better qualifications than before.

Are You Ready for a Change?

On the whole change is good for us. It provides the stimulation our brain cells need to keep on developing well into old age. Think of a job or career change as an opportunity to learn new things and develop your mind.

However, change is also stressful. It's nature's way of forcing us to adapt to changes in our environment. It keeps us on our toes. If life were completely unchallenging and uneventful we would become mentally stunted like the Eloi in H.G. Wells's *Time Machine*. The stress you are experiencing now also provides the extra shot of adrenaline you need to improve your current situation. Without it you would probably be content to vegetate in the same old job rut for the rest of your life. But chronic, excessive stress can be harmful.

Chronic, harmful stress
▶ **What causes it?**
Unemployment causes chronic stress. So can being in the wrong job. This happens when we outgrow an occupation or are incompatible with the one we got into. The stress may be inherent in the job itself such as one that has frequent deadlines. Or it could be caused by features in the workplace such as excessive noise and pollution.

"Plunging suddenly off a well-tended career path is one of life's more devastating experiences," reports *U.S. News & World Report*.[42] And the higher the job level, the harder the fall. Although unemployment makes anyone susceptible to excessive stress, it affects dismissed executives more seriously. Even confident, successful people who see their job loss as an opportunity become depressed from the inevitable frustrating job interviews.

Unemployment also influences the entire family. There is an impulse to vent one's anger and frustration on the nearest scapegoat. Unfortunately, that scapegoat is often a spouse or child. Whether a couple can handle unemployment is the litmus test of marriage, said a psychologist.

"Every pink slip should carry a Surgeon General's warning that it may be hazardous to your health," said Louis Ferman.[43] Even the fear of losing one's job can lead to harmful stress. Whenever there is a significant increase in unemployment, the rate of alcohol and drug abuse, depression, sexual impotence, high blood pressure and other health problems rises. The number of suicides, homicides and first admissions to mental hospitals also rises. The correlation is so clear that some mental health experts say that getting another job can improve a person's mental health more than psychotherapy and medication can.

When we are depressed, we tend to exaggerate the negative aspects of our situation and fail to see its positive aspects. Why blame yourself because you lost your job and can't find another as easily as you thought it would be? Most workers are dismissed for reasons beyond their control — job obsolescence, discrimination, a difficult boss, plant closings, mergers and company relocations. Just being aware of this can lighten your burden of guilt and reduce your depression.

Losing a job forces us to review our priorities. We have more time to make changes that will improve the quality of our lives. In his autobiography, Lee Iacocca writes that after Henry Ford II fired him he was *"coming apart at the seams."* For a brief period he drank more and had the shakes. Finally, he decided to do something constructive about his predicament. *"I had a simple choice: I could turn that anger against myself, with disastrous results. Or I could take some of that energy and try to do something productive."*

Make needed improvements. First, learn how the drastic life changes you are experiencing influence your mind and emotions. Second, identify errors in your thinking which are self-defeating. Third, correct these errors with the self-help methods discussed below or get professional help. Also make plans for your next job or career.

► **Symptoms of Chronic Stress**

If you have more than one of the following alarm signals you may be suffering from excessive, chronic stress.

- You feel irritable most of the time for little or no reason.
- You are depressed for little or no reason.
- You have vague aches and pains for no physical reason.
- You have insomnia.
- You have dizzy spells.
- You are full of fears.
- You are always tired.
- You can't concentrate. Making simple decisions such as what to have for dinner becomes difficult.

► **Harmful consequences**

Excessive stress saps energy you need to get a better job or prepare for a more compatible career.

It harms your health. It's an underlying cause of depression and anxiety, and it weakens the body's immune system.

It destroys your self-confidence.

It prevents you from attaining your career goals. The way you deal with this highly stressful period in your life makes the difference between getting a job or a bundle of rejections. It can ruin your chances of creating a good impression at job interviews. Imagine an actor trying to convey stress without uttering a word — body tense, teeth clenched, brows knitted, shoulders hunched. The interviewer, always alert to such signals, will wonder whether you are trying to hide something.

Anxiety

"Anything that creates tension and causes you to ask, 'Where am I going?' 'What do I want?' is all to the good. Anxiety precedes periods of growth, transformation and development."

— Dr. Michele Berdy, Clinical Psychologist

In this age of anxiety it's normal to feel anxious from time to time. But a persistent, free-floating tension and fear is not normal. There are different kinds and degrees of unhealthy anxiety. There is the mild, chronic, unfocused kind that prevents us from achieving our potential. And there are the strong, almost paralyzing fears that are triggered by a specific stimulus such as airplanes and heights or by a particular event such as a career change or job interview. Many people suffer from social anxiety — feeling uneasy in social situations. If strong enough, it can create panic at the thought of speaking to a stranger, as in a job interview. Such strong fears are called phobias. Phobias can seriously restrict a person's life chances because the feared situation is avoided.

Some of us are anxious from the day we are born. Recent studies show that about 10% to 20% of us are born with highly sensitive nervous systems. For the most part, though, chronic anxiety is mainly a learned response to traumatic experiences. Also, what is learned can be unlearned.

► **Symptoms of severe anxiety**

People who get panicky during a job interview, for example, feel dizzy, perspire heavily, and have clammy hands, increased heartbeat and rapid breathing. These symptoms are caused by an increased flow of adrenaline into the blood stream. They can be so strong that the sufferer feels he is about to faint or have a heart attack. He thinks the symptoms are obvious to the interviewer when often they are not.

There are exercises which help a highly anxious person calm down and camouflage the obvious symptoms. Actors always use them. The great actor John Barrymore suffered greatly from the anxiety known as stage fright, even at the height of his fame.

► **Consequences of untreated chronic anxiety**

You become less productive. The time and energy wasted in unrealistic worries about the future can be put to better use. You can research the job market, assess your job strengths, learn to relax, and develop a positive attitude that leads to success.

A false bravado can alienate people you hope to impress. Personnel interviewers, always attuned to body language, can misinterpret the pretense as an attempt to hide something. They expect you to be nervous. The best approach is to relax and be yourself, even admit you're nervous because you want that job so much.

It's self-reinforcing and harder to eliminate. People with chronic anxiety are always measuring themselves against an unrealistic standard of perfection of how successful, smart, or talented they *should* be. Inevitably they see themselves as failures. Each event in which they fail to measure up to their impossible standards — such as never getting a letter of rejection — convinces them that they will never find a good job. Their expectation of failure becomes more strongly entrenched. Their fear may turn into a full-blown phobia about job interviews. If the fear focuses on a certain object, such as computers, it prevents them from learning an important job skill.

Depression

► **When it's normal to feel depressed**
Everybody feels depressed once in a while. These periods last a few weeks at the most. Even wishing for death can be normal. Most of us snap out of it and get on with life.

But when simple routines become burdensome — buying the newspaper to check the help-wanted ads, getting dressed for an interview — and you still have the blues weeks later, it's time to get professional help.

It's normal to feel depressed after surgery, after a prolonged or severe illness, when you lose your job or have a career setback, or when a loved one dies. In the latter case a depression that lasts months can be normal.

It's also normal for high achievers and risk-takers to suffer bouts of depression because they inevitably have more setbacks. Psychologists see a greater frequency of depression among managers and executives these days. Managers over age 45 who have lost their jobs are especially vulnerable.

These are very good reasons for feeling depressed. Knowing how to help themselves and when to seek help distinguishes people who get on with life from people whose depression becomes incapacitating.

► **When it's time to get help**
If you have at least four of the following symptoms, and they've lasted longer than several weeks, get a medical checkup first. Many physical problems and some medications mimic the following symptoms of depression.

- Decrease or increase in appetite
- Change in sleeping pattern
- Tire easily; lack of energy
- Agitation, hyperactivity
- Loss of interest in daily activities
- Decreased sex drive
- Inability to concentrate
- Feelings of hopelessness, guilt, worthlessness
- Thoughts of suicide

► Consequences of untreated chronic depression

On success in work and life

Psychological studies show that job success and an optimistic outlook are correlated. Optimists even score higher on achievement tests.[44] A self-confident, upbeat outlook increases your ability to make decisions which will improve the quality of your life — in marriage, friendships, as well as career and other areas.[45] Mainly this is because decisions made while you are depressed are usually based on distorted information and emotional reasoning.[46]

Studies also show that optimists handle setbacks better than pessimists do. They've *learned* to view setbacks as challenges to do better next time. They respond to a disappointment, like not getting the job, by improving their interview skills or upgrading their skills. They also are more likely to seek help and advice. An optimist would think, "Each day many people over forty are hired. Many have changed careers successfully and some have had stunning success. If they can do it, so can I." On the other hand, a pessimist would think, *"This proves that nobody will ever want to hire me,"* or *"I'm over the hill. What's the use!"*[47]

An optimistic attitude even helps persons in their seventies get good jobs. A youthful 73-year old woman applied for a job as part-time bookkeeper in a local pharmacy. She lied about her age and was hired. Four years later she was still working there. If you were to sit next to her on a bus, as I did, you would see a well-groomed, mature (not old!) woman with the personality of a young person. When I met her she was planning to take a night course in calligraphy for the fun of it.

Pessimists tend to self-destruct. An unemployed pessimist of forty or more years whose job has been eliminated by new technology would assume that it's too late to change careers or learn new skills. Such a hopeless attitude might lead him/her to take early retirement or accept a lower-level job.

Not only do they spoil their chances of getting a better job or succeeding in their current job, they even appear to be less intelligent and capable than they are. Recent psychological studies show that pessimists scored lower than optimists on achievement tests. *"My hunch is that for a given level of intelligence, your actual achievement is a function not just of talent, but also of the capacity to stand defeat,"* says Dr. Martin Seligman.[48] In another study the explanations insurance agents gave for failing to make a sale distinguished those who later became outstanding salesmen and those who quit in discouragement. The optimists also sold 37% more insurance in their first two years on the job than the pessimists did.[49]

A tendency toward optimism or pessimism is a better predictor of success in jobs where failure is part of the daily routine — like sales — than many psychological tests used in hiring people, says Dr. Seligman.

You can develop the habit of positive thinking. Dale Carnegie's *How to Win Friends and Influence People* has been a huge success for many years because the techniques it espouses work. There are other psychological techniques which have also helped many people. (Read on.)

Its influence on your health
The link between mind and body is strong. Chronically depressed people are more likely to get sick. In one study a group of Harvard graduates were interviewed twice, when they were 25 and forty years later. At age 25 their style of explaining certain events that had befallen them — pessimistic vs. optimistic — predicted their health at age 65. Even at age 45 the pessimists' health began to deteriorate more rapidly. They reported twice as many colds and doctors' visits during the year.[50] Another study found a link between the attitude of helplessness which is common among pessimists and a reduced resistance to illness. On a checklist of health habits, the pessimists were much more careless of their health than the optimists. They smoked and drank more and exercised less than the optimists.[51]

HOW TO RELIEVE ANXIETY AND DEPRESSION

It's natural to feel guilty because you are unemployed, to rage against an uncaring economy. It's easy to give in to depression. You're not crazy. You're going through a stage most of us have gone through. But indulging in self-pity and pessimism immobilizes you at a time you need to take action, to learn and practice healthy mental and physical habits, do a self-assessment, set goals, research the job market and prepare for your new job or career.[52]

How to get rid of harmful stress
▶ **Set priorities**

A simple way to reduce stress and chronic fatigue is to limit the demands made on your life now. Reduce the number of changes you'd like to make by setting priorities. First, make those changes which cannot be put off. The others can wait. Spread the others out in time so they don't all hit you at once. Do one or two at a time so you can adjust better to each change.

▶ **Improve your diet**

Some people get so depressed when they're unemployed that they neglect themselves. They skip meals and grab anything from the refrigerator. They try to forget their problems by over- or under-eating. They don't get enough exercise. Such practices are health risks which increase one's susceptibility to high blood pressure, arteriosclerosis, cancer, and heart attacks. They also contribute to depression and anxiety, and they can make a person look and feel older.

Diet also influences one's chances of getting a job or promotion. Obese persons are rarely promoted from lower management ranks, studies show. Among equally qualified job candidates, the one who is nice and trim wins out. Overweight job hunters are viewed as less productive and as health risks. They are even barred from some professional or trade training programs such as nursing, police and fire work. Obesity is an even greater problem for women job applicants because they are judged more by physical appearance than men are.

A good diet also can make you more mentally alert. A deficiency of certain nutrients — such as the B complex vitamins and folic acid — may cause declining mental alertness as we get older.

Certain nutrients — such as the cholines found in dairy products, grains and legumes and the lecithin found in soybeans — appear to improve memory. A link between calcium deficiency and learning ability is being investigated. Low levels of vitamins C, B_{12} and riboflavin were found to be related to lower scores on tests for abstract thinking in a group of people age 60 and older. Other studies show that low protein levels also influence memory, particularly in older adults who often consume less than the recommended levels.[53]

Diet also influences the rate of aging because the body's capacity to store vital nutrients diminishes as we grow older. Eat more vitamin-rich and high-fiber foods such as raw fruits and vegetables, bran, wheat and other cereals. Reduce your intake of foods that are high in saturated fats, salt and refined sugar. You will not only look better and think smarter, you'll ward off hypertension, heart attack, stroke, arteriosclerosis and a host of other diet-related ills.

▶ **Exercise**

People who exercise regularly have more energy. They also get that "high" which drug users get, but it doesn't ruin their lives and it lasts longer. Laboratory studies show that exercise also releases certain brain biochemicals that ward off depression and anxiety. Many top executives reduce stress through a daily walk, run, or bicycle ride.

"*Use it or lose it,*" advises Dr. James Fries. Just 15 minutes of brisk walking a day keeps the brain cells and the body young. It lowers our blood pressure, weight, and cholesterol level. Many bodily changes that occur as we get older are preventable, even reversible, with exercise. A 55-year old who exercises regularly and eats well-balanced meals can have a younger medical age than a 35-year old who lives carelessly. A study of the cardiovascular system and body composition of an 80-year old marathon runner found that his treadmill performance was that of a man half his age.

Studies also show that regular exercise raises scores on various tests of intelligence and lowers the incidence of memory loss. In one experiment middle-age men were instructed to do 1½ hours of physical exercise three times a week. At the end of the study their performance on tasks involving reasoning and information processing had significantly improved. Another study found that a few months of progressive walking — starting slow and increasing speed over a few months — improved the memory and reasoning ability of persons age 55-70. Moreover, experiments with animals show that the brain shrinks with inactivity and understimulation.[54]

You're never too old to start a moderate exercise program. Ask your doctor what kind is suitable for your age and present state of health. If you have been inactive or suffer from a chronic ailment, starting out with a vigorous exercise program can be harmful.

► **Keep busy and socially active**

Time can be a friend or an enemy. The time spent in our work gives meaning to our lives and sanity to our thoughts. It's an important component of the "cognitive map" we carry around in our heads to guide us through the network of events and social relationships. Unemployment disrupts this "cognitive map." It makes us feel uneasy, irritable, confused, even despairing.

Make a daily and monthly schedule of things to do, no matter how trivial. It will give structure to your days and a sense of direction and control over your life until you find another job. Here are some suggestions.

► Get a part-time job.

► Enroll in an adult education course to upgrade your job skills or learn new ones.

► Plan a weekly schedule of interesting, fun things to do and people to meet. People who are socially active live longer on average than loners. They also have more opportunities to get valuable support and advice. Since unemployment cuts you off from many social activities, force yourself to go out more. There are many things to do close-by that are free or cost little. Go to the library regularly and read about job opportunities. Volunteer at a local community association or help out in the political club. You'll make contacts that might lead to your next job. Helping others who are in need will also give you more confidence to deal with your own problems.

Chronic anxiety: a bad habit that can be unlearned

Among the better known methods for reducing anxiety and depression are relaxation exercises, cognitive therapy and meditation. Studies show that patients who apply these and other self-help methods improve significantly; in fact as much as with psychotherapy.[55] If the thought of changing careers or being interviewed for a job paralyzes you, relax. Such fears are easily treatable.

▶ Visualization

The best way to deal with anxiety is to confront the very thing that causes it. First, practice visualizing yourself in the feared situation, successfully dealing with it. Next, confront the actual event or object. Repeated exposure to it without the imagined awful consequences happening will eventually extinguish the fear.

Visualization plays an important role in the success of top athletes. It can for you, too. Many athletes practice visualizing themselves functioning at peak capacity before a sports competition. Elizabeth Manley, winner of an Olympics silver medal for ice skating, spent much time imagining herself performing perfect triple lutzes and mentally previewing the sort of performance she needed to leave in the minds of the judges.

Practice visualizing yourself at a job interview — poised, calm, dressed for success, articulate, responding wisely to questions. As far as the brain is concerned, visualizing yourself doing something is similar to doing it. Next, go on interviews for jobs you're not overly interested in. With repeated exposure your anxiety will subside. Then you'll be able to tackle the important interviews.

▶ Learn to relax

Just 10 minutes of relaxation exercises a day reduces anxiety and depression, loosens tense muscles, and lowers heart rate and blood pressure. There is also evidence that it increases mental alertness.

Meditation techniques, such as Yoga and transcendental meditation, are also effective. However, hard-driving achievers who like to keep busy all the time may feel a loss of control when they rely solely on such passive methods. It makes their fears emerge, and they become even more anxious. Passive methods should be accompanied by active exercises.[56]

Biofeedback is a high-tech method of reducing anxiety and tension. Electronic sensors display on a screen how your heart rate, blood pressure, brain alpha waves, and muscle tension change as you practice relaxation techniques. Eventually you learn to control these physiological responses. Many hospitals have relaxation clinics in which biofeedback therapy and other forms of relaxation therapy is available.

Are you a depressive person? Test yourself

- Do you waste energy worrying about your real or imagined deficiencies? A healthier attitude is to concentrate on your positive qualities.

- Do you measure yourself against a standard that is near-perfection or one that ill-suits your personality, interests or abilities?

- Do you tend to recall your failures and ignore your successes?

- Do you fail to give yourself credit for successes?

- When a co-worker or manager gives you constructive criticism does it convince you that your entire self is unworthy?

- Do you blame yourself when things go wrong, even though there is insufficient or contrary evidence?

- Do you view yourself as a leaf in the wind, a passive entity with no control over your life?

If you answered "yes" to just one of these questions, the following activities will help.

▶ Seek emotional support

During the recent farm crisis farmers and members of their families were committing suicide at a pace far higher than the national rate. A psychologist noted that a farmer's despair was more likely to grow to intolerable proportions if he refused to discuss his predicament with others.[57]

When we become depressed our view of life and of ourselves becomes narrow and distorted. We tend to see the glass as half empty instead of half full. We fail to see all the possibilities and choices that are available. Inevitably, decisions based on such a distorted perspective become self-fulfilling doomsday prophecies.

That's why we need the support of friends, family members and, if needed, a professional counselor who can help us see things more objectively. They can offer encouragement and helpful information, even job leads.

Avoid people who tear you down, whose negativism discourages you even more. Surround yourself with people who help you maintain a positive self-image. Such people actually help a depressive person function better, recent studies show.[58] Even an "inflated self-regard" helps us to strive against odds because it gives us hope. It makes us work harder and longer, and the perseverance helps us do better.

The following activities will help you identify and correct the irrational, self-defeating thoughts that prevent you from reaching your goal. They will also give you a sense of moving ahead and prepare you for job interviews.

▶ Get rid of your self-defeating thoughts

Write them down. Here are some which especially influence older job seekers:

- I lost the job because I don't have what it takes.
- I'm too old to change.
- Nobody wants to hire me.
- All these younger people applying for the job I would like to have are much better qualified.
- I'll never be able to learn this new technology.
- I don't have the right training/much education, and it's too late to do something about it.
- I've been a housewife all these years. I don't have much to offer.
- I'll probably end my days waiting on soup kitchen lines.

List the facts that disprove each one.
Include events from your personal experience and from what you've heard and read. If at first you can't think of anything, it's because you've acquired the habit of negative thinking. Your pessimism shuts out other aspects that

may be involved. In other words, you're suffering from tunnel vision.

List your positive qualities — your achievements, skills, things you do well naturally. Chapter four will show you how to do this. You probably have forgotten how much you've got going for you. Make several copies of the list and pin or paste a copy in places where you regularly look; like the bathroom mirror and refrigerator door. Read it every time you get into a negative mood. Eventually your assets and successes will become imprinted in your brain and the negative thoughts will be extinguished.[59]

Practice other healthy mental habits

► Each day do at least one thing that brings you closer to your career goal: read the help-wanted ads, mail a resume, go to the library to research an occupation or company.

► Each night, before going to bed, read a few pages of something light and cheerful.

► As you dress or eat breakfast in the morning, as you walk to the supermarket or do other chores, mentally review the items on your list of achievements and personal assets. When no one is around, say them aloud so that they become more strongly imprinted in your mind.

► Think, *"I'm not going to take it anymore,"* whenever someone tries to tear you down. (Constructive criticism is another matter.) Tell that person how you feel about it.

► From now on compare yourself with what YOU have accomplished in the past and mentally review all the improvements you've made. Don't use an impossible external standard to judge yourself.

► Learn to benefit from constructive criticism. Use it as a basis for making needed changes.

► If the constructive criticism dwells on personal habits that irritate others — mannerisms, body language, ways of expressing yourself — write down better habits you need to acquire. Put these in the form of brief, basic rules such as: *"Stop biting your fingernails." "Say as much as possible in as few words as possible." "Don't use outdated expressions."* Arrange them in order of importance and memorize them. Repeat them to yourself, aloud whenever possible, until your behavior has noticeably changed.

▶ Whenever you have an unpleasant thought push it out of your mind by recalling the things that make you feel good, as Maria does in *The Sound of Music*. Psychological studies show that negative events or memories produce a chain reaction of negative memories and happy memories foster more happy memories.[60]

Make needed improvements in your appearance

● Improve your diet and slim down if you need to.

● Even though you feel okay, get a medical checkup so incipient health problems can be treated before they get worse.

● Learn *How To Dress For Success*.[61] Buy a good quality outfit for job hunting.

● Get a more stylish, attractive hairdo or haircut.

● Get a friend, or hire an image consultant, to advise you on a more becoming haircut and makeup for job hunting.

● Throw out your old-fashioned eyeglasses and get a new pair.

A side benefit: your mental alertness increases

Depression can also cause memory problems, especially in older persons. A 63-year-old man began misplacing things, suffered memory loss, and became so disorganized that he could no longer do his job well. A doctor misdiagnosed him as prematurely senile. Later examinations revealed severe depression as the underlying reason. With psychological counseling and antidepressant drugs there was a dramatic improvement.[62]

There is increasing evidence that mentally stimulating activities, in addition to a good diet and regular exercise, keep the brain healthy and developing well into old age.[63] *"It's very much like physical skills. Once you stop using them they get rusty,"* says Dr. Warner K. Schaie.[64] *"Changes in brain cells* — resulting from exposure to mentally stimulating activities — *"have been found in every species investigated to date, including primates. They certainly should occur in humans as well,"* says Dr. Roger Walsh[65]. Dr. Marian Diamond agrees, *"Nerve cells can grow at any age in response to intellectual enrichment of all sorts* — *travel, crossword puzzles, anything that stimulates the brain with novelty and challenge."*[66] The key words here are *novelty and challenge* which imply openness to change.

Neuroscientist Bill Greenough concludes from his animal studies that lack of stimulation, much more than age, limits the formation of new neural connections in adult brains.[67] *"As long as we don't isolate ourselves as we grow older, a very important type of mental faculty may even improve — crystallized intelligence which allows us to draw on our accumulated knowledge to provide alternative solutions to complicated problems."*[68]

► Courses and workshops that teach relaxation techniques and other forms of self-therapy

The adult education programs of most colleges and universities have courses and workshops on how to develop self-confidence, overcome social anxiety, and be more assertive. They are generally held in the evening and on weekends. Also offering such help are:

- Young Men's/Women's Christian/Hebrew Associations
- Dale Carnegie
- Women's centers
- Community mental health centers
- Psychotherapists who teach workshops through private practice

► Self-help books and tape recordings

There are several good books on how to reduce tension, anxiety, and depression. See Appendix A for a sample.

There also are tapes which give instructions on meditation, Yoga, progressive muscle relaxation, and other methods of reducing tension and anxiety. Some merely provide background music and soothing sounds while you practice cognitive therapy or relaxation exercises. Your local library may have a collection of tapes which you can borrow. See Appendix A.

When it's time for professional help

Before the 1960s only rich people could afford psychological therapy. Today there are hundreds of mental health clinics to help lower-income persons who suffer from the stresses of changing times. Many varieties of psychological help exist. In this chapter only short-term therapy will be discussed. This is because the anxiety and depression many job/career changers suffer are not usually the result of deep-seated emotional problems. The most common reasons why people seek help include:

- Abrupt mood swings
- Inability to get along with others
- Alcohol or drug abuse

- Chronic anxiety and phobias
- Eating or sleeping difficulties
- Sexual problems
- Chronic depression
- Physical ailments that have roots in emotional problems. (An anxiety attack can be mistaken for a heart attack.)

► **Psychoanalysis**

This is the traditional "couch" therapy which attempts to find the roots of subconscious emotional problems in early childhood. It's expensive and it takes years of weekly sessions with a psychoanalyst before any improvement is seen. The results can be impressive however. There was a period during which the famous Russian composer, Sergei Rachmaninoff, developed a mental block which prevented him from composing music. After undergoing psychoanalysis from Sigmund Freud he created some of his greatest piano concertos.

► **Short-term therapy**

This comes in several varieties. They all seek to replace self destructive habits of thinking and behaving with healthy, positive habits. There is no attempt to uncover deep-seated emotional conflicts. They work best on people whose problems result from work, marriage or other interpersonal conflicts. Dramatic results usually occur after six to twelve sessions. Studies show they can be as effective as drug therapy in treating depression.

Cognitive behavior therapy views depression and lack of self-confidence as learned habits that can be easily unlearned. Dr. Aaron T. Beck is a University of Pennsylvania psychiatrist whose success with this form of therapy has made it popular. His technique consists of having patients report or write down their negative thoughts, then helping them to see the distortions in these thoughts. Exercises follow that are designed to instill positive habits of thinking. Often the depression clears up in a matter of weeks.[69]

Rational-emotive therapy, a method developed by Dr. Albert T. Ellis, cures anxiety problems. It basic premise is that learned habits, like social anxiety and other fears, can be unlearned. The sufferers repeatedly confront the fear they have been avoiding. Eventually, the fear disappears as they realize the outcome is not as bad as imagined. During the confrontations, they practice techniques to control the terror. These include various relaxation techniques such as deep breathing exercises and visualization. Studies have shown cure rates as high as 80%.

Interpersonal and family therapies view emotional problems, such as anxiety and non-clinical depression, as resulting from poor social skills. A therapist shows persons how the way they relate to others causes conflicts. The treatment focuses on a real-life problem — conflicts with people in authority (such as a boss), with colleagues, or with a spouse or family member. Good results often appear after 12-16 weeks.

▶ Who is qualified to administer therapy?

The Office of Technology Assessment found no difference in the efficacy of therapy by psychiatrists (who, as licensed medical doctors can offer drug therapy) and other licensed professionals: psychologists, social workers, psychiatric nurses and pastoral counselors. Be wary of those who set up a psychotherapy practice without proper training and a license. Ask your prospective therapist where he/she studied. Then check the institution's accreditation from the sources below. Local librarians also can help with this.

▶ Cost of professional help

Studies have found little relation between the cost of therapy and the quality of results. For private therapy, average fees per session vary according to the therapist's location and training. In large urban areas the cost of therapy is two to three times greater than in towns and rural areas. As the 1988 average rates show (see below), private psychotherapists charged an average of $50 to over $150 for one 45-to-50-minute session. Some therapists reduce their fees for people who can't afford to pay more.[70]

Psychiatrists — $75; psychologists — $70; social workers and mental health counselors — $55; pastoral counselors who have graduate degrees in psychology or psychotherapy — $35.

Publicly funded agencies include community mental health centers, university clinics, church centers, and family service agencies. The fee ranged from nothing to $60 per session, depending on ability to pay. However, the waiting list may be long and the number of visits allowed are limited.

Private clinics such as anxiety and stress clinics can be expensive. Rockville's Center for Behavioral Medicine charged about $1300 for a 16-week program in 1986 and about $2,500 for a 5-day program.

The average length of therapy is 12 to 15 hourly sessions and the total cost of treatment is about $1,000. Some individual insurance policies have no mental health coverage. Others pay only part of the fee, often with a $1,000 cutoff. Some only reimburse visits to psychiatrists or psychologists. Generally, however, the coverage for outpatient therapy isn't much.

► **Where to find reputable help**

To find a licensed private therapist contact one of the following:

► Psychology or psychiatry department of the local university, college, or medical school.

► Many small towns now have therapists employed by the state. Check a local hospital. Fees vary according to income. In 1988 they were as low as $9 a session. The nearest human-services agency can refer you. It can also refer you to career counselors and other support people who visit small communities on a regular basis.

► There are also clinics and private programs run by mental health centers, universities, large hospitals and health-maintenance organizations. The sources mentioned here can also direct you to the nearest ones. Many centers treat depression, phobias and milder forms of chronic anxiety. Stress clinics teach biofeedback and other relaxation techniques. Some programs are designed for specific types of persons, such as executives and professional women. The Women's Wellness Center in Los Angeles, for example, helps professional women whose stress comes from problems relating to the female role at work.

The following organizations have branches in many counties. Look in the telephone directory under their county or state names rather than *American* or *National*.

- National Mental Health Association: It has 650 local and state chapters. Look them up in the phone book under your county's Mental Health Association.

- National Association of Social Workers: Look up the local or state branch which is listed under the county or state name.

- American Association of Marriage and Family Therapy, 1717 K Street, NW, Ste. 407, Washington, DC 20006.

- American Mental Health Counselors Association, 5999 Stevenson Avenue, Alexandria, VA 22304. Write for the names of certified clinical mental health counselors in your area.

- American Association of Pastoral Counselors, 9508A Lee Highway, Fairfax, VA 22031.

- National Institute of Mental Health — For free information on the causes and treatment of depression and anxiety, write to: Public Inquiries Section, National Institute of Mental Health, Room 15C-05, 5600 Fishers Lane, Rockville, MD 20857.

How Well Do You Know Yourself?

Now is the time to reassess your work experience, abilities, likes and dislikes, and other job-related aspects of your personality. The increased self-awareness will make you more self-confident. It will help you choose a more compatible occupation, one which you'll enjoy. It is also the first step in preparing a convincing resume. It will guarantee success in your job interviews.

A SELF-ASSESSMENT WILL HELP IN MANY WAYS

It will identify abilities you can transfer to another industry or occupation.

In rapidly changing times a readiness to switch jobs or careers is better than money in the bank as the following cases illustrate.

A woman who was dismissed as staff aide to a foreign mission in the United Nations found a better paying job as administrative assistant in a Fortune 500 corporation. The same basic skills and experience were transferable to the new job; e.g., planning, organizing and scheduling conferences, trips and business luncheons.

Several years ago when music teachers couldn't find teaching jobs many were able to transfer their above-average analytic reasoning aptitude to the rapidly growing computer field. Those with outgoing personalities found success in computer sales, management, and distribution. Those who were introverted found their niche as computer programmers. A high school music teacher who started out as a salesman for Sony corporation later opened his own computer distribution business. He loves his new career, especially the money it brings.

Engineers have a hard time finding good jobs when their training becomes obsolete. Many transfer their superior analytic reasoning and numerical aptitudes, intelligence, and technical skills to other careers — as managers in high-tech companies, as mathematics or science teachers, in computer sales and, more recently, in financial firms.

You might learn you're in the wrong occupation

Did you choose your present occupation for the wrong reasons — family pressure, your friends were in it, it was the first good job offer that came along? Or, was it right for you when you were starting out but your values and interests have changed?. In either case, you're stuck in a career you don't enjoy.

On the other hand you might learn, after completing the following exercises, that *it still is* the right occupation for you. With a few evening courses to update your skills and expertise you'll be on the right track again. You might learn that the reason you are unhappy lies in the company you work for, not the occupation itself.

It can help you find a better job

You'll have evidence to prove that you are the best person for the job. The worst sin of job hunting is going to an interview without knowing who you are, what you want, what your abilities are, and what you can offer the company. It will take you much longer to find a good job, and you're more likely to accept an offer that's wrong for you.

You'll also have evidence that you're worth more than the first salary offer; or, you'll be able to negotiate a better benefits package.

If the vacancy has been filled, you may be able to convince the employer that you are qualified for other job openings in the firm. Employers cannot hire every good person who applies for the same advertised opening.

Most job interviewers ask, "Tell me about yourself." A self-assessment will provide evidence that, besides being compatible with the occupation, you'll fit in easily with the culture of the organization.

A self-assessment will also make it apparent to the interviewer that you really want the job. They see too many indifferent applicants who give irrelevant, hazy answers such as these:

→ QUESTION: *"Where do you think you fit in our company?"*
HAZY ANSWER: *"Oh, I can do anything that involves people. I love working with people."*

→ QUESTION: *"What would you like to be doing in five years?"*
NAIVE ANSWER: *"I'd like to be vice-president of human resources. I'm good at planning and managing people. I was captain of my high school football team."*

HOW TO DO A SELF-ASSESSMENT

If you know the general occupational area you're interested in all you may need to do is read about different occupations and their requirements. But, if you're not sure which direction to take — especially if you are considering a career change — you should do a full-scale self-assessment as described below. It takes time but the results will be worth it. Some people need the advice of a career counselor to do a self-assessment. Others can do it themselves with the exercises given below or from a workbook on the subject. You'll find several in bookstores and in the public library. The basic steps are as follows.

► Assess your strong points: skills, aptitudes, work-related achievements and experience.

► Compare these with the requirements of various occupations. You might discover several that suit you better than the one you're in now.

► Narrow your list of occupations down to those which are most compatible with your interests and personality. No matter how strong your abilities for a particular occupation, if your temperament, interests and values lie elsewhere you'll probably be miserable in it.

► Finally, assess your liabilities; e.g., need for more training or education, restrictions on your career choice caused by health or family reasons.

Major topics for a self-assessment
► **Paid work experience**

List the paid jobs you've had. Include part-time and freelance work. Put them in reverse chronological order, starting with the most recent. Leave ample space under each to include the following:

1. Job title
2. Employer's name and address
3. Supervisor's name
4. Month and year you started and left
5. Starting and final salary
6. Work responsibilities
7. Achievements/accomplishments worth noting

Responsibilities and achievements

Look over your list of work responsibilities and achievements and ask yourself, *"What skills and natural abilities do these involve that make me good at certain kinds of work?"* Look also beyond the obvious ones such as typing, filing, bookkeeping, selling. For example, are your strong points any of the following?

- I learn quickly.
- I'm good at dealing with people.
- I'm creative. I usually find better ways to do my work. When asked, I can think of more ideas than my coworkers.
- I write well. I've received compliments on my letters and reports.
- I enjoy doing accurate detail work.
- I'm a fast worker. I almost always meet deadlines.
- I seem to have more energy than my co-workers.
- I'm well-organized. I can get more done in less time than most people can. People say I write well-organized reports.
- I'm a good leader; e.g., I was chosen to lead a project team at work. People usually are willing to follow my suggestions; e.g., I was chairperson of a volunteer committee; captain of my company's softball team.

"My daddy said to me, 'Honey, if the Lord meant for you to work he'd have given you some skills.'"

— L.F., socialite

Identify skills that can be transferred to another job
DID YOU LEARN TO OPERATE A MACHINE? — e.g., automobile, sewing, drill press, centrifuge, X-ray, industrial robot.
DID YOU LEARN TO USE OFFICE EQUIPMENT? — e.g., computer, fax machine, laser printer, copier, scanner, overhead projector, calculator, software.
DID YOU LEARN A SPECIAL SKILL? — e.g., draw charts and graphs; read maps, blueprints and charts; write computer programs; understand and explain software manuals to coworkers.

List everything you learned at work, no matter how trivial it seems to you. Besides being transferrable to a different organization or occupation, employers value such expertise because it saves them the time and money needed to train a new worker. It also shows that you're not afraid of complex new equipment. Many people don't even know how to use a paper copier or a typewriter. Typing skills are necessary in most occupations these days, including managers and executives. Most modern electronic equipment is controlled by a typewriter-like keyboard.

Let's suppose you have sold real estate, and you want to change careers. First you would identify every responsibility you had in this occupation. Next you would analyze each in detail. Each task involves one or more skills and areas of knowledge. Here are some of the abilities required in selling real estate. As you can see, these and others not listed can be applied to other occupations as well.

→ APPRAISING: Estimating the market value of houses

→ SELLING: Convincing prospective buyers, closing deals.

→ OFFICE MANAGEMENT: Organizing and maintaining accurate records; answering phone inquiries.

→ MATHEMATICAL: Estimating mortgage payments and interest rates.

→ WRITING: Newspaper ads, sales notices, articles for real estate newsletter, letters to clients and members of real estate association.

→ INTERVIEWING: Getting information from and about prospective tenants and landlords.

→ READING MAPS, SCHEMATICS: Studying district and road maps and blueprints.

→ RESEARCHING: Getting information from documents, census reports, survey data. Making on-site observations of a neighborhood. Interviewing for information.

→ OPERATING EQUIPMENT: Typing or word processing; computer operation; using computing software; laser printer; driving a car; detecting defects in boilers, plumbing, etc.

Be generous with action words

Use them to label each learned skill and natural ability involved in your work experience. Here is a list to help you get started. You can add others which apply particularly to you.

Appraising	Problem solving
Budgeting	Public speaking
Cataloging	Purchasing
Directing	Recruiting
Generating ideas	Repairing
Interviewing	Scheduling
Lobbying	Screening
Mediating	Selling
Negotiating	Supervising
Organizing	Teaching
Programming	Teamwork

Next, go through your list and check with a color marker those words which express what you can do especially well.

Go over the list again with a different color marker and check those words which express what you enjoy doing.

Finally, match these words with the appropriate work experiences that illustrate what you mean. For example, when you are being interviewed, instead of saying, *"I'm good at motivating workers under my supervision to do their best,"* you'll be able to cite specific examples of how you accomplished this.

What you liked/disliked

Make a list of what you especially liked or disliked about the following aspects of each job.

► **Job responsibilities**

► **Work schedule:** Night shift, overtime, deadlines, part-time.

► **Physical demands:** Standing, sitting, lifting heavy objects, peering into a microscope or a computer screen, doing detailed eye-hand work, traveling, etc.

► **"Personality" or culture of the company:** Bureaucratic, conservative, fast-paced, relaxed, innovative, democratic, large, small, family-owned

► **Environment:** Indoors/outdoors, city/suburb, cramped-/spacious, own office/shared office, modern/traditional, and transportation facilities, nearby cultural and recreational attractions

► **Add other aspects** that are important to you.

Next, look over your list of likes and dislikes and check off those aspects you would like to have in your next job. Number these in order of priority, from "must have" down to "good to have but not imperative."

Repeat the exercise under the heading *"What I don't want in my next job."*

Your achievements and contributions
List the things you did which went beyond the normal requirements for the job. Here are a few examples. Note the use of action words and phrases instead of complete sentences. You will also use these in your resume.
- Increased sales.
- Invented method for reducing amount of wasted materials.
- Reorganized work schedule and increased productivity.
- Rearranged floor plan and increased usable space.
- Improved product/service quality which reduced number of consumer complaints.
- Improved teamwork and morale.

Describe each achievement in detail — what you did and how you did it. Use measurable or other descriptive terms wherever possible: hours, dollars, percentages, quantity, quality. Example: *"Increased morale and productivity by introducing team projects. Absenteeism declined 45% the first year; productivity increased 300%."* Here are some more examples:
- Increased new orders # percent.
- Increased monthly sales by # dollars.

- Lowered costs by reducing # percent of defects.
- Reduced clerical errors by # percent.
- Simplified (mention task) by # percent.
- Improved quality of our product (describe how).
- Saved # percent of office space for additional use.
- Reduced returned merchandise by # percent.
- Improved delivery to clients Seeby # (hours/days/months).
- Simplified work flow with # (hours/days/weeks) of production time saved.

► Voluntary work experience

On a separate sheet of paper list the volunteer work you have done. Include projects connected with your paid jobs. This says something about you — your initiative, energy level, team spirit, communications skills, social skills, creativity, leadership ability, organizing ability, ability to meet deadlines, and so forth.

Then do the same analysis as you did for "Paid Work Experience," using the same outline. The words and phrases on the abilities list for paid work also apply to non-paid work.

► Job Training and Education

EDUCATION refers to knowledge and skills learned in a formal setting such as high school, vocational or technical school, college, university, and home study programs. It's measured by degrees, certificates, diplomas and credits earned.

TRAINING involves learning in non-formal settings such as workshops, lectures, seminars, and on-the-job. It is generally measured by actual performance instead of grades and credits earned. Even a one-day seminar or workshop should be included on your list if the topic is relevant to the job market. Job-related self-improvement courses, no matter how brief, should be listed also; e.g., public speaking, computer literacy. Courses like *The Art of American Pie Baking* don't count unless you are considering a career in the food industry.

Next ask yourself these questions:
→ Which courses or training did I like best/least?
→ Which did I do best in?
→ Which did I find most difficult?

Also list your extra-curricular activities; e.g., debating society, editor of class newsletter, member of a team project or sport, special interest clubs like science, Spanish, biology, photography.

Include also the special events in your life which served as creative learning experiences, which resulted in personal growth. An example is the case of an older woman who hired a divorce lawyer recommended by a family friend who also was an attorney. This"friend" then represented her husband. Not surprisingly, her own attorney was too busy or unwilling to give much help to her. So she decided to learn a few things on her own. First, she learned how to use the law library. Step-by-step she learned other skills which eventually led to her becoming a self-taught expert in domestic law. Finally, with help from a Displaced Homemaker Center she was able to get on-the-job training which led to a paid job as a legal paraprofessional. Eventually she established a divorce clinic which helps women in similar circumstances.

► *Interests and leisure activities*

The direction of your job hunt or career change will become clearer after you identify a pattern of interests that runs throughout your various experiences, interests and activities. These also will reveal hidden abilities which you can use to select a compatible occupation. A good-looking, single retired insurance executive merged three of his favorite interests — traveling, playing bridge, and women — into a dream job with a shipping line which pays him to teach bridge to wealthy widows who go on cruises. Below you'll find other real-life cases of people who found their dream jobs.

List your favorite interests and leisure activities. Include interests you follow regularly in the newspapers, television and magazines; e.g., stock market, photography, science, technology, foreign affairs.

Next, apply the same method of analysis of learned skills and innate aptitudes as you did for your paid and voluntary work. Note whether your interests and leisure activities involve aptitudes like the following:

→ Eye-hand coordination: sketching, painting, and computer graphics, mechanical activities

→ Verbal analytic skills: debating society, solving word puzzles, editing local newspaper

56

→ Teamwork: team sports, working on voluntary team projects
→ Communication skills: learning foreign languages, writing short stories, writing to a pen pal
→ Computer skills: using computer bulletin boards, creating programs in FORTRAN, desktop publishing
→ Mechanical skills: repairing cars/small equipment, installing vinyl siding
→ Persuasion/Selling skills: acting in little theater group, coaching, playing in team sports

Look for recurring themes

Assuming there has been some consistency in your life experiences, the same themes will recur in all your paid and volunteer work, education and training, interests and leisure activities. Ideally these will match the requirements of the job you want. If not, now is the time to choose a career which will be a joy instead of just a job. Here are some ideas to get you started. Note the use of action words to describe them. This exercise will also prepare you for writing an effective resume.

gnihcaeT Teaching
gnizinagrO Organizing
gnihcraeseR Researching
kroW liateD Detail Work
gniniatretnE Entertaining
elpoep gnipleH Helping people
gnikaeps cilbuP Public speaking
sdrocer gnipeeK Keeping records
smelborp gnivloS Solving problems
saedi htiw gnikroW Working with ideas
smelborp gniyfitnedI Identifying problems
erusserp rednu gnikroW Working under pressure
oroodtuo/sroodni gnikroW Working indoors/outdoors
srehto htiw/enola gnikroW Working alone/with others
slliks laciremun gniylppA Applying numerical skills
Working with my hands
Creating, inventing, designing
Working with plants/animals/objects
Exchanging information, ideas with others

► **Relate the themes to new occupations**

Example: If you're a content accountant or a cracker-jack computer programmer the following themes would recur: well organized, analytic, logical mind; good at detail work; enjoy working alone; good numerical skills; enjoy solving problems.

These and other traits should also appear throughout your list of various interests and leisure activities:

→ Even as a teenager I preferred working at math or crossword puzzles rather than playing on a sports team.

→ I prefer hobbies which allow me to work things out for myself: coin or stamp collecting, inventing things, building model airplanes, building a radio or home computer from a kit.

→ In team sports I preferred to analyze and plan strategies than playing in the game.

→ My favorite game is chess.

If you're looking for a job as copywriter in an advertising agency the following experiences would show your abilities, interests and other personality traits that are consistent with this occupation.

→ I was always creative as a child. I created cartoons, wrote poetry, joined a pen-pal club, wrote articles for the school newspaper, etc.

→ In high school/college I made posters, wrote short stories/articles for the school newspaper.

→ As a volunteer for the PTA I wrote speeches and the copy for ads in the community newsletter.

→ My hobbies include solving crossword puzzles, writing poetry.

→ My favorite game is Scrabble.

→ I still write to my pen pals.

► **If you could start over again**

Picture yourself in the ideal job. Describe it in general terms according to:

• Your responsibilities
• People you would be working with
• Work conditions like work schedule, team/solitary work, few deadlines
• Work environment like indoor/outdoor, spacious/cramped, suburban/city setting

Next, imagine the worst possible job. List the conditions you absolutely will not tolerate in your next job.

The following persons made their dream job come true. See if you can, also.

One woman who loved traveling to exotic places found a second job which pays her to go on luxury trips six weeks a year. The company she works for arranges overseas trips for corporations. Her responsibilities include arranging the trips and seeing that things run smoothly. When she arrives at a destination she stays at a luxury hotel. She confers with hotel managers, caterers, maitre d's of fine restaurants, and gets tickets to cultural events.

A married couple who love outdoor sports and rural living quit their city jobs, sold their home, and bought a 10-cabin resort in a mountaintop village set by a lake. Although their income during the early years was less than the combined salaries from their previous jobs, they lived like vacationers. During spring and summer seasons they spend their free time fishing, boating and hiking and in the winter they ski. They also enjoy all the other amenities of their resort.[71]

------ ⊰⊱ ------

GETTING A JOB
AFTER RAISING A FAMILY

When asked how she became a successful executive (head of Desilu Productions), Lucille Ball replied, *"I ran my studio like I run my home, with understanding of people. . . I've learned to budget my hours and my energies."* The same topics and method of analysis for paid work experience can be done for homemaking and volunteer work. Many of the skills involved are used in paid jobs as well. All you have to do is clothe them in business-like language. Many words on the skills lists for paid work also apply to non-paid work.

Homemaker skills that are used in paying jobs

"Twelve teenagers are having a club meeting in your home and they get into a fight. You learn things about analyzing and removing the causes of interpersonal conflict and promoting teamwork that you can't get from a course in management." — Homemaker being interviewed for a job as administrative assistant

▶ *Many skills needed by secretaries, administrative assistants and managers are also used in managing a home and raising a family*

▸ **Administration** (organizing, planning, managing) — maintaining inventory of home supplies; scheduling and coordinating family activities; supervising and maintaining morale among family (team) members; setting production goals (family plans); delegating tasks; settling disputes (conflict management).

▸ **Money management** — keeping a balance sheet on income and expenditures; preparing income tax forms; managing debts, loan payments, mortgages, investments.

▸ **Clerical** — setting up and maintaining files and records; typing correspondence; proofreading and editing schoolwork.

▸ **Planning, arranging, developing group projects** — parties, meetings, car pool (These skills are important for administrative assistants and conference center coordinators who often plan and arrange corporate conferences, entertainment, banquets and conventions).

▸ **Office equipment and machinery you learned to use** — home computer, copier, printer, VCR, photographic.

▸ **Purchasing** — getting the best price on family supplies, car, home computer and other electronic equipment.

▸ **Manual dexterity** — activities requiring precise eye-brain-hand coordination such as carpentry, arts and crafts projects, sewing, decorating.

▸ **Mechanical** — repair of toys and home equipment such as small engines and electronic devices

Skills developed in volunteer work that are used in paid jobs

Even if you start with an entry-level job, volunteer work experience helps you move more rapidly into a better paying position. Employers especially value committee appointments, leadership positions and other kinds of responsibilities that develop skills in teamwork, problem solving, and leadership. So put these at the top of your list.

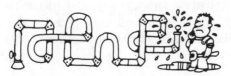

60

▶ **Use action words, measurable terms, detailed descriptions**

Use these to describe your responsibilities and achievements. Instead of saying you were responsible for organizing the yearly PTA garage sale, say you organized a sale that netted # dollars, an increase of # percent over the previous year.

In your resume, under *ADMINISTRATION* you might say that you *supervised* a staff of 15, *increased* membership by 15%, *managed* a $20,000 budget, *formulated* policies or *planned and carried out* a successful fund raising campaign. Under *COMMUNICATIONS* you *wrote* a monthly newsletter, *edited* a conference transcript or *publicized* an annual event.

▶ **Examples of skills that are transferrable to paying jobs**

PRESIDENT/COMMITTEE CHAIRPERSON:
- Organizing conferences and other events
- Recruiting committee members
- Training, managing volunteers
- Maintaining team morale
- Chairing meetings
- Researching, preparing agendas
- Representing organization in public events

Jobs which require some or all these skills include training representative, administrative assistant, restaurant hostess, executive secretary.

FUND RAISING:
- Selling (persuasion skills)
- Planning, organizing fund drives
- Communicating skills — e.g., public speaking, creative writing
- Knowledge of community resources

Jobs which use these skills include telephone soliciting, marketing surveys, receptionist, sales representative, retail sales, marketing.

PLANNING AND DEVELOPING GARAGE SALES, ARTS & CRAFTS EXHIBITS, DINNERS FOR LARGE GROUPS:
- Planning, organizing, coordinating events
- Calculating cost and purchasing supplies
- Hosting events

Jobs which use some or all these skills include administrative assistant, purchasing agent, caterer, restaurant manager.

SECRETARY:
- Maintaining office records
- Screening calls
- Supervising/training clerical volunteers
- Editing/typing reports and letters
- Paying invoices
- Keeping track of expense accounts
- Making travel arrangements
- Organizing schedules
- Keeping track of different projects

The same skills are used by administrative aides, secretaries, and staff assistants. With a broader knowledge of the company and industry they can be promoted to executive secretary or assistant to the chief executive officer. With a degree in business management and knowledge of computer business software there is no limit to how far they can go. Kathleen Kallman rose from executive secretary to assistant vice-president of Beatrice Companies in four years.[72]

Additional volunteer responsibilities and some of the transferrable skills involved:

PUBLIC RELATIONS: public speaking, planning and promoting events, writing advertising copy, interviewing community leaders

TREASURER: bookkeeping, purchasing supplies for large gatherings, preparing budget, paying invoices, maintaining expense accounts

POLITICAL ACTIVITIES: lobbying, public speaking, telephone interviewing, researching, handling pressure situations.

PREPARING NEWSLETTER: writing, editing and layout, art and graphics, using computer and word processing software

CLERICAL: preparing/maintaining detailed reports, typing, word processing, writing letters/notices, organizing/filing documents, using electronic office equipment (fax machine, copier, etc.)

HOSPITAL WORK, CHILDREN'S CAMP, NURSING HOME: counseling, teaching arts and crafts, nursing assistant

DEVELOPING CHURCH/SCHOOL PROGRAM: developing programs, managing conferences, setting priorities.

If you need help

Women's associations such as the Young Women's Christian and Hebrew Associations and Displaced Homemakers help mature women identify the skills acquired from homemaking and volunteer work and negotiate these into paying jobs. Colleges and universities also have special programs and courses for women. These include career planning courses for women who are re-entering the job market; e.g., *Self-Esteem and Image Building for Women; Second Careers for Homemakers*. There are also special programs for working women. New York University's Center for Career and Life Planning has courses like *Advancing Your Career*.

If you need help in assessing your skills, choosing an occupation, and preparing a good resume, contact your local college or one of the associations listed below and in Appendix F.

IDENTIFY COMPATIBLE OCCUPATIONS

"I didn't want to be a performer, and I was always doing things with my hands," said David Burgess, award winning violin and bow maker. As a child he studied the violin but he enjoyed constructing things even more. He found a career which involves both his musical and mechanical aptitudes. In 1984 he won first-prize in the National Competition and Exhibition for Violin and Bow Makers.[73]

The Occupational Outlook Handbook, which is in the public library, has complete descriptions of about 200 occupations. In it you'll find more than one that matches your abilities and interests. Each occupation is described in detail according to the following:

> Earnings
> Job prospects
> Job responsibilities
> Working conditions
> Related occupations
> Tools and equipment used
> What workers do and how they do it
> Education and training requirements

It also gives the following information.

- If the job involves overtime, evening or night shifts
- If much of the work is done outdoors or indoors
- The physical demands of the job (such as crouching or heavy lifting)
- Opportunities for part-time work
- Personality characteristics needed; e.g., someone who likes making decisions, working in a competitive atmosphere, working with people or inanimate objects

The *Occupational Outlook Quarterly* has articles which also describe new and emerging occupations. The Fall 1986 issue, for example, has "Matching Yourself With the World of Work," by Melvin Fountain. It describes 200 occupations according to 17 characteristics and requirements including:

- **Job Requirements**: leadership, persuasion, instructing, problem-solving, creativity, initiative, teamwork, public contact, manual dexterity, physical stamina
- **Work Environment**: hazardous, outdoors, confined
- **Occupational Characteristics**: geographically concentrated (50% or more jobs located in fewer than six states), part-time (many workers employed for less than 35 hours a week), earnings, employment growth, number of new jobs created, educational requirements

Aptitudes and occupations

The following are some examples of aptitudes and occupations which require them.

- **Color, Light, Depth Sensitivity** — artists, surgeons, architects, dress designers, pattern makers

- **Inductive Reasoning** — investigative work, research, writing, medicine, psychology, law, anthropology
- **Mechanical** — good eye-hand coordination as required in the repair and construction of mechanical things
- **Numerical** — accountants, actuaries, bookkeepers, and others who deal with numbers. Also an asset for managers and executives who deal with computer spreadsheets
- **Spatial Visualization** — architects, engineers, map makers, and others in technical, mechanical, and scientific fields

▶ *Occupational clusters*

Occupations can be grouped into clusters or "families" of related aptitudes, skills and training requirements. Each occupation within a cluster combines these in varying degrees. What this means is that your storehouse of skills, knowledge and experience can be applied to more than one occupation.

Soon after Mary E. graduated with a degree in accounting, she got a job in a major accounting firm. After several months she discovered that she hated hassling with irate clients. However, she enjoyed working with the computers and writing software programs. Her training in accounting wasn't wasted. She found a job as computer programmer for a large software firm. Similar aptitudes and interests are involved in both occupations.

The *Occupational Outlook Handbook*, published by the U.S. Department of Labor, should be at your side as you do these exercises. It classifies about 200 occupations into clusters of jobs that require similar abilities and tasks.

▸ If you're good at, and enjoy, helping people, you might consider these two job clusters: (1) teachers, librarians and counselors, and (2) registered nurses, pharmacists, dietitians, therapists and physician's aides.

▸ If you want a job which involves your creative abilities, the job cluster which includes writers, artists and entertainers might interest you.

▸ Let's suppose you're thinking of going into the marketing and sales field. This huge job cluster includes many related occupations — retail sales, cashier, wholesale trade sales, store manager, manufacturer's sales, insurance sales, securities sales, wholesaler, travel agent, real estate appraiser.

▶ The administrative and managerial cluster is even larger — restaurant, cafe and bar manager, sales manager, purchasing agent and buyer for the retail trade, inspector, public administrator, underwriter, assessor, tax preparer, credit analyst, claim examiner, safety inspector, tax examiner and revenue agent.

Personality types and compatible occupations

"What kind of person are you?" If the interviewer doesn't ask this question outright you can be sure it's always on his/her mind. People do better in jobs that match their interests, temperament, values and abilities. Two persons may have an equal aptitude for mechanical work. One is quiet and introverted. The other is expressive and gregarious. The first person would be happier working in an auto repair shop. The second would prefer teaching mechanics or shop.

It's easier to change careers than to change your personality. Psychological studies show that from the late teens until old age people change very little in basic personality. If you are unhappy in your present occupation, or not doing well in it, it may be because you chose the wrong one in the first place.

At age 45 a pharmaceutical research planner — who had a doctorate in biochemistry and a Harvard masters degree in business administration — was ordained into the Episcopal priesthood. He previously worked for a firm whose corporate headquarters is across the street from an Episcopal Church. His career interests began to change after he became active in church activities and was elected to the vestry. Eventually he left his high-paying job to become business manager of the church. This confirmed his decision to study for the priesthood, a career which pays a fraction of what he had been making in private industry.[74]

A 42-year old tax lawyer in Anchorage, Alaska, was earning a six-figure income, yet he was not happy. He gave it up to become a teacher in Harlem, New York City. According to *The New York Times*, he had grown weary of 80-hour work-weeks and the *"cynical view of human nature that tax law nurtured. . . There's a limit to the satisfaction one can earn making a lot of money. . . The world can get along without one more good tax lawyer. But there are a lot of kids out there who might not do so well without a good teacher."*[75]

▶ **How would you describe yourself?**

This may be the hardest part of your self-assessment.

▶ Ask family members or best friends to list your salient personality traits as they see you.

▶ Tape record a brief autobiography covering your childhood, adolescence, youth, and the present. Focus on the following categories of events in each developmental phase: Work, Friendships, School, Leisure activities.

▶ Look for traits that recur throughout each phase; e.g.,

→ *I'm a loner.*

→ *I like to do things with other people around.*

→ *I fly off the handle easily.*

→ *I'm moody.*

→ *I daydream a lot.*

Include traits that you consider less admirable. Even these can be job related. For example:

A person who is temperamental or easily irritated, is better off in a job which has little pressure; e.g., few deadlines, little contact with a demanding public.

Moody? Stay away from jobs which require you to smile a lot, to be gregarious on days when you're feeling rotten.

Daydreamer? Jobs which demand attention to detail and an analytic, logical mind — e.g., bookkeeper, computer programmer, accountant — may not be as fulfilling as jobs requiring imagination and creativity, such as advertising copywriter, graphic artist, illustrator, public relations.

Loner? Stay away from jobs which throw you into the thick of social interaction, jobs in sales, entertainment, management.

Are you an extrovert? Extroverts hate doing things by themselves. They love jobs involving much contact with people. Extroverts who also enjoy helping others are happiest in jobs such as teaching, nursing, customer service, personnel, marriage counselor, entertainer, actor.

Extroverts who are high achievers and enjoy competition make good sales representatives, sales managers, advertising executives, manufacturer's representatives, business executives, regional sales managers, stockbrokers and financial consultants. People in these and related occupations also tend to have much energy. They tend to be self-confident and they view rejection as a challenge to do better. They need freedom and autonomy in order to do their best.

Are you an introvert? Do you prefer to work alone? You would enjoy occupations such as engineer, writer, artist, researcher, and investigative work.

Do you work best under pressure? Do deadlines bring out the best in you? You'll thrive in sales, advertising, public relations, publishing, finance, and other high-pressure fields.

But if you tend to freeze as deadlines approach you're better off in a job that involves little pressure and stress such as a civil service job. You would suffer working as advertising copywriter, software developer or artist in the hectic environment of a small, high-tech company.

Are you curious? Open to change and novelty? You would thrive in research and investigative occupations; e.g., journalist, freelance writer, social worker, psychologist, scientist, private investigator. Many occupations in this cluster also appeal to persons who enjoy solving problems and working alone. They are self-disciplined individualists who don't like being told how to do things and within a specific time limit.

People who score low on "openness" show more interest in occupations such as farming, banking, funeral directing, printing, and other conventional occupations.

Do you have a lively imagination? Are you creative? Then, depending on your aptitudes, you would make a terrific artist, author or inventor. You would enjoy working in fields such as research, computer software development, television, public relations, advertising. Some of these fields also require a high degree of competitiveness, energy and ability to work well under pressure.

Are you a risk taker? This trait generally goes with creativity. You would do well in sales, running your own business, in positions that involve policy making and other kinds of work that involve risk-taking. Studies find that risk takers generally are happier, less lonely, calmer, better adjusted, more self-assured, optimistic and self-motivated than the average person.

Do you like to be in charge? Do you prefer to try out your own ideas, not knowing how they'll turn out? Do you persist in the face of obstacles? Then you would be happy in your own business or as an inventor, researcher, executive officer, teacher.

Do you thrive on order, discipline? Do you feel more secure following the rules? Do you like to plan things in detail before starting a project? Are you more comfortable knowing where you stand in the chain of command? If so, you're not cut out for a job in a high-tech or new-wave company. You would be happiest in a traditional organization where each person has his/her job duties clearly defined. You would be happy working as an accountant, bookkeeper or file clerk.

Aptitude tests and interest inventories

These increase your self-knowledge so you can make a better career choice. But they cannot predict whether you'll be successful or happy in any particular occupation. That's because intelligence, motivation, energy level and other personality-related aspects also play a part. A professional counselor is required to administer some. Others can be self-administered.

If the test results support your other qualifications for a job opening, be sure to tell the person who interviews you. People in personnel appreciate the significance of psychological tests. They often administer them to job applicants.

► Aptitude tests

These indicate what you can do, or learn to do, best. They can uncover abilities you never realized you had, abilities which you'll need in more than one occupation. While skills are mainly learned abilities, heredity plays a large role in determining aptitudes. There are many aptitudes including finger dexterity, musical, artistic, verbal reasoning, mathematical reasoning, mechanical, creative thinking and logical thinking.

Different occupations require different combinations of aptitudes. Teaching, for example, requires a high level of verbal reasoning, creative thinking and other aptitudes besides social skills and knowledge of the subject matter taught.

► Interest inventories

These are like questionnaires which help identify your interests. Knowing what type of work matches them helps you make a wiser career choice. People in the same occupation generally have interests which differ from people in other occupations. For example, a 325-item interest inventory was administered to several hundred successful lawyers who loved their work. The results showed a pattern of interests for 90% of them which differed significantly from the pattern of interests of real estate salespersons, engineers, social workers and people in other occupations. Similarly, nurses share interests that differ from those of successful real estate salespersons, engineers, computer programmers and accountants.

The Strong-Campbell Interest Inventory (SCII) is the most widely used. It must be administered and interpreted by a psychologist. It asks over 300 questions on whether you like or dislike various occupations, school subjects, activities, amusements, types of people, and other categories. It assesses the following patterns of interests.

▸ **Realistic:** Action-oriented pursuits, solving concrete problems rather than abstract ones, nature, operating machinery, reading popular mechanics magazines, mechanical, construction and repair activities, military activities. Matching occupations include carpenter, rancher, cartographer, mechanic.

▸ **Artistic:** Need for self-expression, interest in the theater, art galleries, poetry. Matching occupations include art museum director, author, reporter, librarian, photographer.

▸ **Investigative:** Interest in science, gathering and analyzing information and theories, activities involving self-reliance. Matching occupations include anthropologist, biologist and other sciences, geographer, mathematician.

▸ **Social:** Interested in working with people and sharing responsibilities, need for being the center of attention. Matching occupations include actor, teacher, nurse, playground director.

▸ **Enterprising:** Prefer leadership positions, working with people toward organizational goals, taking risks, competitive activities. Matching occupations include elected public official, life-insurance agent, personnel director, restaurant manager.

▸ **Conventional:** Prefers a subordinate role in a large organization, work that requires attention to detail and accuracy. Matching occupations include dental assistant, proofreader, secretary, statistician.

The following is a widely used self-administered inventory. It has served as a model for several others which are not mentioned here because of space constraints. You can find these in your local library or the college career counseling service. The library may also have a computerized self-assessment service which guides you in identifying your interests and matching occupations.

The Self-Directed Search Inventory by John Holland lists over 1,100 occupations each of which can be classified into one of six basic personality types.

▶ **Enterprising** persons tend to be ambitious, self-confident, domineering, energetic and impulsive. Matching occupations include sales, manager/executive, buyer, media producer.

▶ **Conventional** persons tend to be efficient, conforming, orderly, cautious and persistent. They prefer to carry out orders rather than create and delegate them. Occupations in this category include clerical, bank teller, secretary, tax analyst, banker, accountant.

▶ **Realistic** persons are practical, conforming and stable. They tend to have good physical coordination and enjoy working with their hands. They prefer working with things rather than with people or ideas. They tend to have weak verbal or social skills. Matching occupations include surveyor, skilled trades, technical jobs, farmer.

▶ **Investigative**: These people are generally creative, independent, introverted, curious, analytical and rational. They have weak leadership skills. They enjoy solving problems. They are happy in occupations which involve research and investigative interests such as market researcher, reporter, chemist, anthropologist, journalist, scientist.

▶ **Artistic** persons are imaginative, impulsive, non-conforming, emotional, original, creative and risk-taking. They prefer to work alone. They are happiest working as a writer, photographer, artist, interior decorator, composer.

▶ **Social**: These people are idealistic, persuasive, understanding, tactful, cheerful, cooperative and friendly. They prefer working in groups rather than with things or in solitary problem solving. Such paragons tend to work as clergymen, teachers, social workers, counselors, speech therapists.

Health and physical limitations

After narrowing down your list of occupations ask yourself whether you have any health or physical limitations for doing the work involved.

▸ **Your energy level** should match the demands of the job and the pace of the company. Some companies — those in high technology, finance, advertising, the media — are fast paced and have frequent deadlines. Will you be able to handle this?

▸ **Physical limitations** should also be taken into account. Does the job involve more walking, reading, standing, sitting, writing or talking than you can take?

Suppose you invest time and money studying computer programming and, after getting a job, you find that your eyes can't take staring into a lighted screen five or six hours a day. Having the right skills and interests won't do you much good. Data-entry operators are especially susceptible to eye strain. To add insult to injury, their work speed is often monitored by the computer. At some airlines they are expected to enter information at the rate of 9,000 to 16,000 keystrokes an hour. Some operators develop stress-related symptoms such as headaches, gastrointestinal pain, anxiety and chest pain.

▸ **Biorhythm**: When are you in peak form: morning, afternoon, early evening or after midnight? If your peak hours are not within the traditional 9-to-5 work schedule consider working for companies which operate on flextime schedules or have work-at-home assignments.

SKILLS AND KNOWLEDGE
YOU NEED TO UPDATE/LEARN

Millions of adults are going back to school so they can keep up with changes in their occupation or prepare for a new career. Colleges and universities have special workshops and courses to help them adjust to academic life and brush-up their study skills. Persons who earned a liberal arts degree years ago take business management courses to increase their chances of getting a good job. Executive secretaries who hope to increase their pay or climb the ladder take courses in office automation and management.

It's smart to look ahead and prepare for changes that will occur in your present occupation in the next three to five years.

Many artists, advertising illustrators, architects, interior decorators and draftsmen, for example, are taking courses that prepare them to work with computers, graphics software, laser printers, scanners and other innovations. Managers who know that "artificial intelligence" and management software will soon be doing much of their heavy problem solving are taking computer courses so they'll have a head start over the competition.

There are several ways to keep up-to-date or prepare for a new career. If you have a full-time day job or live far from the nearest college or school you can shorten the time needed to acquire the expertise by combining several of these.

▶ Home study or correspondence courses.

▶ Courses taken by computer, television, radio.

▶ Brief classroom courses that last one day, one weekend, or one evening. These include non-credit courses designed to introduce basic concepts such as *Understanding Computers* or teach a specific skill such as word processing or working with spreadsheet software.

▶ Certificate programs of study are short, intensive programs for people who already have, or don't want, a degree. Depending on the subject area, the programs range from four to ten courses and may require 50 to 200 hours to complete. The certificate shows proficiency in a specific skill or area of knowledge like international trade, training and development, health care management, computer management. A certificate in paralegal studies can be earned in six months by daytime or evening study at many colleges.

Some colleges also have brief, intensive programs for homemakers who are re-entering the workforce and for liberal arts graduates who need specific business or professional skills in order to get a good paying job. Hofstra University, for example, offers *Computer Science Career Retraining*, a 1-year program for persons who have a college degree and need computer skills or want to get into this field. Harvard's Graduate School of Education has a one-year, mid-career math and science teacher training program. It seeks women who earned math or science degrees many years ago.

If you can't afford the tuition, there are sources of scholarships, loans, grants, and free tuition; e.g., employer-paid courses, fraternal organizations, ethnic associations, unions. These offer financial help to students of all ages. In areas recently devastated by unemployment, community colleges were offering tuition-free job retraining courses.

Depending on your particular circumstances, you may not need to go back to school. There are other ways to keep up-to-date:
► Read all you can in your field — professional or trade journals, business magazines, newspapers.
► Join your trade or professional association and attend meetings.
► Talk with professionals in your field.
► Visit Apprenticeship Information Centers. These are usually operated by your State's employment service. The Bureau of Apprenticeship and Training of the U.S. Department of Labor, state apprenticeship agencies, employers and unions also can provide more information about apprenticeship opportunities. (Many programs bar persons over a certain age.)

———∞∞✕∞∞———

CAREER COUNSELING SERVICES
What they can do for you
When you go to a professional career counselor you can expect a combination of the following:
● Several hours of interviews and psychological testing to assess your aptitudes, skills, interests, personality and intelligence.
● A list of compatible occupations to choose from.
● Advice on how to improve your resume.
● Practice interviews which may be videotaped so you can see your mistakes and correct them.
● Referrals to job training and education programs.
● There may also be a psychologist on staff to counsel you on personal and family problems resulting from unemployment.

Career counseling *does not* include job referrals. The main purpose of career counseling is to make you aware of your aptitudes, skills and interests, and teach you how to choose an occupation and find a job on your own. The wisest counselor and the best psychological tests can only suggest options for you to consider. You alone must make the final decision.

There can be no money-back, guaranteed method of assuring that you'll be successful and happy in a certain career. There are too many complex variables involved. A registered representative who was unhappy in his career, despite a six-figure income, underwent expensive, private career counseling. Test results suggested that he'd be happier as a lawyer. So he quit his job and enrolled in law school. Later on he discovered that he could not adjust to the lower standard of living his income as a lawyer provided.

Where to find career counseling services

There are non-profit counseling services and private, for-profit ones. You can find them through the following sources.

- Ask the career counseling officer at the local college or university for recommendations.
- Send a self-addressed, stamped envelope with a request for a free brochure which lists career services nationwide to: Catalyst, 250 Park Ave. South, New York, NY 10010.
- Contact the nearest Job Service office for information on how to apply for their free counseling services.

Non-profit services

There are many non-profit services which operate through the following community organizations. Some charge a fee based on ability to pay.

- Public libraries
- Young Men's/Women's Christian/Hebrew Associations
- Religious associations
- Adult education centers
- Special interest groups — women's centers, senior citizen agencies, ethnic associations.

▶ State and local governments

Many also provide for career counseling through public schools, the local Federal Job Service, vocational rehabilitation offices and veteran's affairs offices.

There also may be special programs for job hunters who are considered to be disadvantaged; i.e., displaced workers, the handicapped, senior citizens, women, minority group members, and people with a low income.

The services generally include several of the following: testing and career counseling, referrals to job training and education sources, and job referrals. They may be offered through group sessions, by mail and telephone, closed-circuit or cable television, or one-to-one counseling. They are either free or cost little. It depends on the type of services requested and the equipment and materials involved.

The North Dakota's Job Service, for example, offers a free two and one half hour battery of aptitudes and skills testing. A computer scores the results and selects matching occupations. After choosing an occupation, the client is referred to a state-sponsored Adult Learning Center for skills upgrading, if needed.

Washington's Employment Security Department has a similar program which also includes help in finding temporary jobs for clients who need income while preparing for a new career.

Missouri's Division of Employment Security has a computerized program which recently helped unemployed farmers find new jobs. The computers grade the aptitude tests and match applicants with available job openings. Job listings for up to 20,000 positions at any one time are in its database. Many farmers who had despaired of ever finding work again found jobs for which they did not know they were qualified.

► **Colleges and universities**

They have career guidance and placement offices which serve students and alumni. Some also offer their services to local residents for a fee. If your local college does not, ask them to recommend other accredited counseling services in the community. They may recommend a member of their own staff who has a local, private practice. This is one of the best ways to get good referrals.

Their adult education divisions also offer workshops, seminars and other programs for special groups of students such as career women, persons who would like to start a business, persons over forty, homemakers. The hours are convenient. The New School in New York City offers *The Sunday Career Center*, a program for working adults who are thinking of changing careers.

Two-year colleges also offer workshops, special courses, career counseling and job placement services. Some offer the services to registered students only. Others open their doors to all residents of the community. The Adult Career and Education Counseling

Center of Duchess Community College in New York, for example, offers its services to workers age forty-plus who are changing careers and to homemakers who plan to re-enter the job market.

Private career counseling services

These usually require you to sign a contract. Ask for a copy to study at home before you do sign. If there is anything you don't understand or not fully described, ask for clarification IN WRITING! Don't sign anything until you have complete information on all the services you'll receive, the length of time these are provided, and the cost.

Look in the current edition of *The Directory of Counseling Services*. It lists accredited members of the International Association of Counseling Services. Then write for the brochures and fee schedules of several private counseling services and compare them. Make an appointment to speak with a counselor in those which look interesting.

Find out the following:

▸ Training and experience of the counselors and whether they belong to a professional association. Members of a professional association are more likely to be up-to-date in their field.

▸ Do they administer psychological tests?

▸ Are the counselors licensed? In some states only licensed counselors are permitted to administer certain psychological tests.

▸ Do they provide psychological counseling for emotional or family problems resulting from unemployment? Only an accredited psychologist or social worker should provide this service.

▸ How much do they charge per session and how many sessions will it take to complete the counseling? Get the time estimate and cost in writing.

▸ Get a detailed list of all the costs involved or you might discover, too late, that several hundred dollars were added to your bill because you asked for the counselor's opinion of your resume.

▸ Will they accept phone calls after counseling to answer any questions you may have while you job hunt? Is there an extra charge for this?

▸ Find out if complaints were filed against the agency. Contact the Better Business Bureau, the Consumer Affairs Department of your city or county, or the State Attorney General's office.

▸ If you plan to enroll in a course or workshop on career changing find out the size of the group. If it's too large you won't get the personal attention you may need.

CAUTION!

▸ The advice you get should not be based solely on tests results. You should also be interviewed on your career goals, work experience and interests.

▸ Reputable counselors will not make a career choice for you. They should give you a list of occupations which match your particular combination of interests and abilities and leave it up to you to make a choice.

▸ Be skeptical of ads that are filled with extravagant promises such as guarantees to find you a high-paying job within a few weeks, contacts with top-level recruiters, a much higher salary than the one you have now. Don't be fooled by promises of guaranteed results or your money back.

▸ Be wary of job placement and resume writing services that also offer career counseling. Career counseling is a profession which requires post-graduate education, the passing of academic proficiency tests, and internship.

▸ If you live in a state which does not license career counselors, check the counselor's training and experience thoroughly. *"In states that don't have licensure regulations, a plumber can call himself a counselor,"* said a librarian for the American Association for Counseling and Development.[76] Check with the Better Business Bureau or the Consumer Protection Agency. For a list of accredited services in your region send a stamped, self-addressed envelope to the International Association of Counseling Services which sets ethical and professional standards — 5999 Stevenson Ave., Alexandria,VA 22304. You may also be able to find its publication, *The Directory of Counseling Services*, in your library or school career counseling office.

FEES charged by private counseling services can range from hundreds to thousands of dollars. They vary widely according to location and the counselor's credentials. The size of the fee doesn't always reflect the quality of service provided. Several years ago consumer complaints were filed against several New York agencies which charged as much as $8,000. College/university counseling centers charge less and the service provided is generally top-quality.

Facts You Will Need

If you want to avoid landing in the wrong job, the wrong company or, worse yet, on an unemployment line again you need some important facts. These facts will also prepare you for the interviewer's questions: *"Why do you want to work for our company?"* *"Why do you want this job?"* Many applicants strike out by giving a vague, uninformed answer: *"It's an interesting job,"* or *"I need the job,"* or *"I like working with people."*

You are more likely to succeed if you know more about the following.
- **Your occupation:** how it has changed; new requirements
- **The company:** products, services, the person at its helm
- **The company's work culture:** values, standards of behavior and job performance, management style
- **The buzzwords**, language of the occupation and industry.

FACTS ABOUT YOUR OCCUPATION
Changes in the occupation and its requirements
Most occupations have already been influenced by changes in technology and management style. Before you go on job interviews find out whether you have the training, skills and personality traits required by these changes. This is especially important if you've been out of the labor market for some time.

Conditions likely to affect its future
Foreign competition and industry-wide economic conditions can reduce or increase career opportunities for you. It's important to

know if an industry is fast- or slow-growing or in decline. The company you are interested in may be planning to relocate. It may start sending sales, managerial and other high-level personnel overseas for a while.

Current need for workers

An occupation which has dismal prospects in one industry may have plenty of openings in another. During the recent recession thriving industries — e.g., health, insurance, high-technology and finance — had many openings for office workers, salespersons and engineers while others — i.e., oil, automobile and steel — were dismissing thousands.

Geographic location also plays a part. An industry which is doing poorly in your part of the country may be booming elsewhere.

Even companies within an industry vary in their need for someone with your qualifications. One company may be expanding while another may be on the rocks. The Fortune 500 company you set your sights on may have a hiring freeze while several smaller companies may be eager to hire you.

Opportunities for advancement

The typical career path may have changed in your occupation. In 1979 the fastest route to a top management position was a staff job in finance and accounting. By 1986 it was in marketing, research, and sales.[77] It's important to know where the next job leads. Is it a line job that can take you places or a support job that will keep you in a rut?

Typical working conditions

How much stress does the occupation and its work setting create? The high-technology era theoretically makes life easier for all workers. Yet some insurers have added job stress to the list of compensable injuries. Excessive stress is also caused by non-occupational aspects such as the following:

- A neurotic or overly ambitious boss.
- Work schedule: Shift work can be particularly harmful.
- Insufficient time out for lunch and other breaks.
- Time spent in commuting; quality of transportation.

The latest buzz words

Employers view older applicants and those who have been out of the job market for several years as being out of touch with the latest developments. This view also applies to anyone who is changing occupations or industries. You can appear up-to-date by learning the latest buzz words in your occupation and industry. Use them, wherever appropriate, in your cover letters, resume and at interviews. Be careful not to overdo it or the recruiter may think you're overqualified or "too smart" for the job.

Even if you're not looking for a managerial, technical or professional job, the judicious use of saavy terminology such as the following will make you appear up-to-date.

- **Bottom line:** refers to dollars and cents
- **On-line:** computer-to-computer communication
- **Software/hardware:** computer essentials, not household utilities
- **Central processing unit:** the brains of the computer, not a company department
- **Quality circles:** a management method, not a geometric figure
- **High technology:** modern office and factory equipment, not aircraft
- **Fax:** not "facts"
- **Scanner:** a high-tech machine, not a worker

A good way to learn the latest buzz words is to read the help-wanted ads. Another is to join a trade or professional association and attend gatherings, talk with professionals in the field, and read its newsletter. Before long you'll be talking like a pro.

FACTS ABOUT THE COMPANY AND INDUSTRY

The main thrust of your research should be to find out:
- Which companies have the best job prospects.
- How the companies compare.
- Whether there are or will soon be new developments that influence the company's future and your job prospects — i.e., merger, reorganization, new technology, new products, new acquisitions, foreign competition.

Products/services

One way to shine at a job interview is to learn about the company's products or services. Too few job applicants bother to find out. It's clear all they are interested in is a paycheck, not their career and not their future with the company.

The work culture

Organizations have "personality" just as you do. They vary in their goals and style of achieving them, in their decision making methods, pace of innovation and change, and code of behavior.

Some aspects of an organization's culture are easier to observe than others — e.g., dress code, job titles, who reports to whom. You can discover these from simple observation, employee manuals, bulletin board notices and organization charts.

Other aspects of an organization's culture, such as its basic philosophy, values, codes of behavior, are more difficult to detect. This is because these aspects are often less clearly defined and communicated by top management. Dismissed employees discover, after it's too late, that the boss dislikes smokers, or miniskirts, or frowns upon secretaries who date their bosses, or that individualists are less highly regarded than workers who blindly follow orders.

Often a new employee has to learn these via the grapevine or by example. In the traditional, hierarchical organization it's clear who is expected to do what and with whom, who reports to whom, and what the codes of behavior are. But often, in the emerging modern organization such standards are less obvious because its culture is still in a formative stage and many positions are in flux.

▶ **Find clues to these "softer" aspects of a company's culture through the following.**

The organization chart also gives strong clues to the hidden aspects of a company's culture. The pyramid depicts the traditional bureaucratic organization. It has a small apex of decision makers and top management, a wider, middle band of mid-level managers, and a broad, bottom band of workers who carry out orders. A flatter pyramid or a circle (or a constellation of circles) depicts the modern organization. Workers have more responsibility for handling and managing their own jobs and greater scope for expressing their ideas.

Written management policies often contain statements regarding proper relationships between co-workers and between different levels of employees.

Statements on corporate goals and philosophy are reported in newspapers, annual reports, and company gatherings.

Type of person at the helm often reflects an organization's culture and even helps mold it. Lee Iaccocca's aggressive, dynamic personality gives strong clues to the type of culture Chrysler Corporation prefers. If you learn something about the head of a company you can guess the kind of people they prefer to hire and who gets ahead. You can learn this from reading the leader's public statements, his published biography (if any exists), and magazine and newspaper articles about the company and its chief.

Annual reports: Companies that are proud of the way they treat their employees tend to brag about this aspect of their culture. Indicators include the following:

► Phrases such as *"fairness/respect for every employee."*

► Signatures of employees throughout the report.

► Comments by lower-level employees.

► Photographs of smiling employees.

► Photographs of top officers that are about the same size as those of "any other"employees: This is also a clue to the company's focus on teamwork.[78]

► Pictures showing how top officers dress and their accompanying statements suggest the type of culture they wish to promote. The annual report of First Hawaiian Inc.'s had photographs of its top officers wearing colorful Hawaiian shirts. It quoted a vice-president: *"We dress like this all year long. We're not stuffy bankers."*[79]

Manager's guide: If you compare the guides of several companies the fuzzy concept of "work culture" or "corporate culture" will become clearer — e.g., Federal Express's guide has a chapter titled "Change" which discusses the priority placed on adaptability and creativity throughout the company.

Employee manual: Look at the section on job performance reviews. What are the criteria for determining good and poor performance? Also read the company's job description for your occupation. Does it refer to team work, flexibility, creativity or other criteria?

At the interview: If you keep your eyes and ears open you'll find clues to the work culture from the following.

▸ The direct questions they ask you.

▸ The gist of indirect questions asked and comments made during the interview: The head of a midwestern company asks questions and makes comments that obviously reflect his interest in applicants who believe in *"traditional Middle American values, people who care about their families and neighbors, people who take pride in their work."*

▸ Does the "corporate uniform" (business suit) predominate? Notice especially how top-level employees dress. In some small, high-tech companies they, also, wear hardhats and overalls or blue jeans and sneakers.

▸ Notice how different levels of employees relate to each other. Do they appear relaxed or formal? Do they call each other by first names or by "Mr." or "Ms.' and other titles? Does the interviewer refer to employees below management level by their titles or as "associates?"

▸ Ask whether workers at all levels share in the profits made by productivity improvements.

The industry it's in: Generally companies in the new, high--growth industries — i.e., computer, information processing, biotechnology and communication — have many characteristics of the new work culture. So do companies involved with creative output, such as advertising, public relations and the media. Hierarchical, or bureaucratic, companies tend to be in the tradition-al industries — i.e., steel, textile, finance, durable goods manufac-turing, transportation and government.

As in all generalizations there is the danger of creating stereotypes which can lead a job hunter astray. An increasing number of companies in traditional industries are overhauling their organiza-tion and culture so they can better utilize modern technology and get more commitment from their workers.

► **Reputation**

How are dismissed workers treated? Has the company cut back its work force in the past few years? If so, were the dismissed employees treated fairly?

► Were they given adequate notice? Or were they told on Friday, *"Don't bother to come in on Monday?"*

► Did they get the notice just before the Christmas bonus or before they were about to retire on a pension?

► Were they given continued health insurance for a reasonable period of time after dismissal?

► Were they given career counseling to help them find other jobs? (Small companies can't afford this.)

► Were excess employees transferred to other positions within the company? Or, were they referred to other companies that had openings?

► Were they given severance pay they could live on while looking for another job?

Some companies have a reputation for dismissing good employees only as a last resort. They prefer hiring freezes, temporary salary reductions, early retirement incentives, putting full-time workers in part-time jobs till things get settled, and retraining them for new jobs.

While thousands of other steel workers were losing their jobs in the early 1980s Worthington, Inc. shifted its production workers to maintenance and construction tasks. Steelcase, Inc. has had only three brief layoffs in its 74-year history. Less than 1% of its workers quit or are fired annually.[80] When Motorola decided to overhaul its culture, it did not order massive layoffs and plant closings. Instead it began an education program to teach new skills to employees at all levels.[81]

Do they hire and promote without discrimination? How many higher-level employees are women or men over fifty-five? Is there a fair mix of age categories throughout the organization? Is the work environment suitable or unsuitable for older workers? (Is it fast-paced, with many deadlines? Does it have jobs with low physical demands? Has the company redesigned jobs or the work setting so older employees can work comfortably?)

► **Key persons**

Who's who in the organization? You can find this information from sources listed in below and in Appendix E. Be sure to get the correct spelling of their names and their correct titles.

Who will interview you? Find out who heads the personnel department. In some organizations it is known as the Human Resources Department. Also find out who heads the department with the job opening. For jobs requiring much responsibility you may be interviewed first by someone in the personnel department, then by others up the chain of command.

It helps to know more about the person(s) than name and title. Psychological studies show that interviewers give higher ratings to applicants who share similar:

● Interests: (You both prefer the Mets, love deep sea fishing.)

● Values: (as shown by the employer who prefers to hire people with "mid-western American values.")

● Backgrounds: (You have the same ethnic or religious background. You both grew up in same community or graduated from the same school.)

► **Where to find this information**

► If it's a well-known organization you can get some of this information from one of the business reference guides listed in Appendix E.

► If it's a major organization, read their published biographies and articles about them in magazines and the business section of national newspapers. Look up their names in the indexes of these publications to save time.

► If it's a local organization read reports about them in the local newspapers.

► Ask people in your network (see chapter seven) who have worked there or can refer you to persons who know.

► **Developments likely to influence its future**

Which industries are thriving?

Focus your job hunting efforts there. If you want a job as secretary, computer programmer, word processor, receptionist, public relations expert or other type of work, companies in expanding industries have more openings.

How much turnover is there?
A high turnover does not necessarily mean bad news. It may be because of aspects that have little to do with its long-term future. Some industries — as in public relations, advertising, entertainment, high-technology — are like revolving doors, with people coming and going. A company or industry may be streamlining and becoming more efficient or it may be declining and laying off workers permanently.

What are the specific areas of growth?
Companies that lay off excess mid-level managers or white collar workers may be hiring people skilled in new technology or new products and services.

Which companies are hiring and why? Is it because they are expanding? Or are they replacing some workers? Are they substituting temporary workers for permanent employees?

Is it about to change leaders? A new chief executive will have an effect on your future with the company. Is the change the result of a normal transfer of leadership? Is it because the company plans to overhaul its culture? Or is it an attempt to rescue a failing company?

If you had accepted a sales position at AT&T recently, just before a new chief executive was appointed, with an eye on a management job soon, your hopes would have been dashed. The new CEO began a massive reorganization which permanently eliminated thousands of mid-level management jobs. If you had done some research before applying for the job, you would have seen news articles which forecast AT&T's new direction.

Ominous signs
The following indicators may or may not be ominous. Find out what's behind them. A sign might point to a declining industry or occupation. Or it might be a temporary condition resulting from a reorganization that will lead to better job prospects.

Are companies in the industry moving operations overseas?
If so, how will it affect your occupation? Thousands of workers lost their jobs when the shoe, textile, computer and other manufac-

turing industries moved operations to countries with a cheaper labor force.

Is there a high worker turnover? If so, is it happening across the board or only in certain occupations or certain divisions of a company or industry? This may or may not be bad news. It might be because of an effort to streamline and improve operations. In 1987 Honeywell-Bull Inc. announced a 10% reduction of its American work force. It also planned to add 200-300 new, important positions.

Has the job loss continued for several years? This could be the death rattle of an industry, company or occupation. In New York City recently many lowerlevel, white collar jobs were permanent lost because of massive computerization. Typists, file clerks, mail room clerks, even secretaries who lacked computer skills, had slim job prospects.

Have profits been declining for several years? This is bad news. See below.

Positive signs
Is the industry or company as a whole growing? If so, is it a temporary growth period or part of a long-range trend? If an expansion does not result in more openings in your particular occupation, there may be openings in new ones for which you might qualify. (While companies in Wall Street were eliminating old-type clerical jobs, they were hiring professionals for new technical positions and office workers who know how to work with computers.)

► *Opportunities/barriers to advancement*
► Which departments and positions are important to the company's profitability? Which would be the first to go in bad times?

► Do you see several promotion positions beyond your current job title on the organization chart? Which positions will move you up the ladder fastest?

► What are the criteria for identifying superior job performance which leads to promotions?

▶ Does the company have a policy of promoting from within or does it prefer to look for talent outside? Help wanted ads often give clues to whether a company nurtures its own talent. *"Paid tuition and in-house development"* are key phrases. In some companies the top people are from the same state, or they are graduates of the same university, or members of the same ethnic or religious group.

▶ Is the person who now has the position you want near retirement age? Is that person a baby boomer who will probably be there a long time?

▶ Does the company have too few positions at the mid-management level and too many eager beavers who, like you, are aiming for such a position?

▶ Fast- and slow-track companies/industries: Your chances of moving up are greater in a small, fast-growing company and in a high-growth industry such as child-care, hotel, travel, biotechnology.

▶ The company's size
Job opportunities

Most new jobs are created by small companies, not by large corporations.[82] A 1988 study of an area of Pennsylvania which was hit hard by a recession[83] found that:

▶ The greatest number of new jobs came from companies that were more than five years old, had 100 employees or less, and were independently owned.[84]

▶ Larger companies were more likely to pull out of a troubled area or a difficult business climate. Small companies generally stuck it out until conditions improved.

▶ New jobs come from high growth, new companies and old ones that are "re-inventing themselves" and creating jobs in the process.

Dismissed older managers are more likely to find a challenging new job, often with better pay, in a small company that needs their experience and skills. Foundations are another good source of jobs because they, also, cannot afford to pay high salaries.

Some employment agencies specialize in finding jobs for retired and dismissed older managers in small companies and in foundations. One agency has filled openings such as chief financial officer for a small subsidiary of a large company, real estate manager for rental units owned by a family company, fund-raiser for a nonprofit organization, manager of a small foundation, and public relations officer for a Chicago office. The salaries in 1986 ranged from $30,000 to $50,000 a year.[85]

Company size and job security
Because of the recent shakeup among large companies, many workers believe there is more job security in a smaller firm.[86]

Company size and job training and advancement
A survey by *INC* magazine found that professional employees — i.e., computer programmers, lawyers, accountants, marketing specialists and others — in smaller companies complained about training and advancement opportunities.[87] Hourly workers said they did not find the jobs as enriching as they had hoped.

This is puzzling. There is so much more overlap in job responsibilities in a small company that an enterprising employee can find plenty of opportunities to learn and practice new skills. And as the business grows, so can his/her career.[88]

However, it is true that small companies are less likely to invest in formal training. This is because they know that the investment will be lost when the trained worker leaves for a better paying job in a large firm. Such aspects make the experienced, mature applicant a more attractive applicant.

Company size and employee satisfaction
Smaller companies are often much better to work for according to the authors of *The 100 Best Companies to Work for in America*.[89] The *INC* survey reaches a similar conclusion. More upper-level employees in the small, high-growth companies than in large companies reported challenging and interesting work, a chance to have their ideas adopted, and a sense of accomplishment. Many also said they were treated with more respect. Hourly workers, however, reported less of these advantages.

Other studies find that employees of small companies generally have higher and more varied responsibilities. They don't have as much red tape. Small companies also tend to be more exciting places to work in because they're more innovative than large ones.

──◆─◆─◆─◆─◆─◆─◆──

"Generally, the harder you work, the luckier you become. "
— Karl H. Vesper

Company size and pay, benefits and perks
Small private companies and non-profit organizations are eager to hire older workers, especially dismissed older managers and executives. This is because their lower pay level makes it difficult to attract younger, top-notch people. Small companies often can't afford pension or other deferred-compensation programs either. They generally compensate by offering stock options, flexible work hours, work-at-home, parental leaves and shared jobs. The non-profit organizations tend to offer more job security as compensation.[90]

In recent years the pay in non-profit organizations has increased significantly. Generally, the ones in urban areas offer the best pay. A 1988 survey of organizations in the Washington, DC area found that entry-level "program assistants" (whose responsibilities range from clerical work to editing newsletters) received an average of $22,600. Executive directors earned an average of $112,501. Job openings in these organizations are listed in their newsletters which your local library probably has on file. You can also write to the nonprofit organizations that are listed in Gale's *Encyclopedia of Associations*.

► *Family-run companies*
Advantages/disadvantages of working for one
Family-owned companies are said to be more humane employers, and their workers have more job security.[91] Tn order to keep top-notch managers and executives from leaving, some of these companies pay above-average salaries.

One expert says the owner is generally *"a strong-willed person who typically rules with an iron fist."*[92] Moreover, non-related employees see little chance of reaching the top. However, the more progressive family-owned companies recognize the need for hiring and promoting top-notch people for the better positions. Furthermore, the chances that non-related staff employees will reach management ranks increase by the third generation. Only 17% of such companies are still family-run by then.[93] Another potential problem is family feuds. These have destroyed several prominent family-owned companies, most recently the Bingham chain of newspapers and the Sebastiani winery. Another dangerous time is when leadership passes from the founder to a son or daughter. About 60% go bankrupt, or they are sold, or rent by rivalries.

How to get information on a family business
Study the company's annual reports for the past several years. Is most of the stock family owned? Look at the names on the list of board of directors. Do the top level persons have the same surname?

Another clue occurs when a company changes its top leaders or promotes someone to a high position. You'll find this information in the business section of newspapers and in business magazines. You'll probably have to look back several years to see who has succeeded whom. If the person promoted to the position you would like to have is mentioned as a son or nephew or has the same surname, then you'll know.

▶ **Companies that have policies favorable to older workers**
Many companies have a policy of hiring older workers and retirees, particularly for part-time or temporary full-time jobs. More of them will as the labor shortage worsens. One of these is Texas Refinery Corporation in Fort Worth, TX. About 88 of the firm's 790 salespeople hired in 1982 were over 60, and 18 of these were over 70. President Wesley D. Sears, who was 67 when he was interviewed for an article in *Modern Maturity*, said, *"Our older salespeople are more disciplined, more self-motivated, and follow instructions better than younger workers. They have enough experience to realize they don't know everything and are more productive as a result."* As proof he named Al Cornelius, 76, who averaged over $60,000 in earnings per year over the previous six years and Allen Shepherd, 69, who led his division in sales in 1982.[94]

Many large company training programs discriminate against older employees, but at Grumman Aerospace workers can enroll regardless of age. In 1985, nearly 60% of its workers who were in a retraining program to develop systems engineers were over forty. Moreover, older part-time employees who work less than 20 hours a week, or 1,000 hours per year, continue to receive monthly pension benefits.

Travelers Insurance Corporation of Hartford is also renowned for its older worker policies. The benefits older employees have include a retraining program, a retiree job bank which supplies many of its temporary and part-time workers, flexible work hours, including job sharing, and a pension policy which allows retirees to work nearly half-time without loss of retirement income.[95]

≪≫✕✕≫≪≫

WHAT YOU SHOULD KNOW BEFORE YOU ACCEPT A JOB OFFER

Local salary range

▶ Read the help-wanted ads in the local newspaper for the type of job you want in order to get an idea of what local employers pay.

▶ Read salary surveys by the Bureau of Labor Statistics and other organizations.

▶ Look in *The American Almanac of Jobs and Salaries* by John W. Wright (Avon Books). It includes job descriptions, salary ranges and opportunities for advancement.

If you have this information **before you start looking for a job** you will not give an outrageous figure when a helpwanted ad says, *"send salary requirement."* Before you say "Yes" to a job offer you'll be able to tell whether the salary is fair.

Standard benefits and perks

▶ Find out whether a company offers one or more of the following and who gets them: pension, medical and dental insurance, paid tuition, job training, flexible work hours, work-at-home jobs, profit sharing, stock options, child care, elder care (for employees who have elderly parents to care for).

▶ Find out what the standard benefits are in the industry. Compare it with the local standard. What are companies in your community offering for the same type of work? (Generally companies that are new or small cannot afford costly benefits and perks. To attract good people they generally offer other compensations such as flexible work hours and work-at-home jobs.)

▶ Rely on your network of contacts who can get this information for you. Scan the help-wanted ads placed by the company and by others in the same industry. Contact the company's public relations or personnel department for this information. Ask questions at the interview.

Commuting

Find out how long it will take to get to a new job and what the transportation facilities are like. Many employers reject job applicants who live beyond a reasonable commuting distance. Such workers generally have poor attendance and low productivity since they're always on the lookout for a more conveniently located job.

HOW TO FIND THE FACTS YOU NEED

A good plan helps you find exactly what you need and no more. Without one you will be buried under a mountain of useless data. It also organizes the information so you can find it right away.

Keep a file of articles from newspapers, magazines and other sources on industries, occupations, and companies that interest you. Read clippings from the file before you go to a job interview, make phone calls, and write a cover letter so you'll know what to say and no more. Employers hate wasting their time more than you do.

When you go to the library take along some index cards or a looseleaf notebook with dividers. Arrange it according to relevant topics. As you come across important facts jot them down under the appropriate topic. This way you'll be able to find what you need quickly. If you have a notebook computer your work will be that much simpler and faster.

NOTE: Don't be overwhelmed by all the topics suggested in this chapter. Not every one is relevant to your particular needs.

Too busy? Hire a clipping service. They will search through computer databases, newspapers, and business, financial and trade journals. They will also scan through help-wanted ads and articles mentioning the name of an employer or occupation. They'll scan out-of-town newspapers for job vacancies, companies, living costs and anything else you need. They can uncover news about a factory expansion, a technological change that might affect your occupation, an impending merger or a reorganization that could influence your chances of finding work. The public library has reference books which list these services.

YOUR PUBLIC LIBRARY

What it can do for you

The library reference department has information on any topic that interests you. It also provides the following services for free or at a reasonable charge.

► A telephone service to find answers to your questions. If you ask for the estimated growth in petroleum engineering jobs in your state within the next five years, or the average cost of living in San Francisco, they will look it up while you wait.

► If they can't find the information they will tell you where you can get it.

► They have a complete list of magazines, journals and other periodicals on specialized topics. There are thousands. Some advertise job vacancies and many have the names and addresses of employers you can contact.

► They also maintain a file of annual reports, past and present, of major corporations and local businesses. The Business and Industry section of your public library is a gold mine of information for job hunters.

► Whatever they don't have they might be able to get through an inter-library loan.

How to find what you need

► **Catalogs and subject indexes**

These are in the reference department.

SUBJECT INDEXES are bound volumes which index articles found in newspapers, magazines and journals. You can look up any topic, no matter how specific, and see which publications have carried articles on it. Indices that are especially useful to job hunters include the *Business Periodical Index* which lists business related publications such as *Human Resource Management, Journal of Marketing, Telecommunications,* and more.

The CARD CATALOG indexes books and periodicals by title and by general and specific topics. You can find the titles of books and periodicals on topics such as Industries and Occupations, Employers, Career Change, Job Interviewing, and Resume Writing.

► **Reference guides and directories**

These have information on employers, occupations, industries, labor market indices, and other helpful topics. Super-directories list all the directories published on every topic of interest. Look here first if you don't know what's available. There are directories of associations, government agencies, private industry employers, industries, publications, and more. The following are especially helpful to job seekers:

- Yellow Pages and out-of-town telephone books
- Private industry directories give brief descriptions of each company's major activities, the names, addresses and phone numbers of top officers, and its divisions and departments.
- Job guides to American corporations
- Directories of trade associations, professional associations, and government agencies.

▶ *Education and job information centers*
These centers have just about everything you need to know about the job market, occupations, self-assessment procedures, education and training, and how to find a job. EJICs can be found in many public libraries. If your library branch doesn't have this service ask for a list of other education and job counseling services for adults in or near your locality.

An EJIC in a New Jersey library helped an immigrant who had a master's degree in business administration find a job in international marketing. They helped him with his resume, provided him with corporate journals, and told him how to contact appropriate employers. A housewife returning to the job market after many years received advice on where to get free computer training and how to apply for civil service tests for word processing jobs with government agencies. A blind woman learned how to apply for a home study degree program at Empire State College. After earning a college degree she received help in starting a new career in human services.

Every state has public library systems with an EJIC where job hunters can get the following information and receive the following professional services.
▶ Notices of job vacancies (local, out-of-state, and overseas): civil service job announcements, national, local and out-of-town newspapers, job newsletters such as *Federal Jobs, Federal Research Service* and *Federal Times.*
▶ A computerized job bank.
▶ Help with resumes and interview techniques.

▸ Career counseling and test administration.

▸ Referrals to appropriate services for testing and counseling.

▸ Books on career changing and a variety of occupations. Some of these also include self-administered tests on interests and skills evaluation.

▸ Information on education and job training resources. In some centers, specially trained librarians help job hunters choose the most suitable educational programs. There is also plenty of printed information — e.g., catalogs and other literature from vocational schools, colleges, home study programs and other educational resources. Information is also available on how to get financial aid.

▸ Prior civil service examinations for study and practice.

SPECIFIC INFORMATION SOURCES

Want to learn what's going on in various industries and in your occupation? Make it a habit to skim the headlines of journals, news magazines and the business pages of newspapers. Soon you'll be able to understand important trends and events which can influence your career. Attend professional and industry/trade conferences or send for their taped or printed proceedings. Read the profiles of companies in reference books such as *Standard & Poor's Register of Corporations*. See Appendix E for a sample of helpful employer directories and guides.

Many published sources of career information, including the ones mentioned in this book, can be purchased in bookstores and by mail. They are also available in school guidance and placement offices and in state employment offices.

Information on occupations

Look through the following publications by the Federal and State Labor Bureaus. Other publications are listed in Appendix B.

▸ *The Occupational Outlook Handbook* describes in detail hundreds of occupations: job responsibilities, skills required, training and education requirements, salary range, opportunities for advancement, where openings are in greatest supply, where to get more information. It also gives the addresses and phone numbers of organizations to contact for more information on a specific career — professional societies, trade associations, labor unions, government agencies, private corporations and education institutions

98

which offer the required training and knowledge.

▸ *The Occupational Outlook Quarterly* describes new occupations — training requirements, salary range, long-term job prospects. It also tells how to choose an occupation that is appropriate for you and how to find a job.

▸ Also look at issues of the *Monthly Labor Review* for current information on salaries, benefits and other items. The March 1987 issue had an article which listed the average salary for workers in 26 occupations and 93 work levels.

State employment agencies also issue reports on the current and projected employment by occupation and industry within the state.

Employers and industries
For information on **a private company** contact the state and local governments where it has operations. For information on **small, private companies in your area** go to the public library. It collects information about local business and industry. You can also contact a company directly and ask for copies of its product and sales literature, annual reports and newsletter.

Trade and business journals
The Wall Street Transcript, for example, reports on a company's plan to introduce a new product or to expand. It contains speeches given by corporate leaders, assessments by stock brokerage firms of listed companies, and more. The public library may have a subscription. If it does not, the business school library of a local college or university probably has one.

Business and news magazines, business pages of newspapers
Newspapers have the most current information on the national job market and industry trends. Weekly or monthly business and news magazines discuss important events and trends in greater depth. Periodicals that will probably be most useful to you include *Business Week, Newsweek, U.S. News & World Report, Time, Fortune, MONEY* and *Forbes.*

Computerized databases

You can get industry news almost as soon as it happens from computerized databases which are listed in Appendix E. There also are several computer data bases that cover the activities of public companies. These business databases can be found in many central public libraries. It costs little or nothing at all to browse through them.

Employee manual

All large companies and many smaller ones have an employee manual which contains one or more of the following items of information.

► Issues that affect employees — e.g., job performance and salary reviews, paid holidays, benefits program, leaves of absence, dress code and other company regulations, policy regarding rehiring former employees, procedures for filing employee grievances, procedure for reading one's personnel file.

► A discussion of (or clues to) the company's culture.

► An overview of the company's organization and activities — - divisions and branches; names, addresses and phone numbers of officers and department heads; services or products; various job titles within the company including the required education, training and skills.

Annual reports

Many companies publish annual reports on their products or services, financial condition, and their divisions, branches and subsidiaries. They may also contain clues to the work culture. The reports usually come out in early spring.

The main purpose of the annual report is to describe the company's activities, earnings and losses, and future plans. Because it also aims to boost stockholder's confidence in the company, it generally focuses on the bright side of things and camouflages negative developments. Usually you must read between the lines and focus on the fine print to find negative information.

As a result, some annual reports are like billboard ads. It's important not to be swayed by their surface appearance. A company which has miserable profit margins may issue a report which is full of flash and hyperbole in order to give the impression of a successful year. Serious problems are often camouflaged by euphemisms. Essex Chemical Corporation's 1987 report had on the front cover, *"Our . . . foresight and determination to believe in a future with spectacular possibilities and be a part of it.*" The following year it was taken over by Dow Chemical, and many long-time employees were out of work. A report by Comsat Corporation contained a letter from its chairman which gave the impression that its telecommunications services was booming. Not until the 22nd paragraph of the 25-paragraph letter did shareholders learn that their company suffered a $47.3 million loss in the prior year.[96]

WHAT TO LOOK FOR:
- Names and titles of officers, addresses of corporate offices.
- Whether it's a family owned or operated company.
- Future plans for the company.
- Results of research and development projects.
- What went wrong in the previous year.
- The company's basic philosophy and goals.
- Red light signals such as a major lawsuit brought against the company.
- Its financial condition.

FOR INDICATORS OF FUTURE JOB OPENINGS study the 5-year summaries. If sales and profits have been rising each year it's a sign the company is healthy and job opportunities are generally bright.[97] If they have been declining or if the company has gone from a profit to a loss it's a sign that belt-tightening measures will be taken. Also read the company's future outlook for mention of new marketing programs, new products, major capital projects, a new subsidiary.

NEGATIVE INDICATORS include the following:
► Overblown phrases that camouflage negative facts; e.g.,
"We are vigorously seeking creative techniques to bring our costs in line." (The company will slash salaries by 20% and cash in its pension plan.)
"We're seizing growing opportunities for global out-sourcing." (The company is moving production to the Far East, where wages are dirt-cheap.)
"The company is now poised for earnings growth." (It lost so much money, earnings can't get worse.)[98]

▶ The law requires that a company mentions pending lawsuits that can significantly reduce earnings. An adverse ruling can reduce job prospects.

▶ Look for mention of discontinued operations of plants and where these are located.

▶ Some companies use statistics the way a drunk uses a lamppost, for support rather than illumination. There may be a legitimate reason for changing the company's accounting system. The change may also be an attempt to make its earnings look better than they are. When a company has made several changes in the past five years, be on guard says Marilyn Moats Kennedy, author of *Office Warfare*.⁹⁹

▶ A sharp drop in its research and development budget is another bad sign, writes Kennedy, especially in these times of intense competition. A company that raids its R&D budget to prop up current earnings *"is like a brain-dead patient subsisting on a life-support system . . . It won't be able to finance new products or market them adequately and . . . it will eventually die or be acquired."*

▶ New products/services that fail for no clear reason.

Kennedy also advises that you look for clues in the independent auditor's opinion on how the company is doing. In Texaco's 1985 report the auditors mentioned a $11.1 billion judgement brought against the company in a lawsuit. You'll find it in the back pages of the report. Generally it's two paragraphs long. Anything longer should be scrutinized. It might be because of a minor change in accounting practices. Or it could mean the company is trying to hide embarrassing facts.

The bad news is usually buried in the footnotes. The company as a whole may be doing well but the division you are interested in may be having problems. The footnotes contain information on how the various divisions are doing and how much each contributes to the company's overall earnings.

You'll also find clues in the chief executive's letter to shareholders. Note the company's plans for the next several years. You might learn the division you hope to work for is being phased out. You might read about plans to acquire another company which means more jobs.

ANNUAL REPORTS CAN BE FOUND in public libraries and school career guidance and placement offices. Also contact the public relations office of a company and ask for copies of its annual reports for the past few years.

Stock market trends

Study the company's recent stock price trends. An increase over several years generally suggests the company is expanding. A downturn may be bad news. It could be part of a normal business cycle. But if the price has declined steadily over the past 5 years it could mean the company is in trouble.

► ### Other sources of information

Contact the experts

► Talk to people you know who have the type of job you want.

► Contact speakers at professional meetings, persons mentioned in newspaper articles, journalists who write business articles in newspapers and authors of journal articles. Don't be shy about contacting important or well-known persons. Super-achievers are generally super-persons, and they're often willing to help strangers. If the person lives out of town write first about what you want to know and ask for permission to phone at a later time.

► Telephone local companies and ask for the name of someone there who can give you additional information. Then phone that person. Richard Bolles calls these "information interviews." It may not be easy to get an interview from a busy person these days but it's worth the try.

Professional and trade associations

These give current information on occupations, their training requirements, salaries and wages, industry-wide job market conditions, and where to locate major employers. Many also maintain job banks for members. Their journals and newsletters are a valuable source of information on matters affecting the industry or occupation. Your public library probably has a file of association publications.

The Encyclopedia of Associations lists thousands of associations which have the facts you need about business, agriculture, law, science, education, social welfare, health, public affairs, direct marketing, data processing and other fields. It gives their addresses and phone numbers, key persons to contact, their publications, and other information.

Conferences, conventions and trade shows

At these regular gatherings you can:

► Get the latest, inside information on a particular field or industry.

► Make valuable contacts. You may meet officers or representatives from major firms. You may even convince someone to arrange for a job interview.

► Learn the latest industry buzz words.

► Obtain evidence to use for your resume and job interviews that your knowledge is up-to-date. If you attended a workshop or seminar held at the conference or show, mention it.

The best way to get information from a trade show is to be there. If you cannot be present you can obtain the proceedings of conferences and conventions. Look in *The Directory of Conventions* to see when and where meetings in your field will be held. Write for a program which lists the topics covered and the speakers and their affiliations. You can write to these experts for more information. Also write to the organization which sponsored the gatherings. They usually publish or tape record conference proceedings and sell them for very little. These contain most of the information presented at the conference.

For the names and addresses of organizations which sponsor conferences and conventions look in Gale's *Encyclopedia of Associations*. You can also learn about meetings to be held in/near your community from newspapers and the Chamber of Commerce. Look in the phone book to see if there is a convention and trade center or a tourist information center, and contact them for information.

Federal/state bureau of labor statistics

Labor bureaus continually gather information on the economy — i.e., job openings nationwide, job vacancies within each industry, the number of new businesses, bankruptcies, healthy industries, dying industries, the number of unemployed persons who are looking for work. You can find these reports in the public library. You can also buy government publications on industries and occupations. See Appendix D.

Write to your state department of labor (or that of another state) for information on local job and business opportunities in any occupation and industry that interests you.

The Federal Bureau of Labor Statistics also issues monthly and special reports on economic conditions in each industry and unemployment and employment figures for major industries by regions and major cities. These are in the library.

Your local chamber of commerce
It has information on the smaller companies in your area.

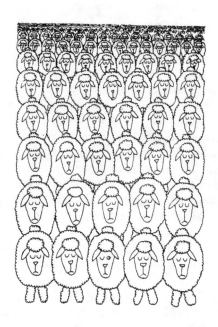

How to Find a Good Job

Persistence pays off

"When you want something, go back and go back, and don't take 'No' for an answer. And when rejection comes, don't take it personally, It goes with the territory. Expose yourself to as much humiliation as you can bear. Then go home and do it all again tomorrow." — Betty Furness.[100]

Don't be discouraged if you get rejections, even many. It happens to most people, including young, highly skilled, well educated persons. In changing times, and especially during a recession, the only certainty is that persistence and the right skills and contacts pay off. As long as you don't make a pest of yourself, persistence is likely to win over an employer when the right opening occurs. Everyone, no matter how high and mighty, falls for flattery.

A college graduate applied, and was rejected, twice for a management trainee job at Macy's department store. On the third try she sent in a one page, well-written letter. She got the job. Another form of persistence was demonstrated by a recent graduate who wanted to be a reporter for a local television news station. Knowing she faced stiff competition, she took a low-paying receptionist job there. After normal work hours, she often volunteered to do odd jobs. This provided additional experience and helped her make valuable contacts. When the right opening appeared her name was at the top of the list.

How long will it take to find a good job?

It varies according to economic conditions and your occupation, job level, and age. Since all these factors interact, statistics based on total averages should be used as rough guidelines. In 1989 it took persons under age 50 an average of 3.03 months to find a job.

Persons age 50-60 took about 3.46 months, and those over 60 took 5 to 7 months.[101] Managers earning $50,000 to $100,000 needed about 6 months to find a new job and longer if they earned over $100,000.[102] Executives age 45 to 54 had to search nearly six months to find a comparable job.[103]

Organize your job hunt and save time

Keep a detailed record of your job search activities in a notebook small enough to carry around. It should have a separate section for each employer you contact. Within each section record these items:

- Resumes and cover letters — date sent out, to whom
- Replies received — date, name of person
- Phone calls made — date, name of person
- Deductible job hunting expenses
- Interviews — date, address, name and title of person who interviewed you, ideas on how to improve your next interview

Best times for job hunting

Send your resume and cover letter as soon as you hear about a job opening. About a week later telephone to see if it was received. If you have access to a fax machine it will be received immediately. Many public libraries now have fax machines for public use. If you want it to get into the hands of a particular person use express mail or registered mail. It will get there faster than regular mail, and there is less likelihood that a clerk will file or throw it away.

January is the best month of the year for hiring. New openings are created in December when employers start working on their annual budget. Scrooge-like, they also announce dismissals at this time. Also, many workers resign after they get a Christmas bonus. An additional benefit is that you'll have less competition since most job hunters are busy with holiday preparations and many don't know it's a good time for job hunting.

The second best time for job hunting begins in mid-August when employers start making interview appointments for vacancies that are expected after Labor Day. Also at this time managers usually give notice that they intend to resign later, and recent graduates quit to look for another job or enroll in graduate school.

Contact the person who makes the hiring decision

Usually managers or team leaders in departments which have a vacancy make the hiring decision, not the personnel officer. They know best what the job requires and are more willing to consider substitute qualifications. They also know more about future openings in the department. The personnel department is generally best for traditional and lower-level jobs.

"Mass market" yourself

Send an all-purpose resume and a cover letter to every employer in a targeted industry and geographic area. Address it to the head of a specific department instead of the personnel office. (It receives so many job inquiries that your resume is more likely to be misplaced or rejected after a careless reading.) Follow up with a phone call about ten days later.

Experiment with a telephone blitz. Although it's more expensive, you'll cover more territory. You also might get valuable information. If an employer has no current vacancy ask for the names of other employers who might have one. Also ask to have your resume kept on file in case an opening occurs later on. Prepare your sales pitch in advance and practice, practice, practice till you feel confident.

Do the following concurrently.

► Send a resume and letter to employers you want to work for.

► Answer help-wanted ads.

► Register with several employment agencies.

► Contact people in your network.

► Experiment with "cold calls" where you simply walk into a personnel office and fill out a job application form. This is usually more effective for lower-level jobs. During a labor shortage it also might work for people who are looking for better jobs. Find out beforehand the best time and day of the week to come in. On a slow day you might get an interview without a prior appointment.

Barriers some job hunters create for themselves

▶ Requesting special conditions the employer can't or won't meet

Some people refuse good job offers which require that they occasionally work late or on weekends. Or they are disqualified because they ask for time off to deal with a personal matter. A proofreader for a Wall Street firm was fired within a month after he was hired because he insisted on a morning off each month to attend meetings of a university club.

▶ Creating geographic barriers

A few years ago there was a sharp rise in the number of women graduates with science and engineering degrees. Although companies were eager to hire them, the women had significantly higher unemployment rates than male graduates. Some women blamed it on sex discrimination but the main reason was that they had placed geographic restrictions on the jobs they were willing to accept.[104]

In our highly mobile society people who are willing to pull up stakes and relocate have a much better chance of getting a good job, and the better the job the farther afield they may have to look. These women thought local opportunities in their high-level occupations were the same as for ordinary jobs. If they had read government reports on the geographic distribution of such jobs they would have known about the poor chances of finding a good job near home.

▶ Problems returning homemakers and retirees create for themselves

"*They make difficult or impossible demands,*" said a Jobs Service counselor. Many restrict their options by saying they want a job that is on a main bus line or near the subway. Some even say they want a job within walking distance.

If they are over 65 or returning to work after many years they need to be more flexible in the type of job they are willing to take. "*Some refuse to face the probability of starting at a lower salary level. They don't realize they are competing with younger applicants who will work for less money and have up-to-date training. Their chances of finding work increase if they take jobs in an entirely different field, or a lower-level job if it's in the company or industry they want,*" he continued. Even if they held a high-level job before, they must prove themselves to a new employer. *"It's easier to get promotions after they shine at a lower level job than to apply for a top position and be turned down because of age.*

"However, if they've been at the management level, accepting a lower-level job with no management involvement may compromise their experience, especially if the company is in the same industry in which they previously worked. They need to know as much as possible about the company, how they fit in, and how many working years they have left. Only then will they know if it's possible to achieve their goal within that time frame. There is no blanket answer that fits all candidates in this category."

"The biggest barriers are the self-imposed psychological ones," said another state labor department official. *"Sometimes older job seekers get the feeling that younger people are smarter and are always breaking records. Nevertheless, if some believe it, it can be a barrier. I don't think older people are any different from others in that the more skills they have the more employable they are."*

Consider other paths

▶ **Consider a lower level job in your first-choice company or an expanding industry.**

As a proven employee who already knows the company and industry, you will be a top contender when the right opening occurs. Opportunities to advance will be even greater if the job you take is in the department you prefer.

▶ **Consider second- or third-choice companies**

It may be difficult initially to find a job in the headquarters of a Fortune 500 firm. It will be easier to find one, and you'll move ahead faster, in a small subsidiary of the same company. After receiving good performance reviews there, it will be easier to move into the parent company. Or, you can get a job in a smaller company and, after proving yourself there, later apply to a major company.

▶ **Consider related occupations.**

Many people who train for an occupation end up using their expertise in another occupation in the same "family," or they take jobs where these skills aren't even used. Many are happy in their unanticipated career.

A history professor, for example, might consider other industries where the same expertise and skills are used. Private companies, publishers and municipal agencies hire people with advanced degrees in the social sciences to work as editor of in-house publications, librarian, researcher, public relations officer, even as company historian. You can look up related occupations in the *Occupational Outlook Handbook*.

It's easier now to transfer to another industry. More employers are hiring people whose needed skills were honed in a different industry. Generally small companies and large companies in progressive industries — such as data processing, financial, and health care — are more likely to hire "outsiders."

More tips

▸ Sharpen your interview skills by first applying for jobs you're not too keen about.

▸ Even if an employer has no opening for the job you want, try to get an appointment for an information interview. The employer may realize the company needs someone with your skills and might even create a position for you. Read Richard Bolles' *What Color Is Your Parachute* for information on how to get and conduct information interviews.

▸ Don't stop looking just because you've been assured the job is yours. Anything can happen (such as an unexpected withdrawal of the offer). Keep other interview appointments and continue reading the help-wanted ads. Also, start mapping out ideas for the new job.

▸ Don't be fooled by a prestigious title for a lower level, low paying job.

▸ Don't panic into accepting an early offer. It takes time and patience to find a good job. A survey found that only 5 out of 100 resumes mailed result in interviews and only one of these might lead to a job offer. The odds depend on the type of job and how much competition there is for it.

▸ If you are offered an unrealistically high salary, find out why. A difficult manager or other problems in the department may be causing employees to leave.

▶ Make sure the person who hires you knows the complete description of the job and your responsibilities. You might end up with too little to do or more than you can handle.

———————•◦◦⊙⊙◦⊙◦⊙◦◦•———————

NETWORKING
Networking can help you find a job.

They used to be known as "old-boy networks" which passed on strategic information — such as who to contact for a top job — to male members of the upper crust. Today networks consist of "just plain folks" who share a common interest and are willing to help one another when needed. There are informal networks of people who live locally and there are regional, national and international networks for special interest groups — women, ethnic and racial groups, professionals, people in a certain age category, and others.

Most people find jobs through personal contacts. These are especially helpful for obtaining higher-level positions. About 75% of mid- and upper-management jobs are obtained this way.[105]

Employers prefer to find new workers through their own employee network. It's less expensive than placing a help-wanted ad, and it's the best way to find people with special skills. The people hired are usually more reliable and are less likely to quit. They also have an easier time fitting in. Employees are reluctant to recommend someone who is not likely to work out because it ultimately reflects on their judgement.

Employers' networks also include other employers in the same industry and leaders of community organizations. Many employers send scouts to adult education classes, church groups and other community gatherings to look for potential employees.

Someone in your network may also be able to get inside information about a company which can be valuable during an interview. If you know someone who lives in another community, he/she can get information for you on the local job market and may be able to make the initial contact with an employer.

Enlarge your network of contacts
The more lists your name is on and the larger your network of people to contact, the more likely you'll get what you want. Make

a list of people who can provide information on job leads, your occupation, a company or industry. Include persons who know about job openings and living conditions in a distant community, or who can refer you to others who do.

A network which is too inbred narrows your possibilities. People you know personally (relatives, friends) tend to have the same information and hear about the same leads. Include people from different circles — e.g., former employers and co-workers, teachers and professors, classmates, former colleagues who now work for another employer. Be friendly with job hunters you meet on the unemployment insurance line, in job placement offices and personnel offices. They often know about job vacancies they don't want. They may also have inside knowledge about an employer.

Talk to people you meet at professional and industry conferences. Many organizations issue a directory which lists the names, addresses and phone numbers of members. Contact some of the people on the list for information.

Contact your school alumni association for the names and addresses of former classmates. Even though you graduated years ago and some of the names are unfamiliar, old school bonds never die. Maybe a former classmate has risen to the top of the corporate ladder.

Get in touch with people in your fraternity or sorority. Some Greek clubs are forming networks to help members advance in their careers. They maintain a talent bank of successful members who can be contacted for information and other forms of help. The New York City chapter of Kappa Alpha Theta, for example, holds informal meetings to help members who are changing jobs or starting a business. They discuss career problems, make business contacts, and help members who are new to the city. One woman got a good job in the catering department of a hotel managed by the husband of a chapter member.

Several large companies — e.g., Proctor & Gamble, General Electric, IBM, Time-Life, Xerox — have alumni associations of former employees, generally those who held higher-level positions. They keep in touch with one another over the years for mutual benefit. They have directories which list the names and addresses of members. Someone said the networking that goes on at the gatherings can be as helpful as a Harvard Business School contact. Members who have become executives in another company or have started their own business seek out new talent at such gatherings.

Find out if a former employer has such an association. You might even start one yourself as Mel Mahler, a former Xerox executive, did. In 1984 he and a former coworker

made up a list of 100 former high-level officers of the company. They sent letters asking each one for 20 more names. Eventually the list included over 1,200 alumni and they had an association.[106]

Recently, employees of plants that have closed down, or who were victims of a mass dismissal, have formed their own associations. You might be in this position. Get in touch with others and start a "dismissed alumni" group. You can hold meetings anywhere — someone's home, the public library — and exchange job tips. A member who learns during a job interview that a company needs accountants, engineers or whatever would share this information.

If you own a computer, you can network electronically.

Many electronic bulletin boards list job openings. It's a great way to get job leads in other communities since you'll be in contact with people throughout the nation and around the world. There is something about computer networking that creates a sense of community, a willingness to help and share information with total strangers. An executive of a small company in Hicksville, NY followed a lead placed by someone in San Francisco which led to his getting a job in Tampa, Fl that paid a six-figure salary. None of the people involved had ever met face-to-face.

How to network

Circulate, keep in touch, and you'll be amazed at how much you learn about job openings and new developments in your field. Attend professional, trade or business meetings. Hang out at places where people in your line of work meet regularly such as restaurants and health clubs. Be an active member of community groups where representatives of local employers are likely to be present. If you are now employed, join an after-hours employee club and attend company get-togethers. When someone in your network hears of an opening, you will be the first to know.

Just being present isn't enough. Make your presence known. Ask people to keep you informed on important developments. But don't ask those you hardly know to help you find a job.

Many people continue networking even after they find another job. *"Wherever I work from now on, my second job will always be to keep networking with contacts in the industry. I don't want to get caught flatfooted if this ever happens to me again,"* said a dismissed manager. They build a support network within their present company, sharing information that can affect their careers.

▶ Contact employers directly

About 25% of all workers find jobs by visiting or phoning an employer and asking for a job, a Labor Department study found. You will probably have more luck with small companies whose business is the same as your specialty — i.e., engineering, accounting, advertising. You can get names, addresses and phone numbers of people to contact from references listed in Appendix E.

First prepare what you are going to say, and practice saying it until you can do it effortlessly. Then contact the person or department head for whom you want to work. If that fails, try the personnel officer. If there are no openings then, call occasionally so you will be remembered when an opening occurs.

The authors of *Capitol Jobs: An Insider's Guide to Finding a Job in Congress* recommend doing this to get a staff job in the Senate and House offices of lawmakers. Just pick up the phone and say, *"I hear you have an opening on your staff."* People are surprised to learn how often an opening actually exists.[107]

▶ Create your own job and convince an employer to hire you.

Many employers won't know how much they need you until you convince them. Some job hunters have convinced an employer to create a new opening for their special skills and expertise even after they were told that no vacancy exists.

This is how a former engineer and school administrator created his post-retirement dream job. He and his wife wanted to live where it is warm enough to enjoy outdoor sports year-round. The job he created was "consultant in residence" — a title he coined — for a resort hotel in the Virgin Islands. He looked up the names and addresses of 106 hotels in that area in the *Hotel & Travel Index*. He wrote to each one offering his services. He even listed the conditions of employment. In return for free lodging, meals and recreational privileges he would work three days a week wherever his skills and expertise would be needed such as training, personnel relations, plant engineering, maintenance. Four resort hotels accepted his terms. He selected one which had a golf course, beaches, tennis courts and a riding stable. Now he quits work about 3 p.m. and swims, golfs or plays tennis the rest of the day.[108]

In times of rapid change many traditional job titles become obsolete and new ones are created to meet new needs. The latter are called "emerging occupations." Employers often don't know about them. All they know is that the old-style job titles on most resumes don't meet the needs of the new workplace. They were not aware — when they bought their first computer systems — that eventually someone would have to be hired to integrate the information from different departments and select new software and hardware to buy. Employees who were paid to deal with these new responsibilities were not officially listed as "systems analyst" or "manager of information systems." Today, most large companies have these job titles on their organization chart.

You may be able to get in on a new job trend and convince an employer to create an opening for you. It's not difficult to spot new job trends. Newspapers are devoting more space to developments in management, science and technology. The daily business section of *The New York Times* reports on new patents and discoveries and how these will affect companies. Another good source of ideas is the Department of Labor's *Monthly Labor Review, Occupational Outlook Quarterly* and *Emerging Occupations and Projections for Growth* which have regular features on emerging occupations. Another method is to combine some of the responsibilities of two job titles, create a new title, and convince an employer that it will cut costs and raise profits.

"Everybody wants a marriage with no misunderstandings. Everybody wants a job with all promotions and no perspiration. I can't deliver it."   — Governor Mario Cuomo

► **How to do it**

1. Select a company you want to work for. Research it thoroughly. Pay special attention to its problems and needs.

2. Think of new or better ways to meet those needs and how your skills, abilities and experience can be used.

3. Look in *The Dictionary of Occupational Titles* and other sources listed in Appendix B for a job title that fits your new responsibilities, or make up a new title.

4. Find out who in the organization is most likely to be receptive to your idea.

5. Plan the best way to convince that person of the need to create a new position for you.

Example: The business section of your newspaper has an article on a company's plans to market its product to the Chinese. You know, maybe even before its executives do, that they will need someone with a knowledge of the Chinese culture who can advise company policy makers. That someone (YOU) will point out how decisions are made by the Chinese, how the American product can be adapted to their smaller physical size and their values and preferences. As a "Culture Consultant" you would also train the company's employees who will be stationed in China on the subtleties of Chinese ways.

► **Which companies are the best/worst for convincing?**

You will probably have more success with a small, innovative company than a large, bureaucratic one. Low-risk, well-established companies rarely create new titles, says Frank H. Cassell of the Graduate School of Management, Northwestern University. Companies at the cutting edge of science and technology are easier to approach. They need *"people whose ideas can help them beat the competition during the turbulent growth period."* Yet, even in small, innovative companies there are officers who are more or less receptive to new ideas. Try to find out, through your network, who those persons are. However, he cautions, new positions often turn out to be projects that eventually end. This is a matter to be decided after you convince the employer to create an opening for you. It also depends on how you define your job title — as having short or long range possibilities.[109]

EMPLOYMENT AGENCIES

Private, for-profit agencies

General employment agencies fill a variety of job openings. Specialized agencies focus on a specific industry or occupation; e.g., health, high-technology, finance. Some of these specialize in a certain family of occupations such as artists, engineers, educators, office workers. They have a better knowledge of the industry and occupation. They are more likely to know the companies you'll be sent to and the people who will interview you.

► **How to find a good employment agency**

→ Contact the career guidance and placement center of the local college or university for recommendations.

→ Look in the Yellow Pages under "Employment Contractors" or a similar title.

→ Read the job listings of employment agencies which advertise in the newspaper's help-wanted section.

→ Look in out-of-state Yellow Pages and newspapers and in the *Encyclopedia of Associations* for employment services in other communities.

Make an appointment with several and compare them.

► Did they take time to ask about your work experience and job related interests, skills and abilities?

► Did they answer your questions fully — types of positions available, how long they've been in the business, success rate in placing people with your qualifications, companies and industries they mostly work with?

► Did they explain clearly their policy, services and fees?

► After they find a job for you are they willing to offer advice if problems arise during your first few months on the job?

Before you sign a contract

► Find out what they will/won't do for you and the charges.

► Ask for a copy of the contract to take home so you can study it. They should clarify anything you don't understand.

► Read it carefully so you won't be shocked by extra charges for advice you assumed would be part of the package. If you ask the counselor to look over a draft of your resume or advise you on how to improve your interview techniques, it could cost plenty.

► Any guarantees or promises of services or information which are not included in the contract should be put in writing.

► Ask how many of its job listings are fee-paid by the employer. If many are, this is a good sign because employers generally avoid paying fees to disreputable firms.

► If you are asked to pay the fee, read the agency's refund policy and fee plan carefully. The fee should be based on a percentage of the monthly or yearly salary. Some states limit the amount of fees an employment agency can charge job seekers. If the fee seems exorbitant, check with the Better Business Bureau and your state's licensing bureau.

A reputable firm collects its fee AFTER you are hired and often in installments.

It will not charge for interviews it arranges for you.

If you find a job on your own while you are registered with an agency you should not be asked to pay a fee.

More tips

► They should not exert pressure or scare you into accepting a job that is below your level of qualifications.

► On the other hand, they should not overstate your job prospects.

► They should back up any promises such as *"access to the hidden job market," "contacts with the right people."* Several years ago a marketing manager filed a complaint against a national search firm which still places large newspaper ads. For a $2,200 fee they promised he would be "steered to the right people." The list of "special contacts" they gave him came from a business directory which you will find in the public library. To make matters worse, the "counselor" knew nothing about the marketing field.

► Be on your guard when they advertise salaries that seem too good to be true. The following excerpt comes from a newspaper ad placed by a "career marketing services company" — *". . . the nation's only 100% guaranteed job changing process . . . salaries ranging from $40,000 to six figures . . . dramatic breakthrough in job changing techniques."* When you see such hyperbole, read the contract extra carefully.

▸ If you are offered a job that is not fee-paid, ask the employer to refund the amount you paid after you have proven yourself on the job. (Fee-splitting is illegal in some states.)

▸ If an employment agency arranges an interview for you and, as a result of the interview, you get a DIFFERENT job, you should not pay the fee. (They refer you to a company for a word processing job and you are offered instead a job as secretary.) Or, the company's interviewer tells you about an opening in another company which you obtain on your own.

▸ You can tell the employment agency that you are only interested in fee-paid jobs.

▸ If the job does not turn out as described you have the right to ask for a refund. A reputable agency will not exaggerate the conditions of jobs it recommends.

▸ If, after you've been on the job for a while, you quit and ask for a refund you must have a valid reason. You must also ask for the refund within the time limit specified in the contract.

▸ If your request for a refund, though valid, is refused, contact the Better Business Bureau or your state's licensing agency.

▸ Don't reveal any job leads you find through your own efforts. The agency might refer other clients to the job before you have a chance to look into it.

▸ Wednesday through Friday are the best days to contact them. Monday and Tuesday are crowded with job seekers who have seen the agency's ads in the Sunday newspaper.

▸ Register with more than one agency.

▸ Be wary when an "agency" offers to sell you a list of job openings, especially through the mail. During the recession in the automobile industry, ads appeared in local newspapers promising job interviews to unemployed auto workers who mailed in twenty-one dollars. They never received a reply. Other ads sold a list of non-existent job openings.

▸ Walk out if they ask you to pay for information about their services.

▸ Don't sit around waiting for an agency to call you. Phone if you haven't heard from them in a week or two.

Check the agency's reputation
Do this even though it has impressive ads in the newspapers and lists branch offices in major cities. Placement services must be

licensed by the city and state in which they operate. There are, however, firms that operate without a license. Past investigations have turned up cases of false advertising, exorbitant charges, and discrimination. If you have a question or complaint, contact your state's licensing bureau and the Better Business Bureau.

Computerized placement services

A growing number of highly skilled, professional and top management people are finding jobs through their home computer. Usually there is no charge to have your resume placed in these databases. Subscribing employers pay. In the few cases where job hunters pay, the fee varies according to salary level. If you have a job and are looking for a better one, you can request to have your resume automatically removed from the list of job seekers viewed by any named employer.

The advantages of this method over traditional job placement agencies are as follows:

► You don't have to go trekking from one agency to another or from one employer to another. You don't have to spend endless hours checking help-wanted ads, making phone calls, filling out applications and squirming through job interviews.

► You can instruct the computer to call up only the specific type of industry, employer, job, salary, and geographic area you want.

► You can apply for jobs in the comfort of your own home, at any hour you please. Computerized job listings generally are accessible 24 hours-a-day. Within minutes you will have access to more job openings than you can have in months using traditional methods.

► Your resume will be seen by employers all over the nation. They can ask for any combination of credentials they want such as type of degree and special skills. They can specify a preference for graduates of their alma mater, as many do. An employer might want to fill a sales trainee position with a college graduate who majored in marketing, speaks Spanish, and is willing to live in El Paso, Texas. The computer brings up only those resumes which meet these criteria. For more details, see Appendix F.

Recruitment firms

They charge employers a fee to find a special type of person for a specific opening. They are known as headhunters because they often raid rival companies for their most talented employees. A large executive recruiting firm found that 98.5% of the people placed in new jobs in 1987 were already employed.

Usually they specialize in a certain industry such as health care, financial services or consumer products. Some specialize in finding persons for professional and mid-level management positions. Others deal only with executive positions. Because of the high fees many small and mid-size companies do their own head-hunting.

As a rule, recruiting firms seek you out; you don't go to them. But some keep a file of unsolicited resumes from promising job seekers in order to have a talent pool to fish from as needed. It won't do any harm, and it might lead to something good, if you send your resume to the recruiting firm which specializes in your field. Follow it up with a phone call to ask for a meeting. Someone you know who is in management may be willing to make the initial contact for you.

Another way to come to their attention is to join your trade and professional association. Headhunters often contact them for names of candidates and ask for their list of members.

For more information look in the *Association of Executive Recruiting Consultants Directory* or the *Directory of Executive Recruiters*. These are in the public library.

Non-profit employment services

▶ **Community organizations and public libraries**

Some offer job placement services in addition to career information and counseling. They may help their clients directly or refer them to other organizations in the community.

Community organizations represent a variety of interests — e.g., religious, educational, ethnic, racial, social service. Employers often recruit new workers through them. Kinder-Care, for example, a national chain of child-care centers, actively recruits through community organizations for the elderly. Local churches often set up job banks and provide other services for unemployed parishioners when a recession hits a community. Many social service organizations offer career counseling and job placement as part of their services. Some help only persons who are disadvantaged in the job market because of age, sex, race or physical handicap.

► Educational organizations

Career guidance and placement offices can be found in vocational schools, business schools, colleges and universities. They are staffed by some of the best professionals in the field. In addition, many colleges have special programs for women and older community residents. Community colleges in particular offer their services to unemployed residents of the community regardless of whether they are, or have been, enrolled as full- or part-time students.

The services provided include a combination of the following.

► Job training and free or low-cost college courses.

► Training in job-finding skills — workshops on resume writing and job interviewing, videotaped practice interviews, a library of information on the job market and employers.

► Job placement: Even if you attended college years ago, you can receive regular mailings of job vacancies in your field for a small fee. However, some experts say the most older graduates can expect is a referral to other graduates who can give them job leads. This omission will probably be corrected as the number of older people attending college for career purposes increases. In 1987 Stanford University started ProNet, a computerized databank of resumes to help companies find *experienced* people for professional and managerial positions. (See Appendix F.) The service is free to alumni. Other schools, such as MIT, Harvard and the California Institute of Technology have started similar databanks.

For information on programs in your area contact your state department of education, the adult education division of a local college or university, or the public library.

► The Job Service

It is funded by the U.S. Department of labor. Each state has a central department which administers offices in local communities. The names of the different state Job Services vary — e.g., California State Personnel Board, Kentucky Merit System Council.

It has more job listings and more information on the local and national job markets than any other source. The rumor that it lists only vacancies at the entry- and semi-skilled levels is not true. The law requires it to list civil service jobs *at all levels*. Moreover, it maintains a national job bank for professionals who are in short supply such as nurses, engineers, librarians, and data processors. However, employers who have a government contract are not required by law to list vacancies which pay above a certain salary.[110]

The Job Service now has a computerized, interstate job bank which can match your qualifications with appropriate vacancies anywhere in the nation. The jobs listed are mostly in the professional and highly skilled categories.

The following additional services may be provided, free or at low cost, by your state's Job Service.

▶ Referrals to local job training programs and information on apprenticeship opportunities.

▶ Career testing and counseling. (You must ask for this service.)

▶ Special programs for certain types of job seekers such as older workers, displaced homemakers, handicapped persons, veterans, dismissed workers and workers who lose their jobs because of imports. Some offices also help displaced executives and professionals transfer their expertise to new occupations and industries.

How to get the most from the Job Service

▶ Read their monthly listing of job vacancies throughout the nation. It's a good way to find a job in another community.

▶ Get to the local Job Service office as soon as its doors open, and go at least once a week. Most job vacancies are filled almost as soon as they are listed. If you phone or write for notices of job vacancies to be mailed to you it may be too late.

▶ When you arrive for an interview be prepared to describe the type of job you want and your qualifications. Bring your resume and any other information you would ordinarily take to a job interview.

▶ State and municipal services

Every state has programs in its cities and local communities which offer job training, job placement and other services for displaced workers, older persons and other types of disadvantaged job seekers. For example, the New York City Employment Committee was created during a recent severe recession to develop job training programs for unemployed residents. Courses were given in financial services, retailing, real estate management, accounting, advertising, food service, building maintenance, data processing, and other skills that were in demand. A Private Industry Council provided the training and the New York State Job Service referred trainees to employers who had vacancies.

In Tampa, Florida, private companies join with the Chamber of Commerce and the Hillsborough County Department of Aging to operate a program called "Working Seniors." The County provides for career assessment and job training, and the Chamber conducts senior job fairs to find qualified persons for openings in the private firms.

In Vermont, a private group, Vermont Associates for Training and Development, coordinates several agencies to prepare older workers for jobs. It offers job counseling, training and job placement. It also hires older persons for its own staff. In 1988 they found jobs for persons who ranged in age from 40 to 86.

▶ **Civil service jobs**

These exist at the federal, state and municipal levels. Most require taking a civil service test. Then you wait, sometimes months, for a notice. Job vacancies are filled according to test score and other qualifications. Many professional and management level openings, however, do not require taking a test. These are filled according to training, education and work experience.

Job vacancies are usually posted in government offices such as the post office, Job Service, and unemployment insurance offices. For an application, contact the appropriate state, county or city government personnel office. Also contact the Office of Personnel Management.

▶ **U.S. Office of Personnel Management**

Once known as the U.S. Civil Service Commission, it places applicants in full- and part-time jobs in a wide range of occupations for the federal government. The jobs are located throughout the nation and overseas. Tests are given several times a year. Civil service examinations for previous years are available in your local library for practice.

You can get information on job vacancies and application forms at your local Job Service office and post office or you can write to: U.S. Office of Personnel Management, Washington, D.C. 20415. Some centers also have information on jobs with the city, county or state governments.

► *Private Industry Councils*

The Job Training Partnership Act (JTPA) requires each state to supervise local programs to retrain unemployed workers for jobs in the private sector. Within each community a Private Industry Council (PIC) sponsors or operates the programs. The Council includes representatives from private industry, education, community organizations, labor organizations and federal and local governments.

Local training centers offer courses in job skills that are most needed in the community. The main goal is to retrain disadvantaged youths and displaced workers for permanent jobs in private industry. Another requirement is that the applicant's total family income in the previous tax year must have been within the poverty range. A small (many say inadequate) percentage of each state's JTPA grant is for training older workers.[111]

For more information on the job training partnership program contact the following.

→ Local Federal Job Service office

→ Unemployment Insurance office

→ State or City Office of Human Resources (or Human Development, Manpower Resources, or similar title)

→ Elected officials in your area

► *Self-help job clubs*

These are associations of job seekers who meet regularly for support and information sharing. If you know other job seekers in your community, it's easy to start a job club. This is how the well-known Forty Plus Club began. You'll have fun, make new friends, and turn the miserable experience of job hunting into a more pleasant adventure. You can use the public library, a church or member's homes as a meeting place.

Forty Plus Club

In 1989 there were 16 Forty Plus Clubs in the nation and the number is growing. Members are unemployed executives, top managers and professionals who are looking for high-level positions. All the work, including managing the club and job recruitment, is done by members who are required to volunteer several hours a week. Members who find a job can remain in the Club as associates. Associates help govern and support the club financially.

They also offer valuable networking advantages. An associate who was about to retire from a senior position in a health service organization hired a Forty Plus member to replace him.

Forty Plus Clubs have a high success rate in helping members find good jobs. In 1988 ninety-nine members of New York City's Club found jobs, usually with small or medium-sized firms. Their average age was 51 and the average salary was $53,000. They found jobs as chief financial officer, director of marketing, controller, chief loan specialist, chief engineer, director of communications, technology manager, sales manager and other high-level positions.

Admission requirements are strict in order to uphold the standards of the Club in the eyes of employers. Applicants must supply at least three references and proof of having earned a salary above a minimum level. This requirement is sometimes waived for women, minorities, and professionals from relatively low-paying fields such as education and religion. The initial membership fee and weekly dues vary from club to club. Members must also live within commuting distance so they can put in the required number of hours of volunteer work per week. See Appendix F for the names and addresses of Forty Plus Clubs.

The services provided include a combination of the following.

▸ **Job recruitment:** Employers are contacted regularly for suitable job openings.

▸ **Resume and cover letter:** New members have their resumes and cover letters reviewed by associates who have experience in the same field.

▸ **Practice interviews** are staged with fellow members. Some clubs have an arrangement whereby members attend workshops conducted by professional career counselors, and some have video equipment.

▸ **Use of the club as a base of operations:** Word processors, telephones, copy machines and, in some clubs, secretarial services are available to members.

▸ **Psychological support:** A major benefit is the mutual support provided by members who have all suffered the trauma of job loss. As high achievers, their job loss has made them especially susceptible to depression. Far too many executives hide the fact from their families while they quietly go mad or dissolve into drink. They leave home in the morning pretending to go to the office whereas in reality they sit in the park or in some bar.

► **Group therapy** is provided by professional psychologists to help resolve or prevent family and psychological problems resulting from job loss.

► **Career counseling**: Members also get help in assessing their skills and work experience and matching these to a new career or industry.

► Senior employment services

Non-profit senior employment services

Most persons who get jobs through senior employment services are over 55, and many are in their 60s and 70s. Over-60 Employment and Counseling Services, for example, are spreading because of the great need for this kind of service. Through them, employers have hired accountants, administrative assistants, administrators and other high-skill workers besides bank tellers, bookkeepers, office workers, receptionists, sales clerks, telephone salespersons, word processors and the like. Many of the vacancies have flexible working hours. Your state or local government's office on aging, the local library and social services agencies can tell you where to find such services in or near your community. Also look in the Yellow Pages.

Operation ABLE

Ability Based on Long Experience is a Chicago based network of organizations who coordinate their efforts to help older people train for and find jobs. It includes local employers, educational institutions, the state's Job Service, senior employment services, religious agencies, and others.

Among the services offered are career counseling, education, job training, a central job bank and an annual job fair. It has become a model for similar programs in other cities in which the central feature is an annual Job Fair. See Appendix F for the address and a list of cities which have similar programs.

Ability Is Ageless

This program is jointly sponsored by New York City's Department for the Aging and the Chamber of Commerce and Industry, New York State's Job Service, private employers, and various community service agencies. It organizes an annual job fair through which local employers recruit older people for their current vacancies. Information on job training, other employment opportunities and preliminary job interviews are also available. The resources at the Fair are used throughout the year to help job hunters who cannot be placed right away find work. There are also workshops on job finding skills, the job market, the concerns of midlife women, etc.

The American Association of Retired Persons

AARP and the National Retired Teachers Association jointly operate a program which places persons who need job training in non-profit organizations. These include the Red Cross, day care centers, Goodwill Industries, nutrition centers, schools, senior centers, veteran's hospitals and environmental agencies. The recruits can work up to 20 hours a week at minimum wage level during training. Afterwards, they find permanent jobs with community organizations — schools, recreational facilities, parks and forests, public works, transportation, social services, housing rehabilitation. They find jobs such as employment counselors, arts and crafts aides, receptionists, secretaries, teacher aides and day care workers.

Another AARP program, the Senior Community Service Employment Program, works with local Private Industry Councils to train older workers. In Humboldt County, CA, for example, they are trained for jobs requiring computer skills and for motel management jobs.

The Senior Community Service Employment Program

SCSEP offers career counseling, job training and placement in part-time and temporary full-time jobs. Many of the jobs are in the public sector. Job training is provided by community service organizations such as Goodwill Industries, the Red Cross, libraries, schools and state employment agencies.

One trainee learned to make dental molds at a university dental school. Another learned law enforcement record keeping. A 92-year-old man, who walked 4 miles to work every day during a bus strike, got a job as assistant director of a job training workshop for the mentally retarded. A retired business owner — who couldn't find a job because of her age (59) and her unneeded skills as owner-manager of several small businesses — was placed as office manager in a center for the performing arts, a job she loves.[112] Other vacancies SCSEP has filled include recreation supervisor, park and museum guide, tribal historian, energy auditor, crime prevention counselor, paralegal aide, housing advisor, vocational counselor, casework aide, clerical worker, and assistant to the handicapped.

To be eligible, persons must be at least 55, unemployed and living at or below the official poverty level. These requirements are sometimes waived when an eligible person cannot be found to fill a vacancy. SCSEP is especially helpful to persons who've been out of the job market for a while, who need to upgrade their skills before finding a job in private industry, and older persons who have difficulty getting jobs.

In 1989 there were about 108 SCSEP sites in 33 states and Puerto Rico. To find the nearest one, write to Senior Employment Service Dept., 1909 K Street NW, Washington, DC 20049. You can also contact local branches of the following.

- State and regional agencies on aging
- American Association of Retired Persons
- U.S. Department of Agriculture
- National Council of Senior Citizens
- National Council on Aging
- National Urban League

The National Council of Senior Citizens

NCSC operates a Senior Aide Program in community service organizations. Many people placed in the part-time jobs go on to better paying, full-time jobs in private industry. A wide range of jobs are filled — e.g., office work, teacher aides, library information assistants, mental health aides. Cities with crime prevention programs employ Senior Aides to do legal research. Aides also serve as police dispatchers for the police department, as investigators for the District Attorney's office, and in city fire prevention programs. The NCSC also trains persons to work as paralegal aides to help the elderly with their legal problems.

To be eligible, persons must be over 55 and capable of at least part-time work. Priority is given to persons 60 and older who are in greatest need. The NCSC refers unemployed persons who do not meet its eligibility criteria to other agencies in the community which can help them find jobs or make ends meet.

Area Agencies on Aging

Every state is required by law to be divided into area agencies on aging to help older residents in a variety of ways. The minimum eligible age varies from 45 to 65. (Some agencies serve only low income persons in the given age category.) Among the many services offered are job training, job placement, and referral to local job training centers. Often they hire older persons for their own vacancies. Their headquarters are located in the state capitols. Within each state there are local planning and service areas, each with its own agency. Look in the phone book under "State," "County" or "City" agencies.

The National Executive Service Corps

It began as a volunteer agency to provide retired executives as consultants to small, nonprofit organizations that cannot afford the services of a private consulting firm. Because so many companies called to find high-level managers and executives to fill their paying positions, a new division was created — Senior Career Planning and Placement. It finds jobs for executives and senior level managers who are fifty and older. There are over twelve ESCs in the U.S. For information contact the national headquarters at 257 Park Avenue South, New York, NY 10010; (212) 529-6660.

► Employment services for women

Most women's centers offer some or all of the following services — career testing and counseling, job training, job placement, psychological counseling, networking and emotional support. Some serve only a certain category of women such as professional and executive level women, displaced homemakers, older women, or women who head families. Others serve women of all ages, at all levels of occupational skills and experience. They may charge a fee based on ability to pay.

They are located in adult education centers and religious and community organizations such as B'nai B'rith, the YWCA and YWHA. Many state and local governments have special commissions or councils to promote women's career opportunities. Here is a sample of women's centers and the services they provide.

Catalyst is a national, non-profit organization which helps all working women, but its major goal is to help women advance to management and executive level positions. It maintains dossiers of qualified women for the use of company chairmen who are looking for women to serve on their boards and for top level positions. There are Catalyst centers throughout the nation. The number and type of services offered vary. All maintain a career reference library. Catalyst also publishes career information books which are helpful to men as well as women. For a free national directory of Catalyst centers and the services they offer contact the national headquarters at 250 Park Avenue South, New York, NY 10010, (212) 777-8900.

W.O.W. (Wider Opportunities For Women, Inc.) offers career counseling for women managers and professionals, training for jobs traditionally held by men, and job placement. It also publishes the *National Directory of Employment Programs For Women* which you can get by writing to W.O.W., 1511 K Street, NW, Suite 700, Washington, DC 20006. It may be in the local library.

Displaced Homemaker Programs are funded by federal and state governments and private foundations. In 1989 about 24 states had a program. Usually its services are free. The program serves women 35 and older who are widowed, divorced or abandoned by their husbands. Women who support a dependent husband are also eligible. They often have no financial resources and are not eligible for unemployment insurance or welfare assistance. They are too young for Social Security benefits (unless they are disabled or have young children), and they have little, if any, income from alimony or pensions. Many have never held a job, or their job skills have become outdated after years of raising a family. Some are professional women who interrupted their careers to raise a family.

The services usually include psychological counseling, career testing and guidance, help in researching the job market, training in interview skills and resume writing, referrals to adult education courses and job training, social support, and seminars and workshops on how to meet other needs such as how to be more assertive, how to deal effectively with a lawyer, and money management.

For information on a Displaced Homemaker's Program near you, contact any of the following.
- Displaced Homemaker Program, 1010 Vermont Ave., NW, Ste. 817, Washington, DC 20005; Phone (202) 628-6767.
- Look in the phone book under your state's department of labor divisions. It might be listed as a Displaced Homemaker Program or as the Division on Women.
- YWCA or YWHA

- The Women's Bureau, U.S. Department of Labor, 200 Constitution Avenue, NW, Washington, DC 20210.

- Older Women's League, 1325 G Street NW, Lower Level B, Washington, D.C. 20005.

Community colleges have special programs to help women and older persons train for and find jobs. The following illustrates the kind of help that is available.

Valencia Community College's Displaced Homemakers Program is one of the first in America. Its success has made it a model for similar programs elsewhere. All of its services are free.[113] The main goal is to help participants become self-supporting. First they have private counseling to assess their personal, financial, educational and vocational needs. Those with immediate needs are referred to food stamp, SSI and other programs and agencies.

Next, they spend two weeks at the College's career center where they take a battery of aptitudes, interests and personality tests and set career goals. They also learn how to fill out a job application, write a resume and perfect their job interview and other employability skills.

An important part of the program for homemakers especially is assertiveness training. Many have been responsive to others for so long that they have forgotten how to acknowledge their own needs. They also learn how to invest and manage money.

Various specialists are invited to speak — e.g., a lawyer talks about legal issues and answers personal questions, a doctor discusses health issues, a cosmetologist gives advice on grooming for the interview. Those who lack appropriate career clothes have access to a resale shop operated by the Junior League.

Job training and skills upgrading are then provided through the College's adult education division and other programs in the community. One of these trains women for nontraditional jobs such as drafting, engineering, soldering and building trades. Participants who want to prepare for higher level jobs can enroll in the college's programs. Valencia's financial aid office helps them get scholarships. Some participants have gone from the high school equivalency program to the Masters Degree level and now have good jobs. A woman with two young sons earned her Bachelor and Master's Degrees at the age of forty-five and is now a college faculty member.

Job training focuses on skills needed by local employers.[114] According to Virginia Stuart, the program's manager, a strong marketing campaign is directed toward employers in the private sector.[115] After the participants find work, they go through an internship program which helps them keep their jobs because, as Ms. Stuart says, *"It's one thing to getting a job; it's another to keeping it."* Other programs include how to start and manage your own business.

YWCAs and YWHAs around the nation usually have reentry employment programs for homemakers. Call the nearest Y for information. The YWCA in New York City, for example, has an 8-week course which trains women for basic office work. The trainees are placed in nonprofit volunteer agencies for a while in order to perfect their skills. The program also teaches resume writing and job interview skills. See Appendix H for more.

► **Contact the following for more information on non-profit employment services**

► Look in the phone book under the name of your city, county or state government and find a title which corresponds to one or more of the following: Job Service, county or state manpower commission, department of human resources, commission on economic development, department of employment services, state department of labor, agency on aging.

► Look in the Yellow pages under the following categories: Employment Services, Community Service Organizations, Senior Citizens' Organizations, religious denominations, Social Service Organizations. (The wording may vary somewhat.)

► Go to the local library. It is a huge repository of information on community resources.

► Write to the Employment and Training Administration, U.S. Department of Labor, 601 D Street, Washington, D.C. 20213.

► Call the local chamber of commerce. In some states it sets up joint operations with Private Industry Councils.

Rural residents can get help from the nearest community college, women's center, or information and referral center. In places where these do not exist there may be an outreach program whereby agency representatives visit counties to conduct programs. Contact one of the sources listed above for more information.

NEWSPAPERS

Although surveys show that help-wanted ads rank below networking and direct contacts with employers as a source of jobs, many people swear by them. How helpful they can be depends on the type of job you want. Ads that call for high-level and professional skills are worth looking into. Over 80% of employers in one survey said they use newspapers to advertise technical, managerial and professional openings. About 70% use the newspaper to advertise white collar and sales openings.

How to use newspaper ads

► Get the newspaper as soon as it's delivered, and answer the help wanted ads right away. Hundreds, maybe thousands, of qualified people may already have seen the same ad.

► Keep a stack of resumes handy. Even better, get a computer which will store your sample resume and cover letter for speedy tailoring to a specific job vacancy.

► If you are late in applying for a job, send your resume and letter by special delivery, express mail or fax machine. Many employers now include a fax number in their help-wanted ads.

► Wise job hunters send a second resume a day or two later just in case the first one is misplaced. It happens more often than you think.

► Learn to read between the lines. You'll see many ads that are filled with flowery phrases such as *"seeking highly motivated person,"* but few that focus on the company itself. A company that is proud of the way it treats its workers will brag about it: *"Our company is listed in 'The 100 Best Companies in America To Work For'."*[116]

Blind ads

These give a box number instead of the employer's name and address. Some people think it's a waste of time to respond to them since a company may place a blind ad to get information on the labor supply and salary levels or to test the loyalty of its employees. Nevertheless, one person's sour experience can be another's dream come true. Abraham Bernstein got a job in 1967 at Aamco

Transmissions, in Bala-Cynwyd, PA, by answering a blind ad. In 1970 he quit because there was someone else in the general manager position he wanted and he didn't want to wait. Six years later, while working as general manager at a different company, he received a call from Aamco saying the position was open. Within a short time he became its president and chief executive officer.[117]

Omnibus ads

These are usually placed by employment agencies. They list many vacancies that pay high wages. They sometimes are used as bait to attract more clients.

Ads that say "gal or guy friday wanted"

These are for entry-level, low-paying job openings. Generally they seek high school or college graduates with little experience. Experienced persons might consider such an opening as a step toward something better if it's in the industry, company or new occupation they want.

Ads that attract/discourage older workers

Magazines and newsletters for "mature" readers sometimes carry help-wanted ads, and not all are for low-level or part-time jobs. The CENTURY 21 corporation recently ran a full-page ad in *50 Plus* magazine calling for real estate salespersons. On the other hand, ads that say *"no experience necessary"* or *"2 to 3 years experience"* indicate the company seeks young, low-paid applicants.

Place your own "job wanted" ad

These are placed mainly by self-employed persons with skills needed in the community, such as tutors, repairmen, word processors and professionals. They are also useful for persons who have impressive or unusual credentials. If you are in this category, place your ad in the section where employers in your field are most likely to see it. Instead of placing an ad in the help-wanted section, for example, an expert in management information systems or an executive should place it in the business section.

Use newspapers to spot employment trends

A simple tally of advertised job openings will give you a general
idea of industries and occupations that are thriving and the salary
range in your occupation.

You also may see job opportunities you had not considered
and for which you qualify.

When a company places a large help-wanted ad that lists
several high-skill vacancies, it may be expanding. Even if your
particular occupation is not listed it's likely that they will need
additional support staff sooner or later — i.e., secretaries, maintenance, guards, word processors, receptionists. Contact the
personnel department and find out. If there is no immediate
opening in your field, send your resume and cover letter and ask
them to keep it on file until an opening comes up. Also scan the
headlines in the business section for news about companies that are
expanding.

National and large city newspapers

They are a good source of advertised job vacancies and up-to-date
business news. They also issue a Sunday supplement devoted
exclusively to help-wanted ads. Most of the advertised vacancies
are local, but you will also find ads for jobs in other states and in
foreign countries. Such ads generally call for highly skilled,
professional and other top-level persons who are in short supply.[118]

Out-of-town newspapers

They are an excellent source of employers to contact by fax, mail
or long distance phone call. *The Washington Post's* Sunday
Help-Wanted section, for example, contains ads placed by employers in the Washington, DC area, some of which list a toll-free
phone number or fax number.

If you succeed in getting an appointment for a job interview,
try to arrive a few days earlier so you can look at business
conditions and living costs in the community. Also look for leads
on unadvertised job vacancies. Call up other companies and ask if
they have any current vacancies or if they expect any soon. Ask
if they know of other employers who might need someone with
your qualifications. Leave your resume and cover letter for their
files. Scan the local newspapers for clues on living costs and the
quality of life — i.e., parks, recreation attractions, pollution, crime,
corruption, educational institutions, cultural attractions. Try to get
an idea of the health of local industries and companies. Study the

business section for clues on industries and companies that are expanding. Then call these employers about possible job vacancies.

Where to find these newspapers

Most libraries subscribe to national and local newspapers. The subscription copies may arrive several days after they appear on the newsstands. Since every minute counts, find out on what day of the week they usually arrive and get to the library as soon as possible. You can buy your own subscription to an out-of-town newspaper. The local librarian can tell you how to do this.

JOB FAIRS

These events are usually held in large cities. Often they are advertised as "Open House" events. Many seek workers for a single industry — engineering, health care, sales — but some are more comprehensive. The participating companies usually seek professional and other highly-skilled people. If there is a general labor shortage they also look at entry- to middle-level workers.

At a recent *"Sales Career Invitational"* job fair, managers from Fortune 500 firms were interviewing for hundreds of vacancies — e.g., executives, managers, market research specialists, engineers, territory representatives, account managers. Jobs were available in the following industries: telecommunications, industrial products, office products, medical/health care, air freight, transportation, consumer products, business services, financial services and computer hardware and software.

Some fairs are sponsored by a group of companies in a specific community or industry. Some are jointly sponsored by colleges and chambers of commerce. Many are arranged by private companies whose business it is to organize such events.

Attending a job fair is the quickest way to get several appointments for job interviews. You also may get information on other occupations and industries that can use your skills. In one hour you will meet more company representatives than you can during months of traditional job hunting. At a recent job fair a drugstore chain got the names of 25 job seekers they planned to call the following morning. A video chain found about 30 people they expected to hire as store managers and other high paying positions. Shipper Management Company was seeking persons for over 100 sales positions (to sell cemetery plots) paying $30,000 to $85,000 in the first year alone.[119]

If you do not live in a city which has job fairs it might be worthwhile to make travel and hotel arrangements and stay throughout an event. A single event lasts one day or two days at the most. First contact the sponsor and ask whether the attending companies are hiring people with your skills. Bring a stack of resumes and any other material you would like to leave with company representatives.

If you cannot attend, send your resume and cover letter to the participating companies. Many fairs have an address where you can send your resume for distribution to these companies.

You can learn about upcoming job fairs from the following sources:

► Look for newspaper advertisements of job fairs.

► Contact your local Chamber of Commerce.

► Ask a librarian how to get in touch with private firms which arrange job fairs. There are several dozen. Among these are Recourse Communications Inc., Career Concepts, Lendman Group, National Career Centers, BPI Inc., and Health Care Careers.

✢-✢

INDUSTRY PUBLICATIONS, CONFERENCES AND CONVENTIONS

Industry publications also carry help-wanted ads. Attending their conferences and conventions is a great way to make valuable contacts and learn about current trends. You may even be able to make a date for an interview. Your presence is tangible evidence of your interest in the industry and should be noted in your resume or cover letter under *Education and Training*.

PROFESSIONAL AND TRADE ASSOCIATIONS

Their newsletters and journals list job vacancies which are often not advertised in newspapers. Many also maintain a job bank for members. Not all the job openings require a license, certificate or degree in the particular field. There is a universal demand for computer programmers, systems analysts and administrators which cuts across professions and industries. The reason why such openings are listed is that they prefer to hire someone who has work experience or knowledge about the profession or industry.

HOW TO DEAL WITH REJECTION

"You can look at life in two ways: You can say, 'Isn't this a dreadful circumstance!' Or you can turn it around and say, 'I'm going to learn something from this.' You have to consciously and determinedly make things work to your advantage. That's an art at any age." — Ruth Mills, broadcaster, at age 93

Just about every high school and college student takes courses on how to choose a career and find a job. They also are told to expect many rejections before finding a good job and to learn from the experience. This puts the inexperienced, older job seeker at a disadvantage. Some become so despondent after one or two rejections they call it quits early in the game. A study of unemployed older women found they used fewer job search strategies than younger women. They were less likely to use personal contacts, employment services and help-wanted ads. They were more likely to walk in cold and ask for a job. They were handicapped before they even started.

If you are in this category, give yourself a chance. Improve your job search skills and learn from each rejection. A 55-year old woman who invested years and money for a degree in computer programming received eight rejections before finding the right job. A stock market analyst who quit a high paying job in order to become an interior designer found the right opening only after he had made about 100 phone calls. Chances are that you'll find a good job far sooner than these persons did. The current labor shortage is in your favor.

Find a Job Through Volunteer Work

Many employers view volunteer work as valuable work experience. It provides clues to your skills, energy level and personality. Of two equally qualified applicants, an employer will hire the one who has done extensive volunteer work. Mary Lou Petitt's 10 years of volunteer service in housing with the New Jersey League of Women Voters helped her get a paid position as housing consultant to the New Jersey Department of Community Affairs.[120]

Volunteer work is also credited for civil service jobs. Several years ago a sex discrimination lawsuit was filed by a homemaker who was denied a job with a New York State agency. Under an old policy, only paid work was acceptable. The charge was that more women than men have done volunteer work. She had listed two years as president of the PTA and the founding and directing of a day care center, activities which required as much as 50 hours a week of her time. As a result of the lawsuit, New York State now regards volunteer work as a legitimate credential.

If you are between jobs, volunteer work will fill gaps on your resume and job application. You'll have a ready answer when the interviewer asks, "What did you do between (X and Y) jobs?"

Volunteer work is also a good way to meet people who can help you find a paid job. About 29% of women in a survey said they had used the personal contacts made in volunteer work to get a paid job. Many had been out of the job market for years.

As in paid work, you usually work your way up to positions of greater responsibilities. This looks good on your resume and it increases your chances of meeting influential persons who can help you find a good paid job. P.R. was a volunteer worker in a community theater group in Washington, DC which raises funds for local charities. He eventually became its president. This brought him to the attention of the Greater Washington Board of Trade which hired him as manager of its membership bureau.[121]

Often volunteers become so valuable they are offered a permanent, paid job by the agency in which they serve. Many non-profit, public service organizations have paid staff members who started out as volunteers.

It's a good way to develop new job skills and upgrade rusty skills

Almost all public service organizations now have computers, laser printers, fax machines and other high-tech office equipment. You will get valuable exposure which can help you find a paid job.

Women who have been out of the job market for years can acquire skills and recent work experience which helps them find better paid jobs. There are more opportunities to develop higher level skills in volunteer work than in a lower level paid job. In 1987 there was a help wanted ad for an executive director: *"Non-profit women's organization seeks candidate with strong administration, leadership and community relations skills. Experience in fund raising and long range planning essential. Salary $36,000."* Homemakers who have held responsible volunteer positions in non-profit organizations have acquired such skills.

It helps retirees and homemakers

▶ *Retirees can find new careers*

After retirement, Louis R. of Malverne, NY, joined RSVP (Retired Senior Volunteer Professionals) to keep busy. They assigned him to the Department of Senior Citizen Affairs where his job was to match employers with older people. One day a call came from a company that audits telephone bills for businesses. They wanted a telephone marketing representative who would sell the service to company executives. Mr. R. recommended himself for the job. At the age of 73 he found a new career at the hours he wanted, from 9 a.m. to 1 p.m..

▶ *Returning homemakers gain self-confidence*

Self-confidence is a key to success in job hunting. Many homemakers mistakenly believe they can't do much of anything except keep house and raise children. Volunteer work gives them an opportunity to develop a sense of self-worth.

It can open doors to a new career

The best way to learn about a new career before you invest time and money preparing for it is to do volunteer work in that area. For example, a large variety of new jobs are opening in organizations which focus on older people and their needs. As a volunteer you'll learn about the types of jobs that are available and their training requirements. You'll make valuable personal contacts that can help you find a job later on. You'll also become familiar with major organizations in the field.

Senior centers offer excellent opportunities for returning homemakers. High school graduation is sufficient for many of the jobs involved, but a college degree is required for professional work. Plenty of financial aid is available to earn a degree because of the great need for geriatric workers. Hospitals, community mental health centers, adult day care centers, home health services, nursing homes, retirement communities, housing projects, public health clinics and the Veterans Administration all need volunteers.[122]

► *You can get 30 education credits or more through volunteer work*

Moreover, the course work will be easier since you'll know about the profession and its technical language. Volunteer work in a social work agency, for example, can shorten the 2-year Associate Degree program needed to get a paid job as social work aide, or a 4-year Bachelor's Degree program which is required of professional social workers. A volunteer legal aide can study for a 2-year certificate and become a paralegal professional. A volunteer nurse's aide can become a practical nurse with a 2-year certificate, or a registered nurse with a 4-year college degree. All these education programs give credit for relevant volunteer experience.

► *You might discover a new field of interest*

A freelance science writer signed up for New York City's School Volunteer Program after she saw a sign in the subway appealing for volunteers. *"I thought it was something I ought to do,"* she said. *"Now I like it so much I'm thinking of a teaching career."*[123]

"The biggest sin is sitting on your ass."
— Florynce Kennedy

Where to do volunteer work

► **Target the industry or organization**

Select the one(s) you want to work for — e.g., radio station, telecommunications, convention center — and offer to volunteer in return for gaining experience and training.

► **Colleges and universities**

Volunteers are needed for a wide range of assignments within the college itself or in the surrounding community. Valencia Community College, in Orlando, FL, uses volunteers in its Displaced Homemaker Program. They do counseling, research, public relations, clerical and other work. At Santa Fe Community College in Gainesville, FL volunteers work in local community agencies to help in poverty areas. They are also enrolled as full-time students in the college's human services program. After graduation the Associate Degree helps them get paid jobs. Contact your nearest community college or write to your state's department of higher education for information about volunteer programs.

► **The Peace Corps**

It needs volunteers of all ages and skill levels to serve from 3 to 27 months in developing nations. The projects they work on include business and public administration, health, natural resource development, and setting up small businesses and banks. A former chemical engineer served as a business adviser to small manufacturers in the Caribbean. His wife, a former homemaker, helped run a library system for the island's high school.

"Even with a master's degree, people who want to do international work need to go out and live somewhere," said Francine D. who served in El Salvador and later became a paid project administrator for a consulting firm.[124] The Corps serves in over 60 countries and teaches about 200 languages and dialects.

It needs persons who have practical experience as well as those with degrees. If you don't have a special skill, the Peace Corps will teach you one or help you develop your rusty skills. There is no upper age limit for eligibility as long as you are in good health. Married couples are eligible if they both serve. Handicapped persons have also served successfully.

Transportation to and from the country of destination is provided. There is a monthly allowance for food, rent, medical needs and travel within the country. Upon completion of service, volunteers receive a readjustment allowance for every month served.

For information and an application call toll-free 1-800-424-8580 ext. 93 or write to the Peace Corps, Room P-301-A, Washington DC 20526.

► VISTA

Volunteers In Service To America needs persons of all ages to serve for one year or more in depressed communities in the U.S. For this reason it has been dubbed the "domestic Peace Corp." Volunteers serve in education, neighborhood revitalization projects, unemployment counseling, day care, drug abuse, health, legal aid, and city planning programs. They may be assigned to work with migrant families in Florida, on an American Indian Reservation or an institution for the mentally handicapped. There is an allowance for food, housing, transportation and other necessities during the period of service and a readjustment allowance after it is completed.

► City/county government agencies and school systems

Their volunteer programs help youths, museums, schools, local government agencies, hospitals, and institutions for the handicapped and the elderly. Volunteers do accounting, research issues like health and aging, set up museum displays, direct group discussions in Senior Centers, help provide recreational and social work services to the homeless, and other kinds of work.

► Social service organizations

They also need volunteers. The Federation of Protestant Welfare Agencies, for example, helps community organizations such as museums, consumer affairs, research and planning agencies, day care centers, and hospitals and homes for the aging. Volunteers have served as budget consultant, member of the board of directors, librarian, bookkeeper, researcher, legal aide, fund raiser, interpreter, counselor, and in other capacities.

► AARP Volunteer Talent Bank

This is a program of the American Association of Retired Persons. It places persons over 50 in other AARP programs and in nonprofit organizations. They serve in crime prevention, consumer affairs, housing, inter-religious liaison, tax preparation, health care, worker equity, women's issues, housing and other activities. For information write to AARP Volunteer Talent Bank, Dept. MB7, 1909 K St. NW, Washington, DC 20049.

► **Conservation groups**

There are local and state chapters which employ accountants, ecologists, economists, writers, editors, educators, lobbyists, researchers, organizers, bookkeepers, and more.[125]

► **National Executive Service Corps**

It offers consulting services to small businesses and charitable or government organizations that can't afford the services of a private consulting firm. Volunteers usually are retired business executives who help with business plans, fund raising, communications, financial controls, labor negotiations, management information systems, marketing, strategic planning, and other issues. Volunteers who have no consulting experience are given special training. For information contact National Executive Service Corps, 257 Park Avenue South, New York, NY 10010; (212) 529-6660.

Where to get more information

Ask your former or present employer to steer you to a program. You can also contact one of the 400 clearinghouses in the nation which have volunteer job listings. They are listed in the phone book as Voluntary Action Center or Volunteer Information and Referral. In the Yellow Pages they are listed under Social Services or Community Organizations. Ask for assignments which will help you learn new skills or upgrade those you already have.

So Long, 9-to-5

Flexible work styles are becoming more prevalent in the new workplace. They include flextime, part-time, temporary full-time, work-at-home and job sharing. In 1989 the states of California and Washington started work-at-home programs for their employees to reduce the traffic congestion and pollution associated with driving to work. Other states and private businesses are expected to follow. Probably within your lifetime you will see traffic jams vanish and fewer hours wasted in commuting.

PART-TIME AND TEMPORARY FULL-TIME JOBS

Part-time work is officially defined as less than 35 hours a week. It can be done on a permanent or temporary basis. An assignment may last one day, several months, or a whole year. Permanent part-time jobs generally pay better than the temporary kind, especially at the higher skill levels. They often have fringe benefits, too, which temporary part-timers generally do not get.

Register with more than one employment agency and you'll be able to work as long as you like, whenever you like. You can work for a variety of employers or stay with one employer, coming in whenever they call you. Many companies and government agencies keep a permanent roster of part-timers who are on call throughout the year. Engineers, for example, can make a good living from temporary jobs that last from a few months to several years.

Advantages

▶ **It's a good way to get job leads.**

▸ The people you meet at work may know about full-time job openings elsewhere.

▸ Often a temporary assignment can lead to a permanent job with the same company.[126] The permanent jobs offered are not always the same ones performed as a temporary worker. Scott Lane quit his job as artistic director of a theater in Los Angeles to write musicals in New York City. To support himself he worked part-time as a word processor. A one-day assignment at Citibank stretched into several weeks. A manager who had heard about his artistic background asked him to help with a presentation. The results were so impressive that he was hired as a full-time creative assistant in the bank's communications division.[127] A woman who worked as a temporary secretary for a trade association heard about an editorial opening on its publications staff. She applied for the job and was hired.

▸ Employers prefer to hire people who have proven themselves to be reliable and capable. They often hire promising applicants as temporaries to test them or while awaiting approval to hire them as permanent full-time workers. In 1978 Stacey V. got a temporary job at Metro Goldman Mayer in New York City. Four weeks later she became a full-time secretary. Six years later she was assistant to the president.

▶ **It's a door-opener for people who have difficulty finding full-time work.**

The difficulty may be due to age discrimination, a physical handicap, or some other reason. If you are in this category, a temporary job is an opportunity to prove yourself. When a permanent opening occurs in the company, you are more likely to be hired than if you were to apply for the same job as an untested stranger.

A woman who had no work experience because of a congenital heart condition and a brief period of mental illness began her work career at age 32. While recuperating from heart surgery she studied stenography. After the recuperation she was able to build up her resume with temporary job assignments. One of these developed into a permanent, part-time job at Texaco in New York City. There she received excellent job performance reviews which helped her get a full-time job as secretary at a United Nations mission.

A senior employment agency sent a 74-year-old retired marketing manager on a temporary assignment to analyze a company's sales force. Without being asked, he recorded his observations on ways to improve the productivity of its sales force. The report — which revealed a sharp mind and invaluable experience — was so impressive that he was offered a full-time job.

▶ *If you plan to move*

Temporary work enables you to earn money while you learn about the job market in the new community.

▶ *If you are between jobs*

Temporary work will prevent embarrassing gaps on your resume and job application.

▶ *If you want to start a business*

Working temporarily in a similar business will give you valuable experience which will help reduce the risks involved.

▶ *If you are returning to the job market after a long absence*

Working in different companies and industries will help you to understand the changes in the new workplace. You will see, and maybe work with, the latest technological equipment. It's no big deal to learn how to use a fax machine, but it will be a big deal if you include such experience on your resume and job application.

▶ *If you are changing careers or upgrading your skills*

Temporary work will help pay the rent while you take adult education courses. You can even learn new skills free of charge or at low cost from a temporary employment agency. The larger agencies offer training on word processing, spreadsheet and desktop publishing software. If your office skills are rusty, you will be sent on job assignments that match your level of performance. As your skills improve you'll be given more complex assignments and better pay.

► **If you want to travel**

You'll be able to take off whenever you like without worrying about being fired. You can even work your way around the world as the Australians do. Some large employment agencies have branches throughout the U.S. and in foreign countries. They can help you find work wherever you want to go.[128]

Disadvantages

► **Lower than average pay**

Although an increasing number of temporary jobs pay the going rate, far too many still pay less. Some employers pay only a third of the full rate, reports the Association of Part-Time Professionals.[129] In fact, sometimes they ask a temporary worker to take work home at no additional pay.

► **Few or no paid benefits.**

Few temporary workers receive paid vacations, holidays, social security, medical insurance and pension plans. They are also excluded from company training programs. Large companies are more likely to offer paid benefits to temporaries who work 20-29 hours a week. Small firms generally cannot afford it.

The labor shortage is improving matters. More companies are luring highly-skilled temporary workers with benefit packages that include health and life insurance, paid vacation, and child-care allowance. More temporary placement agencies are offering vacation pay, cash bonuses, medical and dental insurance, profit sharing and tuition reimbursement to their regular temporaries. Recently, new legislation was proposed to extend such benefits to most temporary workers.[130]

► **"People dump on you when you're just a daily temp."**

Thus complained a woman who naively believed that her Masters Degree in Fine Arts would open doors for her in the business world. After months of futile job hunting, her savings were nearly depleted. She had two choices — go on welfare or become a temporary clerical worker. The low pay and unchallenging work were bad enough; she also got the heavy workloads. She also complained about being *"treated like dirt."* This is not unusual. Temporary workers are often given peak work loads and assignments with frequent, heavy deadlines.

▶ *Job security is poor.*

Many employers, including government agencies, keep temporary workers on call for years. When business is up, the workers are called in. When it goes down, they are the first to go.

▶ *Out of sight, out of mind*

When it's time for career advancement, many permanent part-time workers are forgotten. Often, they are not considered for short-term, challenging projects. However, those whose skills and work habits are valued get good assignments, reports the Part-Time Professional Association. They need to make themselves seen, heard and available where the action is.

Many people stay in a temporary job for years in the futile hope that it will lead to a permanent, full-time offer. Meanwhile, they get no benefits and no pay increases. There were temporary clerical workers in one state government agency who had been there for as long as seven years, earning little more than the minimum wage and receiving no paid holiday or medical insurance.

What kinds of jobs are available?

Medium- and lower-skill occupations which have a lot of part-time and temporary jobs include the following.

accounting clerk	machine operator
computer operator	medical secretary
convention	proofreader
hosts/hostesses	product demonstrator
data entry operator	promoter and tester
general office work	receptionist
interviewers	sales clerk
legal secretary	telephone salesperson
light industrial worker	typist

High-skill and professional part-time and temporary full-time jobs are increasing for executives, financial officers, engineers, designers, marketing specialists, physicians, lawyers and others. A lawyer, for example, can get assignments that range from a single courtroom appearance to a full year's service at a law firm. For years several engineers have been working as temporary employees of Pitney Bowes. They get the same or higher pay than the staff engineers but no benefits.

The demand for managers to work on a short-term or project basis is also growing. Former middle- and upper-level managers with 10-20 years of experience are often hired for such assignments. Many are near retirement age. In 1988 they earned from $30-$100 per hour.[131] New, small companies also need part-time chief financial officers to provide control when financial crises or organizational problems arise.[132]

Opportunities are increasing in the health, engineering and high-tech industries. If you have a degree or certificate in an occupation which has a shortage of workers — e.g., physical therapy or nursing — you can find work whenever or wherever you like at good pay.

Specialists in the following occupations can also find temporary or part-time work at good pay.

accountant	paralegel
advertising copywriter	pharmacist
auditor	management consultant
computer graphics	market researcher
computer programming	money manager
controller	researcher
desktop publishing	statistician
direct-mail specialist	training and development
human resources generalist	writer/researcher
laboratory technician	X-Ray technician

How much is the pay?

Temporary and part-time workers in high-demand, high-skill occupations often get more pay than permanent workers. Workers with lower-level skills, or skills that are in low demand, generally get less than regular workers. If they work at odd hours such as night shifts, weekends, and during high volume periods they can earn higher hourly pay than full-time employees. Such work can be found in banks, insurance companies, department stores, airlines, accounting firms, resort hotels, and other industries which have high-low cycles of business.

Where to find temporary and part-time jobs

▶ If you are an executive or professional you can more readily find such work in small firms and in nonprofit organizations such as trade and professional organizations and foundations.

▸ If you join The Association of Part-Time Professionals — See Appendix F — you'll receive its newsletter, *The Part-Time Professional*, and have access to its Job Referral Service. Many jobs are listed in the newsletter, but more are obtainable through the Job Referral Service. Some of the jobs listed involve working at home via telecommuting or telephone.

▸ Executives can also find temporary work through local small business associations.

▸ The help-wanted ads placed by large employment agencies often include temporary assignments. Call and ask whether they have work in your field. If they do not, ask if they know of any local employers who do.

▸ Look in the professional and trade publications. These also have help-wanted ads which include temporary assignments.

▸ You can also write to employers directly, offering your services. Nearly all U.S. companies use temporary workers. Many large corporations rehire their retired employees as temporaries. They often hire executives, top managers, and professional employees as consultants. Some also maintain work pools of retired technicians, clerical workers, and skilled blue-collar workers. Even though you were not on their payroll, it's possible to get your name on their list of badly needed, skilled workers.[133]

Many small companies also need skilled retirees to come in a few hours a week or to work on special projects. They need bookkeepers, computer specialists, researchers, managers and other high-skilled workers.

▸ Federal, state and municipal governments hire many people for a wide range of temporary full-time and part-time jobs. You can get information at the local Jobs Service office.[134]

▸ Register with several temporary employment agencies. Unlike the traditional employment agencies, they hire you and then assign you to employers who need temporary workers. They pay your salary, taxes, social security and certain fringe benefits. Besides part-time day work you can get full work weeks, evening and weekend assignments. If you register with several agencies you can make a full-time career as a temporary worker.

Some temporary agencies specialize in a particular occupation or industry. If you have specialized skills it's best to register with one of these so you'll get more steady work.[135]

Some temporary agencies specialize in finding work for persons over a certain age. The largest of these, Mature TempsAmerica, has offices in several cities. Many of these agencies, however, are small. Senior Resources, in New York City, for example, finds permanent, part-time office jobs for older persons. Some of these are job share positions. (See below.) It has placed persons ranging in age from their late fifties to late seventies.

You also can find temporary or part-time work through the following sources.

- Look in the Yellow Pages under *Employment Contractors, Temporary Help.*
- Look in out-of-state Yellow pages and newspapers and the *Encyclopedia of Associations* for temporary services in other communities.
- Contact the Association of Part-Time Professionals, Flow General Bldg., 7655 Old Springhouse Road, McLean, VA 22102; Phone: 703-734-7975.

JOB SHARING

This is a form of permanent part-time work in which two or more persons have the same job. They share the responsibilities, pay, benefits and working hours. Unlike temporary part-time workers, job sharers can more readily advance in their careers.

According to the Part-Time Professionals Association, any job can be shared. Those that have been successfully shared include secretary, lawyer, school administrator, teacher, school librarian, economist, personnel executive, research assistant and engineer.

However, job share positions are rarely given to newcomers. You have to be a valued, trusted employee with needed skills, someone who is viewed as too good to lose. It's easier to get a job share position if you're in a field where there is a worker shortage or if you have a unique ability or skill.

How to get a job-share position

A few employment agencies, such as Senior Resources (see above), have job share assignments. You can also ask agencies which specialize in your field of work if they have, or expect to have, such positions. If there is a labor shortage in your field it will be easier to convince them to refer you and someone else to share one job. But first do some homework. There are some potential problems in job sharing — especially with a stranger — which you should know about. The sources listed in Appendix F can help you.

Contact a federal, state or local government agency, and ask if there are job-share positions available. They are more likely to experiment with various forms of flextime work.

FLEXTIME WORK

Labor experts predict that by the year 2000 more than 50% of workers will be involved in these new work styles, and many will be at, or beyond, the retirement age.

The most common form of flextime work is the 8-hour-a-day, 5-day-a-week schedule in which YOU, not someone else, decide when to start and stop working. However, you must be present during a certain period each day, usually from 10 a.m. until 3 p.m. You can work between 8 a.m. and 4 p.m., 10 a.m. and 6 p.m., or any other schedule that is convenient.

The second most common form squeezes 35 or 40 hours of work into less than five days a week. A 5-day, 40-hour week can be squeezed into four days of 10 hours each, or three days of about 13 hours each. Or you can work 4 or 5 hours a day, 7 days a week, or 10 hours a day for 3 days and 5 or more hours the next.

Flextime work can be arranged in many ways. An industrial relations specialist in a federal agency begins work at 6:30 A.M. and leaves at 2:30 P.M. every month except in summer when he works longer weekdays and takes three-day weekends. The Federal Government's alternative work schedule program allows thousands of full-time employees to adjust their schedule to suit their needs.

A compressed month or year works in the same manner, but the longer workdays are balanced by a shorter month or year. Under this plan you can attend school full-time for a semester, start a home business or do something else and still keep your job.

The flexyear contract, as it is known, has been popular in Europe but is rare in the U.S. A plan is made for the entire year which determines how much time you want to put in each day on the job and how much vacation you will have. The proportion of work and vacation time doesn't matter as long as you complete the yearly quota of work. You and your boss may agree on an overtime workweek for eight months a year, giving you four months of vacation. Or, you may agree on five hours of work each workday all year round, or work 12 hours a day for a year and take a year off, or any other variation which suits you both.

Advantages/disadvantages

The obvious advantage of flextime work is that it allows you to choose a schedule which suits your lifestyle. You'll also save in commuting time and expenses. A less obvious advantage is the elimination or reduction of job "burn out." However, some employers have abandoned flextime schedules because their workers suffered from chronic fatigue, irritability and poor job performance. There were other problems such as conflicts in scheduling.

Where to find flextime jobs

Flextime hours are better suited for the following types of work.

→ Occupations that involve creative work such as artists, editors, writers, computer programmers, software developers and designers.

→ Those that require little supervision as in many professions and managerial positions.

→ Occupations where there is a shortage of skilled and professional workers such as nurses and computer specialists.

Certain types of industries are more likely to have flextime positions.

→ Federal, state and municipal governments are pioneers in flextime schedules, particularly for high-level, high-skilled employees.

→ Companies that are open for business 24-hours a day such as car-rental firms, hotels, catalog retailer.

→ Companies that have heavy-light work cycles — e.g., banks, retail stores and mail order firms.

→ Home-based businesses also are more likely to offer flexible schedules and work at home jobs.

TELECOMMUTING JOBS

How would you like to work at home, by a lake in the mountains, in the sunny Caribbean, or wherever else you want? Computers, fax machines, portable telephones and other technological miracles now make this possible. Instead of taking a bus or subway, many white collar workers "telecommute" to a central office. A growing number of executives and professionals also telecommute for at least part of the week or month. Employers now can hire good workers anywhere in the world where these new machines can be installed. A New York-based corporation, for example, can assign word processing and other data-entry work to employees who live in El Paso, Texas or even in a foreign country.

How does it work?

Some employers require their telecommuters to be in the office during certain days of the week. Others only require that they come in occasionally. The amount of time a telecommuter can work at home is also determined by the type of job. Many graphic artists, writers, computer programmers, and software developers can work at home full-time.

Who benefits?

▶ *Residents of small, rural communities*

More job opportunities are available as companies open satellite offices in distant communities. Recently a claims processing office opened in International Falls, a tiny town near the Canadian border. The employer, United Health Care Inc., is an insurance company based near Minneapolis. The owner made an arrangement with the nearest community college to offer courses in office technology so the residents could train for the new jobs.

▶ *Certain professionals and high-level employees*

With a fax machine, lap computer and spreadsheet software, corporate accountants and financial executives can work on company files at home or at the beach. A growing number of chief executive officers are able to plan their company's policies in the mornings and evenings and play golf in the afternoon. Graphics artists, corporate designers, public relations experts and other professionals can also be blissfully absent during the morning commuter crunch.

▶ *Handicapped persons*

The computer now makes it possible for thousands of severely disabled persons to earn a good living. A paraplegic, who formerly subsisted on a $312 monthly Social Security check, was earning over $1,100 a month as a word processor for American Express. Several other large companies hire severely disabled persons to do programming and other types of computer work. A non-profit organization called Lift in Northbrook, IL trains qualified persons for such jobs.

How much does it pay?

Highly skilled and upper-level telecommuters generally get the same salary and benefits as their counterparts who work at the office. For example, Aetna Life & Casualty's systems programmers who work at home receive the same salary and overtime pay as those who work full-time in the office.

Generally it's the entry-level workers who are not paid well. Data entry workers who work at home, for example, receive about 25%-30% less than regular office employees who do the same work, and often they get few or no benefits. But some companies — e.g., Levi Strauss, Travelers Corporation, Pacific Bell, J.C. Penney — pay their home workers the same as their office employees and offer paid benefits as well.

Some work-at-home programs have been accused of being "electronic sweatshops." Several insurance companies have been accused of paying workers who process claims at home by the quantity of work done rather than by the hour. This practice of piece work was condemned in factory sweatshops at the turn of the century.

Advantages

Many retirees, students, and persons with home responsibilities accept the lower pay and lack of paid vacations and benefits so they can work at home. Telecommuters also save in commuting time and expense. In 1989 a person working full-time at home could save more than $2,000 a year in commuting costs, restaurant meals, business clothes and cleaning bills.

Disadvantages

Some experts say office employees who work at home are more easily exploited because they work alone and have no labor unions to represent them. If business turns sour they are the first to lose their jobs. Often they work long hours without overtime pay.[136] In 1987 a group of claims processors sued a Sacramento life insurance company. One of their complaints was that they had been pressured into working as much as 16 hours a day at home and the company had misrepresented the working arrangements.

Legislation was proposed recently to give home workers the same rights as other employees — unemployment insurance, worker's compensation coverage, paid vacation, overtime pay and other benefits.

Difficulties to expect

This type of work is not for everyone. How will YOU deal with the following, typical problems that might occur?

► The temptation to take time off can be irresistible when no one is looking over your shoulder. Persons who do boring, routine work, such as data entry or word processing, are especially susceptible. Working at home requires good organization, privacy, and a lot of self-discipline.

► Your work schedule is easily interrupted by neighbors, spouses and children who make demands on your time.

► Cabin fever can creep up on you before you realize what's happening. A recent study found that working alone at home increases stress, possibly because of the lack of emotional support from office workers.

► If your work is engrossing, you can easily become a workaholic.

► You are cut off from the valuable office networking that can help advance your career.

► Certain occupations — those that require client contact, supervision of others and teamwork — are especially ill suited.

► Too much togetherness can increase family or marital strife.

These and other minor problems can be prevented If you are seriously considering a work-at-home job. See Appendix F for the titles of several books which give tips on how to set up a home office, ensure privacy, resist temptation and — most important — ward off the "out of sight, out of mind" peril that keeps you off the promotion ladder.

How to find a work-at-home job

Opportunities will vastly increase if you own a computer, modem and fax machine. You also need typing skills to do computer work at home. Low-cost adult education courses can teach you how to type, work with computers and use word processing and spreadsheet software. In some communities persons who are unemployed or over a certain age can take such courses for free or at reduced charge. Many temporary employment agencies offer free or low-cost training in these skills.

▶ **Jobs that are suitable for working at home**

One or more of the following characteristics are common:

- They require little face-to-face contact.
- They can be processed on a computer and the output transmitted by computer or fax machine.
- They are not tied to a specific address.
- They involve working in the evenings and weekends — e.g., credit card processing, travel reservations, bookkeeping, data-entry, word processing, insurance claims processing, forms and applications processing, telephone order taking.

High-skill and professional work which can be done at home include the following:

accountants	graphic artists
broadcast technicians	lawyers
budget analysts	managers
computer technicians	marketing specialists
computer programmers	planners
desktop publishing	proofreaders
editors	researchers
engineering projects	statisticians
executives	stockbrokers
financial analysts	writers

A Wall Street stockbroker — who wanted to live and work in the Berkshire mountains — asked her boss for permission to work at home on a trial basis. To test whether the experiment would be cost-profitable, she at first paid for the phone, secretary, rent and utilities. By the end of the trial period her productivity had increased so much that she was in the top 10% of her firm's brokers in total commissions. This convinced her employer to pay all the bills from then on. She was so good that eventually she was promoted to senior vice president. *"People say you have to be close to the throb and pulse of Wall Street, but this is a phone business,"* she explained. The computer gives her access to stock information at the same moment it reaches brokers on Wall Street. *"As long as I have this, I can sit in an igloo."*[137]

Companies that have telecommuting programs

An increasing number of companies employ telecommuters. The following companies and industries had such positions available recently and probably still do.

▸ Information processing, high-technology and telephone companies have been the most active experimenters in the new work styles. They include Mountain Bell, IBM, Digital Equipment, Xerox, AT&T, New York Telephone, Southern New England Telephone, Pacific Bell, Rising Star Industries and Control Data.

▸ Financial and insurance companies have recently jumped on the telecommuting bandwagon. These include Citibank, Equitable Life, Manufacturers Hanover Trust, New York Life, Chase Manhattan Bank, Blue Cross & Blue Shield, Aetna Life & Casualty and Travelers.

▸ Some retail companies like J.C. Penney.

▸ Other employers include Johnson & Johnson, Levi Strauss, the U.S. Federal Office of Personnel Management, Los Angeles County, the states of Hawaii and Washington, and the California Public Utilities Commission.

Beware of work-at-home schemes

You probably have seen magazine and newspaper ads that say you can make a lot of money "right in the comfort of your home." According to the U.S. postal inspector, there is little chance of making much money from such schemes. These usually are rackets which involve stuffing envelopes, assembling small equipment from overpriced parts — which you buy from the company that promises to buy the finished equipment from you or guarantees that you will make a profit selling them by mail — and buying expensive camera equipment from a company that offers to buy your photographs.

Their ads promise unrealistically high profits and are filled with hyperbole: *"Earn hundreds of dollars a week at home in your free* time!" "Guaranteed huge market!" "No experience necessary!" There may also be glowing testimonials from anonymous persons. Often they require you to buy an expensive starter kit or send money for more instructions. An ad might say, "Earn $350 a week stuffing envelopes at home! For instructions and materials, send $10!" A Government investigation found that only 2 out of 50 companies actually paid people for this kind of work. After paying the fee they received only a plan for doing the same thing they were instructed to do — place a classified ad to solicit envelope stuffers to whom they sent similar plans.

Why Not Be Your Own Boss?

This chapter has enough information to help you decide whether owning a business is a better alternative than getting a job. It's not the whole story, not by any means. If it whets your appetite for entrepreneurship, Appendix G has sources of information on how to start a business and where to get help.

Opportunities to start a small business are increasing rapidly as a result of the following:

▶ Modern technology — inexpensive computers, printers, copiers, fax machines and other electronic marvels — makes it possible for one or two persons to run a profitable business from home or from a small, rural community.

▶ Large companies are shutting down entire departments in order to cut costs. They need small businesses to provide the services and products that were formerly available in-house.

▶ More American companies are establishing operations in, and doing business with, foreign countries. They need new types of services that small businesses can best provide, like language translation and arranging the details of overseas travel.

▶ Demographic and cultural changes in the nation are creating many more opportunities. A home-based business can easily provide personal services and products that two-career couples, working mothers and the elderly cannot provide for themselves.

The 65-plus generation is increasing at twice the rate of the general population. They need services such as health care, home repair and shopping. Products need to be redesigned and new ones created for them.

Moreover, Americans are retiring at a younger age. Small businesses can provide travel services, guided tours, fitness clubs and other ways to fill their leisure time.

Ethnic communities and other fast-growing market segments are creating exciting new opportunities for small businesses.

As American consumers become more affluent and sophisticated, they acquire a taste for specialty items. Thirty years ago in Columbia, SC, it was hard to find gourmet foods that were readily available in major cities like San Francisco. Today there are many small specialty stores and mail order businesses that sell exotic foods such as egg rolls and macadamia nuts.

Rebecca Matthias spotted a business opportunity after searching in vain for maternity clothes that were suitable for her management level job. She started "Mothers Work" in Philadelphia to manufacture maternity clothes for executive women. At first she sold her products by mail-order, then through retail stores, and finally through franchises. That was in 1982. By 1986 her business had become a $2.5 million dollar company.[138]

WHY PEOPLE START A BUSINESS
For more independence

Many people who've lost their jobs or other means of support in recent years have started a business. Betty Isaacson began making wood-and-fabric home decorations in her kitchen to supplement the family income during the farm crisis. Five years later her business, Betsy Bobbins Inc., employed 40 workers and had moved into a 2,800 square foot building on her farm in Loomis, Nebraska. Gross sales were about $1 million.[139]

Many people, including high-salaried workers, quit their jobs to start a business because they grow tired of the 9-to-5 routine or the rat race. Others decide to take a risk and apply their talents, skills and experience to earn profits for themselves, not for someone else.

"When you are on your own, you get paid what you are worth, not what your job is worth," said Mary Kay Ash, founder of Mary Kay Cosmetics Inc. She started her company in 1963 after resigning from a direct mail company where she had continually been passed over for promotions. In 1983 her company earned $600 million in sales.

When Barbara Haas learned that her male colleagues were earning $25,000 a year more than she was getting, she quit her job at a law firm, withdrew $2,000 in savings, and started a consulting firm, Pension Parameters Inc., in New York City. That was in 1971 By 1985 she was managing over $600 million in pension funds for over 1,500 corporate clients.[140]

To live and work where they want

Others want to live in a different climate or to flee urban pollution, crime and traffic congestion. A woman in her fifties left the blizzards of the Northeast to open a leather crafts shop in the airport of a Caribbean island. Others who love snow sports have set up a mail order or service business in or near a ski resort area.

For more time to do what they want

Some people start a part-time business so they'll have more time for fun or pet projects, not to make a lot of money. Usually they work as freelancers. Ginny K., at age 58, quit a high-paying job as systems analyst because she wanted to paint and help her husband run a home-based export business. *"My income suddenly plunged and my standard of living skyrocketed. I've never been happier,"* she says.

Some people plan to develop their business to the point where they can take only the amount of orders that gives them more time for leisure. Others plan to develop a thriving business, sell it for a hefty capital gain, and take it easy.

To do more creative work

Many people who are bored with their jobs start a business with no intention of striking it rich. They subsist on an uncertain income in order to do work they love and for variety and challenge. For some, wealth comes as an unexpected side benefit. Mitch Kapor's hobby of creating computer programs has made him a multimillionaire. He started the Lotus Development Corporation to sell one of his creations, the Lotus 1-2-3 spreadsheet.

Others have gone into business after their idea to improve a product or service, or to create a new one, was rejected. Thanks to their employer's short-sightedness, some have become very rich. In 1956 H. Ross Perot was a successful IBM computer salesman in Dallas. One day he noticed that many of his corporate customers didn't know how to make the best use of the computers he sold them. He had an idea to package data-processing and consulting services together with the hardware. After it was rejected by IBM, he resigned, withdrew $1,000 from his savings account, and started a business to provide the new service. EDA is today a major corporation.[141]

To supplement an income, maybe even get rich

Usually it's not the professionals and executives who become millionaires; it's the owners of small, run-of-the-mill businesses. If your goal is to be rich, you have a better chance of succeeding as an entrepreneur than as an employee. You need a hot idea for a product or service which is in demand and the willingness to put in most of your time, energy and capital investment.[142]

This is especially true for management-level women who still face career obstacles in the business world. The proportion of self-employed women who made $75,000 or more in 1984 was seven times greater than the proportion of women making that much in salaried jobs, according to a survey by *Working Woman* magazine.[143]

Because they can't get or hold a job for some reason

If you can't work a 9-to-5 job because of a physical handicap or some other reason, a home business is a terrific way to earn a living or supplement an income. Coralee Kern started her home-based MAID TO ORDER service after developing a disability which forced her to quit a job that barely paid enough to feed herself and her children. Within a few years it was grossing $300,000.

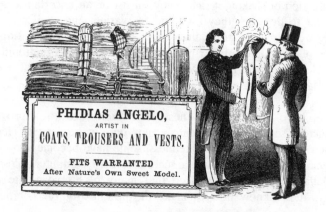

PHIDIAS ANGELO,
ARTIST IN
COATS, TROUSERS AND VESTS.

FITS WARRANTED
After Nature's Own Sweet Model.

QUALITIES NEEDED FOR SUCCESS

At first glance, statistics on the high failure rate of new businesses look grim. The Small Business Administration reports that three out of four small businesses fail within the first year, and nine out of ten fail within ten years.

The figures don't show how many failures were due to business owners quitting too early in the game. They don't reveal how many started over again and later became successful. Most successful entrepreneurs, like Henry Ford, had two or three failures before they learned to do it right. Many entrepreneurs who eventually succeed say their earlier failures were valuable learning experiences.

Many successful entrepreneurs began with no college degree, no prior business experience and no big bank account. All they had was a good idea at the right time and the personal qualities to make a go of it. Do you recognize yourself in the following personal criteria needed for success in business ownership?

Are you self-reliant?

Winners don't need anyone to lean on when there are problems to solve and decisions made. They enjoy taking risks, solving problems and doing the creative work themselves. If you feel more secure working under supervision, think twice about starting a business. Consider a franchised business where everything is pre-arranged for you.

Are you willing to take calculated risks?

Successful entrepreneurs, like successful corporate executives, are gamblers. They gamble on the future. But first they learn all about the market for their product or service. Then they take action. Not all small business ventures involve taking a substantial risk, however, and there are proven techniques for reducing the risks involved.

Are you creative?

Some of the most creative people have mediocre I.Q. scores. What they do have is an uncanny ability to generate a lot of ideas, many of which seem crazy, impractical and unworkable at first. People laughed at the idea of flying in the air like birds. Another hilarious inspiration which will soon become a reality is trains speeding at several hundred miles an hour on a cloud of electrified air.

Creative persons see opportunities where merely intelligent people see nothing. They are able to spot a consumer need that nobody else is meeting or find ways to improve an existing service or product. They view obstacles which discourage most people as fascinating problems to solve. The man who invented the cotton swab after watching his wife laboriously wrap absorbent cotton around a matchstick made millions. Many of the best money making ideas are ridiculously simple.

Do you like change and variety?

A business operation rarely runs on a straight line. It goes up and down like a roller coaster. You have to be prepared to revise your business plan periodically in response to the inevitable surprises and changes that occur while doing business.

Do you have some talent or expertise in what you plan to sell?

Some people became successful beyond their wildest dreams working at what they know and like to do best. Many others with a great idea failed because they lacked experience in, or knowledge of, the field they were in.

Mary Farrar, a Kansas City homemaker with five children, got a job as bookkeeper for a local steel contractor because she needed extra money. Soon she was also supervising the fieldwork. In 1978, with $500 in savings, she started her own steel-contracting business, Systems Erectors. By 1987 she was selling about $5 million worth. *"There is nothing special about me. I had no family members in the business, little formal education, no business training, no money, no genius."*[144]

In 1976 Joan Barnes, mother and former dance and recreation teacher, developed a preschool exercise program for the local community center. It became so popular that she started Gymboree Inc., in Burlingame, CA. By 1979 she was selling franchises and by 1986 it had grown into an $8 million company.[145]

Margaret Rudkin was the best cook in the neighborhood. The demand for her pies, cakes and cookies was so great that she began selling them by mail order in 1937. Twenty years later her Pepperidge Farm business was sold to the Campbell Soup Company for $28 million.

Are you self-confident?

Are you willing to wait, probably years, before the big payoff? Someone asked a millionaire how he made his fortune during the Great Depression while everyone else was going broke. He replied, *"Good judgement."* And how does one acquire such good judgement? *"Experience,"* was his reply. How did he get such valuable experience? *"By making mistakes,"* he said. Learn from your mistakes. Don't be clobbered by them.

Many new owners quit before giving their business a chance to succeed. They underestimate the time it takes to break even. Winners, on the other hand, know it can take up to two years just to complete the preliminary steps to start a business. Some quit because they get tired of 60-hour work weeks and the feast-famine income their business generates during the early years. They long for the good old 8-hour workdays and a steady paycheck. Others find that starting a business disrupts their family and social life more than they are willing to accept. Still others panic when they face unexpected problems they must solve alone.

Self-confidence enables new business owners to surmount the inevitable disappointments and emergencies. *"For every business success I've had there have been five setbacks. You just have to keep pursuing what you want until you get over the barriers,"* said the owner of a small bath shop in Greenwich Village, NY.

Self-confidence is more than a passive belief in your abilities. It comes from careful research, followed by a detailed plan of actions to take before you start the business and during its initial phase. It involves making preparations in case things go wrong when you least expect them to, such as a breakdown in vital equipment or an unexpected expense. It involves devising ways to boost your morale whenever exhaustion and unexpected setbacks make you feel like giving up.

Are you a workaholic?

A curious thing happens to people when they start working for themselves. They put in longer hours and more effort than when they worked for someone else. They are even willing

to sacrifice their social life to get the business going. In a recent survey of 3,000 newly formed or newly purchased businesses, 53% of the respon-dents said they spent 60 or more hours a week working at their business. Almost 20% also had a full- or part-time job.[146]

Are you well-organized and attentive to details?

For want of a nail a shoe was lost; for want of a shoe, a horse was lost; and for want of a horse, a battle was lost. A major reason for business failure is that people don't put in the time required to attend to details and work out an efficient plan of action *before* starting the business, says the Small Business Administration. It's the only way to keep from getting swamped by the mountain of things that were due last month.

Every detail of producing, packaging, and marketing a product or service needs planning, no matter how trivial it seems. Even choosing the right package color can make the difference between winning or losing out to a competitor.

In 1981 two former guitar teachers started a bakery, The Well-Bred Loaf, with the idea of using only natural ingredients. By 1985 revenues had climbed to about $4.5 million. They attribute their success to the attention paid to details and marketing. For example, they prod store owners to keep the items refrigerated and return stale items without charge. If a cookie is over-baked, or the color on the brownie doesn't look right, it is pulled out. Instead of using powdered eggs they cracked fresh eggs by hand until they found a machine to do it. They were not tempted to cheat by thinning the brownie batter, even though it was so thick it couldn't be poured by a machine.[147]

HOW TO GET A GOOD BUSINESS IDEA

Do you have a skill or expertise that will sell?

Make a list of all the things you know or can do well that you can sell or teach others — e.g., a school subject, a craft, computer programming, landscaping, playing a musical instrument, a foreign language. McAdoo Rugs, in North Bennington, VT, started out as a retirement hobby in 1975. In 1986 it employed nearly three dozen craftsmen and sold about 1,000 rugs a year at prices ranging from $270 for a 34-inch rug to $72 a square foot for large rugs. More than a third of the rugs are custom orders for which there is an additional fee of $50 to $200.[148]

Find an unmet business need

Look for a needed service or product which no one else is providing. Laura Newman ran into an unexpected problem soon after starting a home business. (Her ingenious solution may have earned her a small fortune by the time you read this.) When clients phoned they could hear her baby crying, dog barking and other non-business noises in the background. This dilemma inspired her to tape record and sell a cassette with typical busy office sounds. It is so realistic that clients often apologize for calling at a busy time.[149]

In 1982 there were about 1,000 small manufacturing firms in Long Island, NY, each grossing at least $500,000 yearly. Some were started by mid-life career changers in a garage where they assembled or manufactured items — e.g., fiber optics and computer chips — needed by the new and rapidly growing high-technology industry on the Island.

Valerie Freeman of Dallas taught business administration until the day she noticed that her students got jobs as soon as they learned word processing. In 1981 she started Wordtemps Inc., a temporary personnel agency. By 1985 her gross sales had reached $6 million.[150]

Rita Addison left her psychotherapy practice to start Clean Air Associates, a Boston-based business which serves Fortune 500 companies. In 1986 they were paying up to $35,000 to learn how to set up no-smoking policies and for advice on the legal, economic, and health ramifications of the policies. She also runs training sessions for supervisors who will enforce the no-smoking rules.[151]

Find an unmet personal need/interest

► As prices come down, sales of "smart" home appliances, computers, copiers, fax machines, printers and the like will soar. Their owners will need low-cost repair services and help in learning to operate them.

► The current national concern over food additives and other contaminants that cause health problems is creating a demand for natural food products which can be sold by mail order.

► The computer has created a need to supply all kinds of products and services to homes and organizations.

When Gail Ray worked for IBM, she received many calls from customers who wanted to rent computer equipment. In those days computer rentals were unavailable. In 1983 she quit her job to start PCR Personal Computer Rentals in Coral Gables, FL. In the beginning, she dealt with the customers and suppliers, and she picked up, delivered and installed the equipment without help. A stockbroker who was looking for a tax shelter gave her the financial backing to franchise her business. By 1989 her firm had become the nation's largest chain of computer rental stores.

► America is becoming an increasingly multiethnic society. There are many opportunities to satisfy their diverse cultural needs and preferences, as the following case shows.

A unique business idea came to Taylor Barnes and Wayne Wilson when they couldn't find an suitable birthday card for Wilson's grandmother. First, they searched through many stationery stores to see if any upscale ethnic greeting cards existed. After finding none, they hired a local printer to print 2,000 Christmas cards which focus on African imagery and art-deco designs that Barnes had designed. The hard part was convincing local stores to put the cards on display. The cards sold out within days. That was in 1983. By 1987 their company, L'Image Graphics, had become one of the fastest-growing card companies in the U.S. with expected sales of $600,000.[152]

Create a new need

Several years ago everyone seemed to want a Pet Rock. The person who got the idea of advertising and selling four huge Idaho potatoes nestled in a cedar lined box for $20 plus shipping and handling also made a small fortune.

Ed Lowe created a more enduring new need. In 1948 he was operating a struggling coal, ice, sawdust and hauling business in Cassopolis, MI. One day a neighbor asked for some sawdust for her cat's box. He gave her granulated, dried mineral clay which he had been trying to sell unsuccessfully to chicken farmers as nesting material. Soon she and her friends were coming back for more. Lowe filled ten brown paper bags with clay, wrote KITTY LITTER on each bag with a grease pencil and began selling, and selling. By 1988 Edward Lowe Industries had become a $350-million-a-year cat box filler industry.[153]

"The difference between doers and dreamers is that the latter wait for the mood before taking action while the former create the mood by acting." — Daniel Green

Improve an existing product/service

Buy a competitor's service or product. Look for ways to produce and sell it better and cheaper. Or, get a job in a big company that produces and sells it. Find its weak points and think of ways to make improvements. Then sell it yourself.

When Tom M. was an IBM manager, he thought of a way to provide better service for its computer terminals in banks. After his idea was rejected, he got a $20,000 loan, quit his job, and started Technical Support Service to service IBM equipment. It took 18 months to get an account, and the business lost money for five years. By 1985 it was earning $12 million a year.[154]

Two housewives started a wallpapering service in a community which already had this service. They beat their competition by providing greater reliability and a willingness to do rush jobs.

"Domino's Pizza" earned $1.4 billion in sales in 1986 with a promise to deliver pizza in 30 minutes or let you have it free.

An air traffic controller was subsisting on unemployment insurance until one day a friend's complaint about garbage collection in the neighborhood sparked a business idea. He phoned the residents to ask if they would like a more efficient service that would be $1.50 a week cheaper. About 200 said yes. So he and two other unemployed traffic controllers bought a used garbage truck and started picking up trash. Three months later they bought a second used truck and expanded into other neighborhoods. The first year they barely made ends meet. He borrowed money from relatives to keep afloat and his wife made her own clothes to cut expenses. Three years after the business began it was sold to a giant solid waste cleanup company for a seven-figure sum.[155]

Find a "gold mine" in your community

If you live in a city which attracts business conventions or in a community with interesting geographic features, think of a service or product that visiting tourists and business persons will buy. Organize and operate tours to ethnic restaurants, museums, discount shops, factory outlets, scenic spots or other places of interest. Start a singles gourmet club which meets regularly at fine restaurants. Organize camping, backpacking, horseback riding or skiing weekends for small groups.

Does it have abundant, free or low-cost natural resources that can be transformed into a useful, exotic or gourmet gift item? A resident of the Northwest creates unusual Christmas wreaths from the pine cones in her area. She also sells instruction kits on how to make them. Another person sells fragrant fireplace starters made of pine cones. A woman living near the English Channel creates beautiful, one-of-kind night lights made of sea shells mounted on driftwood. Southeastern Minnesota's abundant forests feed a thriving lumber industry. The Maust Fuel Corporation was started in 1986 to manufacture firewood from its byproducts.

Find a niche

Some of the success stories mentioned above are also good examples of a special market niche that has little or no competition. Here are more examples:

During the trucking industry's post-deregulation shakeout a small company was thriving while many big ones were going bankrupt. It specialized in newsstand deliveries and transporting theatrical sets.

As a young actress Barbara Walden could not find cosmetics suitable for Afro-American women, so she decided to make and sell her own. Before long her company was selling annually over $5 million worth of personal care products in major stores.

Lyle Sugerman's LS&S Group Inc. in Northbrook, IL, locates and markets high-technology aids — like talking calculators, clock radios and watches — for the blind. He started the business after learning that few products other than canes, magnifiers and similar items were sold to this consumer group. First he checked with the American Foundation for the Blind and learned there were 500,000 legally blind Americans and another 1.4 million who were severely impaired visually. Within three years his sales more than tripled.

Caution: avoid fads, unless . . .

Very few businesses based on fads last longer than three years. In 1985 when Halley's comet flashed across the horizon many small businesses were started to exploit the unique event commercially. When the comet disappeared so did the demand for items such as Halley's glow-in-the-dark caps. Several entrepreneurs, however, had made plans to stay in business. Their experiences provide tips on how to succeed after a fad dies down.

▸ Tap a special market that will continue to buy after the fad has passed. Astroline Products in Albuquerque, NM started out selling Halley's T-shirts. The founders planned to continue selling astronomy-related products to museums and planetariums.

▸ Sell a product which will continue to have a demand after the fad disappears. Burton Rubin started Halley Optical Corporation in 1981 to sell Halleyscopes for comet watching. After the comet disappeared he sold telescopes and optical products.

▸ Establish marketing networks. Owen Ryan, founder of General Comet Industries, planned to use the contacts made in his comet business as a base for an international marketing business. He licensed an "official Halley's logo" to other businesses for use in jogging shoes, cocktail mixes, cereal boxes and other items. The business was operating in seven countries and expecting sales of $10 million the following year.[156]

—— ·⋛≫✳≪⋚· ——

RECIPE FOR SUCCESS
Do you really know what kind of business to start?

Many people fail because their idea of what kind of business to start is not specific enough, reports the Small Business Administration. Someone opened a small radio and television store which thrived as the neighborhood grew. One day a major appliance store opened a branch there and began taking away his customers. If he had persisted in thinking of his business as a retail store he might have gone broke. Instead, he correctly predicted an increased demand for quality repair work and decided he was in the electronic repair business. His profits skyrocketed.

Is there evidence that it will succeed?

Having a good idea is just the beginning. You need evidence that people will want to buy what you intend to sell. Some of the women who go to the Women's Economic Development Corporation in Minneapolis for advice on how to sell their great idea are advised to come back when they have a more marketable idea.

Are the economic conditions ripe?

Some ideas are more vulnerable than others when the economy dips. During the good times Yuppies (Young, Upwardly Mobile Persons) viewed maid service and gourmet takeout dinners as necessities. After the stock market crashed in October 1987 they were doing their own housecleaning and cooking their own dinners. If you plan to start a business when the economic forecast is cloudy, make sure it will weather the downpour. Some businesses, such as gift retail stores, are more susceptible to economic swings. Others, like pet food and home repair services will always be in demand.

Do you have enough savings?

At least until your invoices are paid? If demand for your product or service drops? If an important piece of equipment fails, as it usually does, at the worst time? When some other unexpected emergency occurs? Most new business owners discover that sales in the early years are much lower, and expenses much higher, than expected. One way to get around this is to start small, at home if possible. People who run their business from home are more successful over the long term. One reason is the lower start-up costs.

Do you know how to start and operate a business?

"Eighty-five percent of small businesses in this city fail. It's not just the difficulties with the economy. So many people don't know the basics of running a modern business," — Sidney H. Kushin, former commissioner in New York City's Economic Development Administration.

Several midwestern farmers who started small businesses after losing their farms were earning over one million dollars within a few years. Before taking the plunge they read everything they could about similar businesses. They contacted people who were doing what they planned to do. They learned how to market their service or product by telephone and how to find distributors. They bought and learned to use computers to keep accounts, develop mailing lists and handle correspondence. They learned how to make their products accessible to distant customers by using toll-free phone numbers and overnight courier services.[157] Some even got a job in the type of business they were planning to start so they could learn first hand how a successful business should be run and what mistakes to avoid.

► **Set up a good record keeping system**

A new business is fragile and vulnerable. It must function more efficiently than a mature one. You'll need a record-keeping system to help you get more done in the same amount of time and to avoid waste and loss. You'll also need a business plan to get a bank loan if you need one. All this should be done before you start the business.

A good record-keeping system shows profits or losses each month. It prevents delays in providing services and ordering supplies and inventory. It reveals errors and waste. It shows whether you are paying bills on time, how much tax money to set aside, and when it should be paid. You can learn how to set up a good system from the Small Business Administration.

▶ ### Do you need a business plan?

Not everyone needs to start out with as detailed a plan as is described in *Business Plan For Small Service Firms* which you can get free from the Small Business Administration. It depends on the type of business, how much you plan to invest in it, the expected volume of sales, how much money you need to borrow, if any, and whether you plan to hire workers or rent an office.

Some people start out with less than several hundred dollars for printing business cards and flyers, and the rest of the operation is fueled by their ingenuity. They usually have small local businesses such as private tutoring and home repair services. After business picks up, a more detailed business plan may be useful. Many successful companies never even followed a formal business plan. They started with an idea and just took off. EDA, Banana Republic, David's Cookies and Cuisinart are a few examples.

A business plan will help you estimate the cost of setting up and running the business during the first year and determine whether you need to borrow money. It shows an estimate of major costs such as fixtures and equipment, overhead costs, fees for an accountant and lawyer, and licenses or other local taxes. It will also help you estimate the costs of promoting and advertising your business which many new owners grossly underestimate.

▶ ### Run the business part-time at first, if possible

If you do this before quitting your job you will:

- Know if you really want to own a business before investing more time and money in it.
- Learn from your mistakes.
- Learn from your customers what improvements your product or service needs, whether your price is too high or too low, and how to improve your package design and advertising.
- Build up a customer base and a mailing list.

- Know what your best/worst selling periods are and when and how much inventory to order.

- Learn how much time it takes to complete a service and set the price accordingly.

CAUTION: Do you have the stamina to work 35- or 40-hours a week at your job plus an additional 14 or more hours running your own business? Are you willing to give up time spent with your family and friends?

Do you know who your customers and competitors will be?

Another common cause of business failure is not learning enough about its market. To promote and advertise a product or service successfully, you should know many personal things about your potential customers — income level, sex, age, occupation, educational level, preferred reading material, hobbies and interests.

You also need to know who your competitors are, and how to provide a better product or service. You might discover — despite a promising customer base — your chances of competing successfully are slim. One woman thought she had a good market for her resume writing service in a nearby college town. She had demographic data which showed there were many graduating students who would need such a service. But she failed to learn about the college's placement bureau which provides the same service for free.

You need to ask the right questions, to break down large questions into more specific ones, like the following:

→ Who is more likely to buy my product or service — Working couples? Couples with children under the age of five? Single parent households? The young-old (65-75)? The old-old (80-plus)? Persons with incomes above $100,000?

→ What is their ethnic, racial, religious background?

→ How many potential customers are there?

→ Where do they live?

→ What clubs, associations and other groups do they join?

→ How many businesses are providing the same service/product?

→ How many appear prosperous?

→ Are there too many competitors for my market size?

→ What advantages will my service or product have over theirs?

→ What price do they charge?

→ How many businesses of this type failed in the past few years?

→ Why did they fail?

Do some market research

Market research firms charge a fortune to find answers to these questions, but you can get some essential information on your own, inexpensively. Suppose you want to start a home repair business for elderly home owners in your community. First you would look up how many people above a certain age live in your census tract. (The library has this information.) Then you would walk around the area to get an idea of the age of the housing. The older it is, the greater the need for your service.

Suppose, instead, you want to start a tutoring service for grade-school children in your community. You need to estimate how many middle and upper income families live there. (Lower income families can't afford this luxury.) You also need to know how many children there are in this age category. A simple walk through the neighborhood, schools and playgrounds can give you an overview of your potential market.

You also need to know if there are others who sell the same service and, if so, how you can improve on what they are doing. There is no sense starting a tutoring service if the community is saturated with them *unless you have a way of excelling the competition.* You can find out how many there are by looking in the Yellow Pages and studying local newspaper ads. Send for their brochures or phone to inquire about their service. Take note of what is being done, how it's being done, and where it's being done. Think of ways to make your service better than theirs.

► Census reports and other market data

The library has census reports and other survey data which contain the following information:

► The number of people in various categories such as income, age, sex, marital status, number of children, ethnic background, race, religion, education.

► Where such persons are located nationwide — by region, state, city, and local census tracts. You can look up, for example, the geographic distribution of Spanish-speaking persons. You can get even more specific such as Spanish-speaking residents in a certain census tract who originate from Honduras.

► Average housing costs in a locality.

Let's assume you want to sell by mail order gold-plated toothpicks as a gift item for "people who have everything." In order to estimate the disposable income in a given census tract you would look up the number of households above a certain income level, the localities where they tend to cluster, and the average housing costs in these localities.

If you intend to serve the local market you will need answers to more questions:

► Is there a strong economic base? Are there many low-income families? If so, how well do you think piano lessons, gourmet foods or maid service would sell in such a neighborhood?

► Are nearby industries operating full- or part-time? Have any businesses or industries moved out or closed down recently? Are some of the larger department stores moving out?

► Are new ones scheduled to open soon?

► Do you see many houses that are boarded up? Does the area look run down?

► Where is the traffic flow greatest? Count the number of people and cars passing by. Then you'll know where to set up your business and distribute your business cards, flyers, free samples and brochures.

Information the census reports do not provide:
A more sophisticated study may be required. You may even have to hire a professional. This can be expensive. However, you can get a nearby university business department to "rent" you a student at very low cost.

Another method involves creating and mailing questionnaires to selected samples of potential customers. This can be more expensive than you realize.

Another involves purchasing data from an organization which has already done survey studies on the particular population you are interested in. Suppose you have a great product for mothers of quadruplets. You plan to sell this nationwide by mail order. First, you need to check whether this product is sold in local stores or by mail order. Next, you need to know if there is a reasonably large market out there. The census reports only give the number of babies born, regardless of whether they are single or multiple births. Specific information such as this can be found in surveys conducted by market research firms, hospitals, consultants and other organizations.

Other sources of valuable market data include the following:
► Consult accountants about the industry.
► Talk to suppliers. They know what sells.
► Join the trade association. They have answers to questions that apply specifically to the industry. A man who planned to open a men's quality clothing store got answers to these questions: How much do small specialty shops spend on advertising? What is their average rent? How bad is the problem of theft?
► He also saved much money by doing much of the grunt work himself and then giving his findings to a market research firm for analysis.

Your information must always be up-to-date.
A nationwide census is done every ten years, so you'll need information on demographic changes that occur in off-census years. You must be continually on the lookout for unexpected changes such as an economic crisis, a plant closing, even foreign political events that can affect your business without warning. During the recent farm crisis many farmers who foreclosed had to move away. This left many small businesses which catered to their needs without a market.

You can get such information in various ways like the following:
● Make periodic, on-site observations if you're serving the local market.
● Keep up with events as reported in business periodicals, newspapers and trade or professional journals.
● Regularly contact the local Chamber of Commerce and Small Business Administration office.
● Join your trade, business or professional association.
● Get to know your local real estate broker, banker, and others who know about the latest events in the community.

-※-※-

DECIDING ON A LEGAL STRUCTURE

There are three main types of business structure: sole proprietorship, partnership, and corporation. The following brief descriptions cover the sole proprietorship and partnership only since these apply to most newly established businesses.

The sole proprietorship

This type has just one person as owner and operator. It is recommended for people who are just starting out. When the business expands, a partnership or corporation may be more advantageous.

There are fewer legal restrictions than the other two types. All you may need is a license or two. Little or no government approval is required, and it's less expensive. As sole proprietor, you keep all the profits and make all the decisions. Another advantage is that there is no special taxation.

However, you must file a separate income tax return for your business. (If you have a full-time job while you manage a part-time home business, you can write off some business expenses and losses.) Another disadvantage is that a sole proprietor usually has more difficulty getting a long-term loan. Also, there is unlimited personal liability in case of a lawsuit. You alone are responsible for all debts. Someone who is injured or loses income because of your business can file a claim against your personal assets and your business. That's why it's important to get insurance.

The partnership

A partnership involves two or more persons as co-owners of the business. There are two kinds, general and limited. In the general partnership shareholders participate in the daily operation of the business. They also share the liability. In the limited partnership the partners do not participate directly in business operations nor do they assume any liability.

A written partnership agreement should be drawn up to avoid or settle conflicts that may occur later. It should cover such matters as how to divide profits and losses, each partner's responsibility for business expenses and debts, what to do if a partner dies, sale of partnership interest, and limits to each partner's authority.

Two businessmen attribute the success of their partnership to a written contract in which they also agreed to share equally the duties of chief executive officer. The responsibilities in each partner's area of expertise were stated, and each was given complete authority for decisions in that area. Mutual agreement in marketing, legal, and financial operations would be required. Other features that contributed to the successful partnership were mutual agreement on the business plan, long-term strategy and an equal share in the company.

The main advantages of a partnership are the combined assets of the partners, the fact that two heads are involved in decision making (lessening the chance of error), and each partner can deduct a loss up to the amount she/he has invested in it for income tax purposes.

Among the disadvantages are the following:

► Buying out of a partnership can be difficult unless the matter has been covered in the written agreement.

► If one partner leaves, the partnership ends. However, a new partnership can be created. There is insurance to minimize such risks.

► Compared to a corporation, long-term financing is more difficult to get, but it is easier than for a sole proprietorship.

► A partner can be held liable for the actions of the other partners and their business debts. If the business fails you could lose your home and personal assets.

► Many partnerships fail because of misunderstandings and personality conflicts. If you must take a partner, experts advise taking extra precautions. E.Y. started an electric equipment manufacturing firm with nine partners, none of whom had any business experience. The early years were a nightmare, with ten loud voices to listen to, each representing a financial stake. There was too much conflict and too little flexibility. Conflicts can be avoided or minimized by planning how to resolve potential conflicts at the start and putting it in writing — i.e., who does what, how much time each partner puts in, how to resolve conflicts.[158]

·--·‡·ᴍ·‡·--

SELECTING THE SITE
It's more important for some businesses than for others

Some businesses — such as restaurants, service stations, retail and convenience stores — must be located where they can be seen and where customers are always passing by.

A young couple opened a gourmet delicatessen in a middle class neighborhood. Even though it was around the corner from a busy boulevard, few people saw it. To make matters worse, the store lacked a large window, and people could not see the luscious display inside. It folded within a year.

Within seven years Temps & Co. became the largest temporary help firm in Washington, DC. The founder says *"image"* was important to its success. The offices are located in storefronts, and four of the company's twelve locations are in retail space (which is more expensive than office space). He also lavished attention on the design and decoration of the reception areas. These features helped increase the recruitment of skilled job seekers by as much as fifty percent.[159]

For other types of small service businesses — accounting, printing and copy shops, home repair, etc. — location is not as important as having a product or service that attracts loyal customers. For some businesses, such as mail order, it makes no difference whether their base of operations is an attic, garage or basement. Computers, fax machines, laser printers, copiers and other electronic equipment plus reliable parcel delivery service make it possible to operate a business even in isolated places. The only disadvantage is that you won't find all the support that is available in large metropolitan areas — i.e., bankers, accountants, lawyers.

The home based business

There are two points to consider before you even think of doing it: 1) How will it affect your family's living arrangements? and 2) What will you do when the business outgrows your living space?

If you plan to have customers come to your home there are more matters to consider.

▸ Are the physical facilities attractive and comfortable?

▸ Is there adequate lighting, heating and air conditioning?

► Is parking space available?

► Does it have an authentic business image? The owner of a travel service who served customers in her living room was doing poorly until she converted part of her basement into an attractive, wood-panelled office with a separate entrance. She also placed a commercially made sign outside. The professional decor assures her customers that this is a reliable, well-run business.

► How far is the nearest main street, bus or subway stop? Your customers are not likely to go out of their way if the drive or walk to your door is inconvenient. A better way is to sell by mail or provide a pick-up and delivery service to customers' homes. Some products can be sold from a brightly painted station wagon parked near a busy highway or shopping mall. Flea markets and garage sales are other alternatives.

If you lack the space or if you need a more attractive, accessible site, there are ways to get it without going broke on commercial rents.

► Meet clients and schedule conferences at a restaurant or a client's office.

► Borrow, rent or share someone's home. A teacher who lived in a small apartment with her elderly mother wanted to open a reading clinic. Since she could not operate from her apartment, she formed a partnership with another teacher who lives in a large house in the center of town. They converted an entire floor of the house into a classroom, testing room, reception area and two offices. Then they hung out a sign, "Reading Clinic and Testing Service." The business eventually grew into a highly recommended learning center.[160]

► Rent or share space in a community center or business incubator (see below). Suppose you want to start a catering business. You lack the space and you can't afford an expensive kitchen oven and other equipment. One woman solved this problem by renting the local church kitchen. Other community organizations might be willing to rent, at reasonable cost, their facilities during their "down time" periods.

Small business incubators
They provide space, office services and advice in financing, marketing and other matters at reasonable rates. In 1989 there were 375 business incubators — most of them less than three years

old — that were members of the National Business Incubator Association. Of these, 52 are linked to universities.

Even newer are "shared factories" where small manufacturers get training in, and the use of, the latest technologies such as computer-integrated manufacturing. The cost of this very expensive equipment is shared by the participating manufacturers. In 1988 there were about 40 shared factories, most of them in the early stages of development.

Incubators are financed and operated by state and local governments, nonprofit groups, venture capital firms, private companies, universities, and chambers of commerce. Each entity has its own reason for doing so. The private companies operate incubators for profit. Some require payment of royalties on their tenants' new products and equity on their business. This is in addition to, or in lieu of, rent and consulting fees. Seagate Associates in Paramus, NJ rents a separate area of small private offices as an incubator. For an additional fee it provides secretarial, consulting, and market research services. They also make referrals to legal and accounting services and sources of loans.

State and local governments — usually working with local colleges and universities and private companies — expect the new companies to provide an additional source of taxes and new jobs. Space is available at special low rates. Office and administrative services are available, also training for employees of the new businesses. Often, in return, the new business owners agree to hire their employees through government funded job training programs.

▶ **What they provide**

Incubators help increase the success rate of small businesses as much as 60 to 80 percent, reports the National Business Incubation Association. This is because they have low overhead costs. They also offer valuable business advice, a more professional image than a home-based business provides, and services and equipment which many startups cannot afford to purchase by themselves.

Those located on, or near, university campuses also provide laboratory and research facilities, access to the university's business library and business courses, graduate student workers, and advice from professors. A biotechnology company which couldn't find affordable laboratory space to develop a new product was able to rent the laboratory of an incubator at the Georgia Institute of Technology.[161]

Some incubators only provide office space. Others also offer a combination of the following — office furniture, electronic and computer equipment, secretary, receptionist, typist, copy machine, a conference room, market research, and advice on matters such as developing a business plan and a loan package. Many government sponsored incubators also provide a local industrial development expert for finding customers, suppliers, financing experts, and other necessities.

Persons who want to test their business idea first can rent a small cubicle for part of the day. When the business expands it can be rented full time, or the owner can move into a private office which costs more. Conversely, a tenant whose business is doing poorly can go back to running the business from home until it picks up again. Meanwhile, telephone answering and mail-holding services can be kept at the incubator for a small monthly fee.[162]

► **The costs**

Rents are often below market rates, and the fees for business services are low compared with their usual cost. Recently, space at the Minneapolis Business and Technology Center cost about 30% less than at downtown locations. However, leases usually do not run more than five years because the purpose of an incubator is to help a fledgling business grow strong enough to fly off on its own.

► *How to get into one*

Multi-purpose incubators accept almost any kind of business. Others specialize in a certain industry. The Fulton-Carroll incubator in Chicago, for example, is for industrial companies. Those in Atlanta prefer high-technology businesses. Incubators jointly operated by a local government and private groups accept only businesses which have the potential for helping the local economy. Usually, they all ask to see a business plan.[163]

Some questions to ask:

→ How long can you stay?

→ Are you required to relocate in the same geographical area after leaving the incubator?

→ What services are included with the rent?

→ How much will the additional services you need cost?

→ Are you required to give the sponsor part ownership in your business? What will you get in return? (Some sponsors provide consulting services and/or financial help as part of the deal.)

→ Does the incubator make referrals to loan sources?

→ Does it offer counseling, information, or any other type of help on how to run your business? (University affiliated incubators use professors and graduate students from their business, science and engineering departments as advisors.)

→ Talk to other tenants. Are they satisfied with the services? Is security protection adequate?

Contact the following to find the nearest small business incubator

→ Small Business Administration, Office of Private Sector Initiatives, 1441 L Street, NW, Wash, DC 20416

→ Local economic development agencies

→ City hall

→ Chamber of Commerce

→ Business department of the nearest university

→ National Business Incubation Association, Ohio University, Athens, OH 45701.

FINANCING YOUR BUSINESS

Do you have enough money to start?

A major cause of business failure is insufficient capital. Most people underestimate the amount needed to get a business going. They need money to start it, keep it running until it becomes profitable, and cover all business and personal expenses for at least six months.

▶ **Estimating costs**

The Small Business Administration suggests that you first estimate the cost of the following one-time expenses:[164]

→ Fixtures and equipment and their installation
→ Decorating and remodeling
→ Beginning inventory
→ Deposits for utilities
→ Telephone and installation
→ Professional fees: lawyer, accountant, etc.
→ Licenses and permits
→ Insurance

Next, you need to estimate recurring expenses — rent, advertising and promotion, inventory renewal, delivery costs, supplies, telephone and utilities, insurance, taxes (including Social Security), interest on loans, maintenance. Finally, estimate how much cash you need to keep the business running for the first three or four months. Experts recommend adding 20% to your cost estimate for unexpected expenses.

Raising money without a loan

▶ Look into your bank accounts, stocks, bonds and other investments. Sell some belongings.

▶ Your relatives and friends may be willing to invest in your business or go into partnership with you and share the costs.

▶ Small business investors give loans ranging from five- to six-figure sums to businesses that are too new to attract venture capital. It isn't easy to find people who are willing to invest in a new business. Nonetheless, there are private investment groups of wealthy people who will consider small startups which have the potential of growing. The Center for Entrepreneurial Management Inc., for example, has chapters in several major cities.[165] The problem is locating them and, once you have found them, persuading them that your business is worth the risk involved.

► **Where to find investors**

• Write to the Investment Division, Small Business Administration, Washington, DC 20416 for the *Directory of Operating Small Business Investment Companies.*

• Ask your banker and accountant.

• Contact the business school of the nearest university.

Getting a loan

It will probably take much longer than expected to find the money you need. Some people panic and grab a loan offer before they check it out. They overlook the fine print which says they will give up control over part of their business. Or, an unexpected setback makes it impossible to pay the loan, and they go bankrupt.

Beware of private, unlicensed loan companies. You could lose plenty as thousands already have. Before signing anything, check with the Small Business Administration and the Better Business Bureau. Read the loan contract carefully. If there is a clause that allows the lender to call his loan for any reason, do not accept the offer.

Some experts advise taking a second mortgage on your home, but it's best to wait until interest rates stabilize. Use this as a last resort and only if your business is a sure winner or if your spouse is working and can cover possible increases in monthly payments.

► **Loans from family and friends**

You may be able to work out a deal whereby you pay less interest than a bank loan and they get more return on their money than from a savings account. No matter how close the relationship, you should both sign a letter of agreement covering payment terms. It should also specify how much prerogative the lender has in running your business. Sweet relationships have gone sour because the lender assumes he/she has the right to interfere.

► **Help from the government**

Small Business Administration (SBA)

The nearest SBA office will give you free information on low interest government loans. These generally have better terms than bank loans. Your banker can also help you apply for a loan under the SBA's Loan Guaranty Plan. Also ask about tax breaks and low interest loans offered by your city and state governments.

Small Business Investment Companies (SBIC)
SBICs are private credit companies which are licensed by the Small Business Administration. They give credit-style investment loans in return for a share of the profits. Interest rates are low and there are few or no collateral requirements. Some invest only in businesses owned primarily by women, minorities, and Vietnam War veterans. For a list of SBICs, write to the Small Business Administration Investment Division, 1441 L Street NW, Washington, DC 20416.

Small Business Innovation Research (SBIR)
SBIR is a government program which authorizes federal agencies to give up to $50,000 to entrepreneurs whose ideas have the potential of solving technical problems the agencies are having. If the results of the trial period are acceptable, an additional loan of up to $500,000 may be given for the following year. For information contact the Small Business Administration.

▶ Job Training Partnership
Many JTP programs train and help unemployed persons start their own business. Programs like the following exist in many communities and are expected to multiply.

The Council for Economic Action, in Boston, identifies industries a community needs and provides training and technical help to persons who want to start a small business that will meet these needs.

The BID Resource Center in Beaumont, TX helps entrepreneurs obtain contracts to sell their goods and services to the federal government.

At the Anne Arundel County Department of Aging in Glen Burnie, MD, JTPA funds are used to help persons 45 or older start small service businesses such as home repairs, hair care and respite care. They also learn general bookkeeping, and are given self-employment tax information and advice on marketing and contracts.

WAMY Community Action, Inc. in Boone, NC uses JTPA funds to run a self-employment program for people 55 and older. Agency staff and local community colleges provide the training. A lending organization under contract to the program provides for loans, and the ASU College of Business provides consultants.[166]

► **Help from community organizations**

Ethnic, religious, minority and women's groups will help out when a bank will not give a loan. Three friends opened a restaurant in Ann Arbor with $28,000 in savings. It became so popular that they had to expand. Yet, every bank in town turned down their request for a loan. They finally got a low-interest loan from an ethnic organization.

► **Help from foundations**

You might be eligible for a grant or a low-cost loan from a foundation if you are a member of a group which is classified as disadvantaged. You can look up foundations in Gale's *Directory of Foundations* or you can contact the Small Business Administration for a list.

► **Credit union loans**

Credit unions are cooperatives which function like banks. They offer loans at a lower interest rate and on easier terms than banks. Many are employee cooperatives. If you are unemployed, it may still be possible to join a credit union owned by persons who share a common characteristic such as a profession or trade, residence in a community, even a common surname. The SBA can tell you how to get such information.

► **Bank loans**

It has never been easy for a new business to get a bank loan, and the recent outbreak of bank failures has made it almost impossible. Bank regulators now require more stringent lending requirements, especially to risky new businesses. Persistence might pay off, however. A woman was turned down by thirteen banks before she found one that gave her a loan.

It's easier to get a bank loan if:

► Your business is already operating.

► You put up your own money or collateral, usually at least 30% of the amount needed. (The more you are willing to risk in your business the more assurance the creditors have that it will succeed.)

► You learn the buzzwords of the financial world so you can appear to know more than you do about running a business.

► You fill out the loan application COMPLETELY, ACCURATELY, and IN DETAIL.

► You are candid. The worst thing is to be evasive.

► Find out why a bank turns you down. If it's because of a flawed business plan, correct it.

► At the interview, be prepared to answer more questions and clarify information you gave on the loan application form. Bring along your financial statements and business plan. The banker wants to have a clear idea of how you will use the money.

Questions you may be asked at the interview
→ What kind of business are you planning?
→ How much money do you expect it to earn the first year?
→ What experience do you have in business and management?
→ What makes you so sure it will succeed?
→ Have you made a preliminary market survey?
→ Have you chosen a business location?
→ Why do you think this location is good for your business?
→ How much money will you invest in your business?
→ How much money do you need to borrow?
→ How will you use the money?
→ What collateral can you put up?
→ When do you expect the business to begin paying for itself?

Learn how to apply for a loan application.
Enroll in a Small Business Administration's pre-business workshop. Have a SCORE volunteer — Retired business persons who work with SBA offices — look over your application. Read their free or low-cost publications.

► Commercial credit companies
These are easier to get loans from since they are not governed by the same regulations as banks. Many are reputable. For fast action they are better than a bank. They impose less restrictions that can hamper your business. However, because they generally make loans against inventory or accounts receivable, businesses which lack substantial assets have more difficulty getting a loan.

194

LEGAL NECESSITIES

Business license, seller's permit

You may be required to get a business license or seller's permit. The regulations vary from state to state and according to the type of business. A family day care license in New York requires on-site inspections for health care, fire safety, sanitation and other possible problems. In some other states only an application form and a fee is required. In most states professionals like contractors, marriage counselors and real estate brokers must have a license. In addition, the federal government regulates mail order operations and many other businesses. The Small Business Administration can tell you what is required for your business.

Zoning laws

Local zoning regulations set restrictions on a home business such as the number of employees allowed to work there and how much space to use. There are also federal and state laws which restrict the type of commercial goods produced at home. The federal Fair Labor Standards Act, for example, forbids the manufacture of some items of apparel. Some local zoning laws limit or prohibit bringing deliveries or clients to the home.

Ignoring the laws can cost you plenty, even put you out of business. In 1980 three farm wives in Clarinda, Iowa started Bordeaux Inc. They hired other farm wives to applique trimmings on jogging suits. The business grew to 150 seamstresses working in their own homes. In 1987 the Department of Labor sued the company, citing legal restrictions on hiring employees to work at home on certain garments. Besides the lawyers' fees and other expenses, they lost sales during the long court battle. They also were required to drastically reduce the number of seamstresses working in their own homes.[167]

Insurance

Some types of businesses, such as day-care centers, cannot afford to operate without insurance, and it can cost plenty. The annual insurance premium of a learning center in Colorado jumped from $5,000 to $13,000 in May 1985 because of publicity and lawsuits stemming from recent child-abuse scandals.

Basic property insurance protects a business against theft and damage. Liability insurance provides protection from a lawsuit brought by someone who is injured on your property. It also covers hospitalization and treatment. Life and disability insurance is needed by a partnership. After a partner's death it allows the remaining partners to buy shares of the company which might be passed on to the heirs of the deceased.

There are other types of insurance which can eat up your money.

► Business interruption insurance which pays overhead expenses and lost profits while your business rebuilds or recovers after an accident.

► Supplemental perils insurance which covers loss of inventory following a fire.

► Credit insurance for uncollectible bad debts.

► Accounts receivable insurance to cover debts that are uncollectible if your records are destroyed.

► Bonding insurance for protection against embezzlement if an employee who handles your money turns out to be a crook.

► You have to pay your own social security and medical insurance.

The IRS

Probably the most unpleasant aspect of running a business is the government reports that must be filled out on a quarterly and yearly basis — personal income tax, business income tax, possibly state sales tax, and Social Security self-employment tax.

The IRS gives extra scrutiny to tax returns from people who operate a home business in addition to working at a regular job. This is because many people use a home business as a tax haven.

IRS deductions are allowed for home business expenses. But you must prove they are necessary to your business and that the part of your home used for the business is exclusively used for that purpose. Among the items you are allowed to deduct are phone service and utility bills, furniture, remodeling expenses, home repairs and similar expenses. You can also claim the value of your work area is depreciating and take a deduction for loss. And you can charge yourself rent for the percentage of your home used for business, and deduct that also.

The Small Business Administration can help you estimate the costs and deductible expenses of working at home. The local IRS office has free tax guides such as *Business Use of Your Home* and *Tax Guide For Small Business*.

GETTING THE BUSINESS GOING:
PROBLEMS THAT MIGHT OCCUR

Long hours/short income

The owner of "Nibbles," a multimillion dollar business which sells all-natural cheese spreads and snacks through supermarkets, earned her success. At the start she put in 80-hour weeks of hard work. *"If the baker didn't show up, I was the baker. If the dishwasher didn't show up, I washed the dishes. My accountant finally told me, 'You're gonna work your ass off and never make money.' "* She finally decided to hire helpers.[168]

Most new business owners run out of gas trying to be everything and do everything. And the more successful the business becomes, the greater the pressure. Some marriages fail after years of being on the road frequently. Many of these unhappy entrepreneurs say the success wasn't worth it. At some point they should have hired a manager so they could have more time to plan their company's future and be with their families.

It takes a lot of self-discipline

Working for yourself brings temptations. No one is looking over your shoulder, so why not take off now and then? But a few minutes off here and there will add up until you won't be able to meet important deadlines. There are ways to cheat temptation.

▸ Establish a routine and stick to it until it becomes a habit.

▸ Make the environment in which you run your business inviting. A woman who operates a research and editing business from her tiny city apartment pasted an entire wall with a wooded scene, hung potted greenery from the ceiling, and keeps her cassette recorder tuned to woodland sounds with birds chirping and breezes blowing.

▸ Reward yourself each time you resist the temptation to cheat on your schedule. Punish yourself whenever you do.

▸ Move your workplace to a quiet part of the house.

Your social life becomes a fading memory

After you get over the initial euphoria of being your own boss, you'll feel isolated. You'll miss the social interaction at the office. Here is how some people have dealt with the problem.

- Do some of your paper work at the beach or park.
- Make frequent trips to the library to read business forecasts and the latest news on your type of business.
- Take lunch breaks in a local diner or shopping mall.
- While on these trips, distribute your flyers, business cards, and other promotional material. Pick the most exciting corner of main street and watch people go by as you distribute sales materials. One enterprising entrepreneur "parked" in Grand Central Station 2in New York City during rush hours and handed out her flyer.
- Take a course on how to run a small business.

A home business can interfere with your family life

As it starts expanding, the family's living quarters can be taken over by an accumulation of equipment, supplies, part-time employees and inventory. Here are some solutions which have worked for others.

→ Add an extension to the house.

→ Rent additional office space nearby — a neighbor's garage or basement, a desk in a local real estate or insurance office.

→ Move your business to the garage, basement or attic.

→ Get a camper and park it in the yard.

It might not be taken seriously

Women especially have found this to be a problem. It can be serious enough to cause the loss of potential clients. A professional image is important, even when you are working from your garage. You can't expect clients to take your business seriously if you greet them dressed in hair curlers and old clothes. Instead of meeting clients in your living room or kitchen,

→ Borrow an office from a friend until you can afford to rent your own.

→ Rent a desk in the local insurance or real estate office for such occasions.

→ Meet clients in the lobby of a hotel or take them to lunch.

→ Never have children or teenagers answer business calls for you.

→ Announce the name of your business after you pick up the receiver. Don't answer with a "hello" or "(name) residence."

→ Have business cards made and quality stationery with your business logo on it. Use the logo on everything: business cards, stationery, mailing labels, order forms, etc.

SELLING IS A SCIENCE AND AN ART

Having a good idea that will sell is not enough. You must know how to reach the people who are most likely to buy your product or service. It was ten years before the inventor of the typewriter, Christopher Sholes, made a profit. He made the mistake of targeting private consumers instead of business owners as his market. He invented it in 1868. In those days clerks wrote letters by hand, including copies. Employers would have saved a lot of money by having the letters typed with carbon copies. Yet only a few thousand typewriters were sold in the first decade.

Promotion and advertising

Advertising includes direct mail, space and classified ads, and radio and television commercials. It's very expensive, so it must be done right. You need to know who your potential customers are, which publications they read, how to pitch the wording of your ad to their interests and needs, and the best months in which to place an ad.

Promoting a product or service takes more time and energy but it costs less, often nothing at all. Free and low-cost promotion methods include word-of-mouth advertising by satisfied customers, getting feature stories about your business in the local newspaper, appearing on local radio and television shows, speaking before local community groups, and distributing fliers or free samples.

▶ Newspaper/magazine ads

These include the inexpensive, small classified ads and the very expensive space ads. Some experts think newspaper ads aren't worth the cost for a small business because the audience is too general. This is especially true of big city newspapers. But an ad in the local newspaper can reap rich rewards for a business which serves that community. One woman who started a house-cleaning service received hundreds of orders immediately after placing a seven-dollar ad.

While space ads in newspapers may not be worth the expense, a space ad in the Yellow Pages, in a business or professional directory, or a community newsletter will probably draw a continuing response. A professional looking space ad created by an advertising agency can cost hundreds of dollars. There are books in the library on how to create your own.

Classified ads have made a lot of money for some persons. But many have gotten few or no responses at all. The secret, experts say, is in repeat advertising. they can be used to acquire names for your mailing list. The important thing is to findout which publications your potential customers are more likely to read. People of a certain income and educational level — the two are correlated — read certain types of newspapers and magazines. High-income professionals, managers and executives, for example, are more likely to read *The Wall Street Journal, The New York Times, Washington Post* and similar newspapers. Advertising rates in these publications are very expensive.

There are also thousands of special interest magazines and newsletters where advertising space is much cheaper than in a national newspaper. Fred Wolferman, of North Kansas City, MO, created a 2-inch thick English muffin which he thought was bigger and better than anything on the national market. He started out in 1978 with no mail order experience and one self-written ad in *Bon Appetit* magazine which, he admits, was dreadful. Still, orders poured in and his business grew dramatically. In 1986 he sold his business to Sara Lee for an undisclosed amount.[169]

▶ *Free or low-cost advertising and promotion*

▶ You can place an ad in the community newsletter, on community and church bulletin boards, in school newspapers, give--away shopper's guides, and other local publications.

▶ Distribute flyers and free samples at community events. These include flea markets, fund raising events, conventions and trade shows, exhibitions, street and school fairs, church bazaars, shopping malls and supermarkets.

▶ If your business serves the local market, ask friends, neighbors and relatives to recommend customers and spread the word about your business. Talk to real estate brokers, the local policeman, bus and cab drivers and others in your community who know about potential customers for your type of business.

▸ Carry your flyers and business cards wherever you go, and distribute them. One woman who started a tutoring service got all the clients she needed by distributing her business card to teachers and parents at local schools. She also handed out flyers to children getting off school buses. Two women in their sixties started a multi-service business for two-career couples who live in the wealthy part of their community. They got all the customers they needed by placing a flyer on cars parked in front of the more expensive homes.

▸ Another gimmick is to give out free samples of your product or service. A piano teacher recruited additional students by auctioning her services at a local arts center and by giving free concerts in the local shopping mall.

▸ Telephone sales can be used effectively by a business which caters to the local market, and it's cheaper than direct mail. You can get addresses and phone numbers of local residents from the reverse telephone directory. You can buy it from the telephone company or find it in the library.

▸ Feature articles in the local newspaper, community newsletter, company newsletter and anything else which is distributed locally also provide free advertising. Some people write their own article and send it in, knowing it's more likely to be accepted if it saves the editor time and effort.

Direct mail

It's expensive, but worth the cost if done right. It involves mailing a letter, brochure or catalog, order form and reply envelope to a selected list of persons.

Mail order businesses have been booming recently mainly because so many women are working. Millions of people don't have the time or easy access to transportation facilities to shop, especially for specialized goods and services. Specialized markets are the answer. How else can a Boston resident buy Cherokee Indian bread? Giant companies like Sears are no threat to this type of product.

Direct mail cuts out the middlemen so you can afford to offer a better quality product or service at a more reasonable price. However, the field is getting so crowded that a catalog and its advertised items must be unique and of good quality in order to bring in orders. Just look at the catalogs coming to your home that try to sell you the same cheap, tacky things.

Getting a bank loan is more difficult because a mail order business is regarded as risky. Experts have estimated 50 to 100 failures to each success. Test the market for a product before you invest a fortune. A man who was thinking about starting a fiber optics manufacturing business in his garage rented a mailing list of 8,000 potential buyers. He wrote a simple flier which described the product and mailed it. When 6,000 replies came, he knew he had a winner. Then, and only then, did he invest the money and time to open his business.

Take your product or service directly to the consumer

This technique made Avon, Tupperware and Mary Kay successful. It's especially popular with businesses that cater to working mothers and affluent professionals who have little time to shop in stores. Others use ingenious approaches such as selling handcrafted items from a decorated pushcart. K&N Mobile Distribution Systems, of Fort Worth, TX, uses trucks to sell electrical parts to industrial firms.

THE EASY WAY TO GO INTO BUSINESS
BUY A FRANCHISE

If you want to go into business without much financial risk, invest in a franchise. The US Department of Commerce reports that 8 out of 10 franchised businesses succeed. Although buying an established franchise is safer than starting your own business, much depends on the franchise.

Franchises that cater to fads tend to be risky. The risk is also higher for new franchises which haven't worked out all the kinks. On the other hand, you'll get a better location and more personal attention from the franchisor. Those that are first in a market with a product or service generally do best because there is not much competition. To be safe, investigate any business that is less than two years old. Contact the Better Business Bureau to make sure the company is legitimate.[170]

Choices that are available

Franchises exist in a wide range of fields. Among the fastest growing in 1989 were small business services, home services, ice-cream stores, automotive outlets, fast food restaurants, video rental stores, furniture and equipment leasing, child-care centers, health and fitness programs, well-known restaurants and specialty food shops.

Franchises that follow demographic trends are fast-growing because they are usually the first to meet new needs. These include home and personal services that save working couples' time and energy — e.g., inspecting houses for prospective buyers, matching home buyers and sellers, shopping, housekeeping, doing errands. An unusual, but necessary, service for an increasingly mobile nation is Critter Care Inc. It cares for pets in their homes while the owners are traveling.[171] Franchised diet programs are booming as a result of the current health craze. In 1989 there were about 12 diet franchise companies, and the top 5 were selling more than 100 units annually. The typical investment for a diet franchise was in the $25,000-$75,000 range, and incomes of $40,000-$75,000 were reported.[172]

The following is a small sample of franchise businesses and their cost in 1989.

▸ *Home services*: Molly Maids — $22,000; Merry Maids, Inc. — from $25,000 to $30,000.

▸ *Automotive*: Jiffy Lube International (quick oil changes) — $130,000; 5 Minute Oil Change — $6,975; Midas Muffler — $140,000 plus working capital; Precision Tune — from $101,000 to $120,000 plus real estate costs.

▸ *Food*: Domino's Pizza — $84,700 to $134,500; Howard Johnson's Restaurants — $1 million; McDonald's — from $300,000 and up. Lesser known food franchises are much less expensive. These include Jo-Ann's Nut House — $45,000, Subway Sandwiches & Salads — $34,000, and grocery stores and soft drink bottlers.

▸ *Leisure*: Ever since the cost of video cassette recorders dropped, video rental franchises have opened in most neighborhoods. National Video sold 1,350 franchises in 48 states in 1987. The start-up costs were $350,000 to $450,000 depending on inventory and location.

▸ *Pets*: America's love affair with its dogs and cats has attracted pet franchises and mail order pet businesses. Docktor Pet Centers (pets and related products) — $149,800 to $192,500.

▸ *Business*: There are numerous business franchises offering a vast range of services. Many serve the needs of small businesses: Butler Learning Systems (training programs for executives, sales, office personnel) — $10,000; Computer Maintenance Service (services, repairs microcomputers) — $1,000; H&R Block, Inc. (income tax preparations) — from $1,000 to $4,000; Simplified Business Services (business management control for small businesses including income tax preparation, consultation) — $500.

Shipping franchises have low start-up costs and are easy to operate. Services include check mailing, redirecting mail to another city by phone, 24-hour access to mail boxes, packaging & shipping parcels, phone message service, copying, printing, typing, Western Union transmissions, facsimile, and telex. Mail Boxes Etc, cost $40,000 to $60,000.[173] This and Packy the Shipper were among *Venture* magazine's 100 fastest-growing young franchises.[174]

Advantages of owning a franchise
▸ You get plenty of support

A franchise contract generally includes advertising, accounting, hiring and training services. The better ones also help with financing, legal assistance, site selection, managing construction, and the hiring and training of employees. Some companies provide financial help during the difficult early period. Jiffy Lube International — which ranked 12th on the 1988 Franchisor 100 List — established a Small Business Investment Company for that purpose. Generally, the bigger and better-known companies offer the most support, but they are also the most expensive.

Subway Sandwiches ranked first in *Venture* magazine's 1988 Franchisor 100 List. The founder's continuing management assistance and frequent contact with franchisees has contributed to its success. To motivate and educate them, he distributes weekly and monthly publications. When they have a problem they can call one of the firm's 50 coordinators who have the authority to resolve most problems[175]

▸ Operating costs are lower

Franchise companies buy in huge quantities and the savings are passed on to their franchisees.

▶ *It's a low-cost way to learn how to run a business*

When you invest in a well-run franchise you get a proven formula for success. It's the best training ground for learning to manage your own business later on.

Disadvantages

If you prefer to have others make most of the decisions for you then franchising is the best way to go. But if you are a free spirit who likes to try out your own ideas, who resents being told how much to charge and how to decorate your store, a franchise will seem like a straightjacket.

Needed for success

It helps if you are a workaholic. Expect to put in 60- to 70-hour weeks in the early stages. Life will be easier if the franchise is in a field you prefer and are familiar with. If you don't know much about the industry you can learn by reading extensively and taking evening courses or by working part-time in an existing franchise.

Major reasons for failure

▶ Failure to investigate the franchise operation before buying.

▶ Insufficient reserve cash for unexpected business setbacks. You need enough cash to cover contingencies and meet all your expenses for at least six months or until the business turns a profit.

▶ Expensive, unplanned expansion.

▶ Buying a franchise from a new company which has not worked out its problems.

▶ *Investigate before you buy*

There are many sad tales of people who bought a franchise in a failing company or in a fraudulent company without investigating first.

In 1986 Carol Brothers' Pop-Ins, Inc. maid-service franchise filed for bankruptcy. The chain owed over $82,700 in back taxes, $12,400 in back wages, and $745,000 in unpaid bills. Many franchisees lost thousands of dollars. They had been given promises, expensive poor-quality supplies, and little else in exchange for their investments. Yet, Brothers continued to sell franchises. Eventually, the franchisees forced her to bring in a new president in exchange for an additional $250,000. Before long, the new president left, filing suit for the salary she was never paid.[176]

Before you buy into a company you must know the following.

- Its financial history, growth rate and profit margin. How many of its franchises have failed? Are any of them selling out? If so, find out why.

- Are there at least 3 to 4 *successful* company-owned outlets? That's a sign the company wants to see its franchisees succeed. On the other hand, a company that makes most of its money selling franchises instead of a product or service shows a lack of interest in how well its franchisees are doing.

- Is the field it's in getting crowded?

- Is the industry it's in growing?

- What are the hidden costs?

- Will you be able to buy merchandise from the franchisor at reasonable prices?

- How can the franchise be terminated, renewed, sold, traded or converted?

To avoid disaster experts advise that you do the following:

▸ Have a lawyer who specializes in franchise law examine the franchise agreement and any other documents before you sign.

▸ Check the background of the company's owners. Some states require a company to file a disclosure statement which lists its business dealings in recent years and names of its franchisees.

▸ Have an accountant investigate the company's financial health and profitability.

▸ Write to the International Franchise Association to see if the company is a member in good standing.

▸ Contact the state attorney general's office to see if any complaints about the company are on record. Get a list of all pending lawsuits against the franchisor. Also check with the Federal Trade Commission to see if the company is registered and if any complaints have been lodged against it.[177]

▸ Get customers' opinions about the product or service.

▸ Visit and talk to people who own a franchise in the company.

Make long-distance calls if you have to. Ask them the following questions.

→ Did they get any training? If so, how good was it?

→ For how long did they train?

→ Does the company provide continuing services such as advertising and periodic visits to see how things are going?

→ How helpful are the company's staff?

→ Has the company kept its promises?

Endnotes

CHAPTER 1: Changes

1. InfoWorld, 6/11/84, "Smalltalk with Alan Kay," by Jim Bartimo.
2. U.S. News & World Report, 7/2/84, "Dynamic Elderly."
3. A 1989 survey by the Daniel Yankelovich Group found the largest companies interviewed had a less overall positive attitude toward older workers than did the smaller companies (those with less than 100 employees). They viewed workers age 50-plus as less flexible and less able to adapt to new technology. They also were more likely to have early retirement programs.
4. U.S. News & World Report, 12/23/85.
5. FORTUNE, 2/13/89, "What Flexible Workers Can Do," by Norm Alster.
6. Business Week, 9/29/86, "Management Discovers The Human Side of Automation."
7. WorkAmerica, June 1988.
8. The New York Times, 8/11/89, "From Milking Cows to Manning Computers," by Felicity Barringer. A new data-processing business in Linton, North Dakota — population 1,500 — began in 1989. Farm wives work with computers, earning $5 an hour, for Rosenblut Inc., a Philadelphia-based travel agency. In South Dakota thousands of data processing jobs have been created since Citibank moved its entire billing operation from New York City to Sioux Falls in 1981. Almost all are data-processing or telephone-based jobs.
9. The New York Times, 2/9/86, "A Machismo That Drives Women Out," by Marilyn Loden.
10. Too often older employees make the mistake of assuming that a new, younger boss will appreciate their wisdom and experience gained from 25 or more years with the company. The best way to win the respect of younger managers is to keep the relationship on a professional level and not give old-fashioned, fatherly advice, according to Mike Lombardo, a psychologist at the Center for Creative Leadership in Greenboro, NC, as reported in 50 Plus, October 1988.
11. FORTUNE, 3/14/88, "How To Be a Global Manager."
12. U.S. News & World Report, op. cit., 12/23/85.
13. U.S. News & World Report, 9/25/89, "Best Jobs For The Future." Many companies are expected to hire M.B.A.'s who are fluent in the language and culture of the country in which they have overseas offices. They will also hire more professionals who have international backgrounds in law, accounting and finance for their U.S. offices.
14. Whyte, William F. The Organization Man, Simon and Schuster.
15. U.S. News & World Report, 2/29/88, "America's Blue Collars Get Down to Business." At XEROX Corporation, plant-level workers are taught to conduct meetings and solve problems. They work in small "family groups" with little or no supervision. Former supervisors are called "advisors." Ad hoc teams are formed to solve special problems or to improve quality and productivity. The teams may include production workers and professionals.
16. U.S. News & World Report, 3/7/88, "The 21st Century Executive."
17. Business Week, 6/6/88, "Motorola Sends Its Work Force Back to School." Motorola's assembly line workers now must be able to read

computer graphs and understand the new statistical process control method of monitoring production. Monitoring by computer screen takes a new set of skills — ability to read graphs, change percentages to decimals, etc.

18.   Business Week, 7/7/86, "IBM's Fancy Footwork to Sidestep Layoffs."
19.   Personnel Administrator, February 1989, Vol. 34(2), "Hiring Job Spirit," by Jeffrey J. Hallett.
20.   Inc, December 1986, "Printer Harry Quadracci."
21.   The New York Times, Careers special edition, 10/16/88, "An Improved Outlook For Manufacturing," by Jennifer Stoffel.
22.   EXXON USA, Third Quarter 1985, Vol. 24, No. 3.

Business Week, 5/25/87, "GM Is Spreading The Gospel According to Toyota."

23.   As quoted in EXXON USA, Ibid.
24.   Inc, op. cit., December 1986.
25.   FORTUNE, op. cit., 2/13/89.
26.   U.S. News & World Report, op. cit., 2/29/88.
27.   Inc, op.cit., December 1986.
28.   More frequent shifts in machinery requires greater employee resourcefulness and flexibility. See Business Week, op. cit., 6/6/88 and The New York Times, 9/26/89, "Companies Stepping in Where The Schools Failed."
29.   A widely held myth is that midlife and older women especially are "stuck in their ways" and therefore difficult to train and supervise.
        A 1984 survey of 363 companies by the Conference Board found that 69% of managers agreed with the statement that older workers in general "tend to be less flexible and more resistant to change."
30.   FORTUNE, 4/11/88, "Tomorrow's Jobs Plentiful, But ....," by Louis S. Richman.

Business Week, 2/4/85, "Suddenly The World Doesn't Care If You Live or Die."

31.   The New York Times, 2/21/88, "US Industry's Unfinished Struggle to Compete," by Claudia H. Deutsch.
32.   According to Richard Ferry, president of Korn/Ferry International, as quoted in Business Week, 2/6/89.
33.   The New York Times, 10/7/84, "What's New With Executives Abroad," by Philip S. Gutis.

CHAPTER 2: Choices

34.   FORTUNE, 5/9/88, "On The Rise."
35.   From a survey done by Jack Erdlen of Costello Erdlen & Company, a Boston outplacement and human resources firm. It was reported in The New York Times, 12/23/86, "Getting aid following dismissal," by Elizabeth M. Fowler.

The higher the pay the longer the job hunt, writes Timothy Schellhardt, The Wall Street Journal, 12/15/89. Expect to search one month for every $10,000 of salary you want.

The following figures are from a Bureau of Labor Statistics report in November 1989:

Occupation	Average Number of Weeks Unemployed	% Weeks Unemployed	
		Less than 5	15 or more
Managerial, professional	14.3	38.2	26.9
Technical, sales, administrative support	10.6	51.4	19.5
Service occupations	10.8	52.4	18.7
Precision production, craft, repair	12.2	52.2	20.3
Operators, fabricators, laborers	10.9	49.6	18.3
Farming, forestry, fishing	12.6	55.3	20.7

36. The New York Times, 11/16/86, "From Farmer to Collegian."
37. According to Richard Gould, author of Sacked: Why Good People Get Fired and How to Avoid It. Wiley, 1986.
38. Industry Week, 1/2/89, Vol. 238(1), "Managers on The Move," by James Braham.
39. Business Week, 6/4/84.
40. The New York Times, 5/9/86, "How a Blind Ad Led to Aamco's Presidency."
41. The New York Times, 4/16/89, "Industry-Hoppers Move Ahead," by Peggy Schmidt. Not every type of employer hires industry outsiders. Those that are willing include service industries such as financial services, data processing, health care and employee training. "The less bureaucratic the organization the more open-minded management is likely to be about moving in people from different company cultures."

CHAPTER 3: Are You Ready For a Change?

42. U.S. News & World Report, 3/23/87, "You're Fired!"
43. Of the University of Michigan's Institute of Labor and Industrial Relations.
44. The New York Times, 2/3/87, "Research Affirms Power of Positive Thinking," by Daniel Goleman.
45. Journal of Rational-Emotive and Cognitive Behavior Therapy, Spring/Summer 1988, Vol. 61, "Cognitive Career Counseling for Women," by Diane Richman. An attempt was made to change the self-defeating beliefs and role conflicts held by many career women. The results showed that cognitive therapy significantly reduced these barriers in women who sought help because of job-related problems.

46. The New York Times, 7/21/88, "For People Prone to Depression, Danger Signals on Bad Moods,"by Daniel Goleman.

47. Many psychological studies show results similar to the following studies which are briefly summarized:

Gerontologist, December 1988, Vol. 28(6), "Aging of the brain: How can we prevent it?" by Lissy Jarvik. The results of this 20-year long study of twins shows that intellectual ability after age sixty is not inevitable. Declining scores on several cognitive tests were correlated with poor health and with dementia. The mental performance of normal, healthy twins remained within normal limits except for speed.

Psychology and Aging, December 1988, Vol. 3(4), "Continuity in intellectual functioning: The role of self-reported health," by Dorothy Field, K.W. Schaie & Victor Leino. The subjects in this study were tested with the Wechsler Adult Intelligence Scale in 1969-70 and again in 1983-84 when their ages ranged from 73 to 93. Although many showed a decline in intellectual functioning, there were substantial individual differences at all age levels. More than 50% of the subjects showed no reliable change and a minority showed an increase in scores for verbal intelligence. The results point to the important role of health in maintaining intellectual functioning in advanced old age.

Social Behaviour, June 1988, Vol. 3(2), "Microcomputer proficiency in later-middle-aged and older adults: Teaching old dogs new tricks," by Adam Carfein, K. Warner Schaie & Sherry Willis. In this study 56 adults ranging in age from 49 to 67 years, who had no computer experience at all, took several kinds of intelligence tests. Then they were given training on how to use computers. After training was completed, they were given a test on the computer tasks. No significant age difference was found in intellectual ability or in computer proficiency.

48. Journal of Personality and Social Psychology, March 1989, Vol. 56(3), "Explanatory style across the life span: Evidence for stability over 52 years," by Melanie Burns and Martin Seligman. Dr. Seligman and his colleagues have done several studies on cognitive style and its link to depression, low achievement and physical illness.

49. Journal of Personality and Social Psychology, April 1986, Vol. 50(4), "Explanatory style as a predictor of productivity and quitting among life insurance sales agents," by Martin Seligman and Peter Schulman.

50. Journal of Personality and Social Psychology, "Pessimistic explanatory style is a risk factor for physical illness: A 35-year longitudinal study," by Christopher Peterson, Martin Seligman & George Valliant.

51. The study was done by George Valliant, a psychiatrist at Dartmouth Medical School, and Christoper Peterson, a psychologist at the University of Michigan.

Leslie Kamen and Martin Seligman also found a link between pessimism and a weakened immune system which left the sufferers more vulnerable to ill health. Also, the pessimists were passive with regard to helping and caring for themselves and meeting life's challenges. See "Explanatory style and health" in Current Psychological Research and Reviews, Fall 1987, Vol. 6(3).

52. International Journal of Aging and Human Development, 1988, Vol. 27(4), "Social interaction and depression in elderly individuals," Ken Rotenberg & Jocelyn Hamel. This study found that depression was significantly related to the quantity of social interactions that involve frequent conversations. The researchers' interpretation of the results is that a healthy social life, with close relationships, wards off depression.

53. The results of such studies do not prove that poor nutrition lowers mental capacity, says James D. Goodwin of the University of New Mexico School of Medicine. It could be that persons who are less alert forget to take their vitamins or do a poorer job in meal preparation.

54. Canada Journal of Psychology, June 1987, Vol. 41(21), "Environment and the aging brain," by James Black, William Greenough, Brenda Anderson & Krystyna Isaacs. This is one of several studies made on this issue. Their findings show that physical exercise has positive effects on the aging brain. In this particular study, young and old animals showed increased synaptic connections between brain cells after exposure to some types of enriching experience. The conclusion is that "neural plasticity" persists into old age and that the brain is vulnerable to the effects of poor physical health.

55. Recent studies of severely depressed patients who received cognitive therapy with and without drug treatment have found a significant improvement over those who were on drug therapy alone. The improvement persists one year later. Other studies comparing drugs and psychotherapy have shown they are equally effective for treating major depression, but psychotherapy is more effective in preventing relapses. The reason appears to be that therapy teaches patients more constructive ways to deal with future problems. See the American Journal of Psychiatry, October 1989.

    Journal of Applied Rehabilitation Counseling, Spring 1988, Vol. 19(1), "Beck's cognitive therapy: An overview for rehabilitation counselors," by Wayne A. Bowers; Nordisk Psykiatrisk Tidskrift, 1988, Vol. 42(6), "Cognitive controlling factors for mood," by Gunnar Götestam & Tore Stiles.

56. Psychology Today, April 1985, "Relaxation: The Storm Before The Calm," by Frederick J. Heide.

57. The New York Times, 8/17/87, "Suicides Show That Farm Crisis Goes On," by Keith Schneider.

58. The New York Times, 11/26/87, "Trying to Face Reality? It May Be the Last Think That the Doctor Orders," by Daniel Goleman.

59. Scandinavian Journal of Behaviour Therapy, 1987, Vol. 16(4), "The role of evaluative self-schemata in self-talk: Some predictions and explorations," by Micael Bruch, Victor Meyer & Edward Chesser. This study examined the effect of self-talk on anxiety and performance in subjects who were administered coping and achievement tasks. Persons who engaged in self-defeating talk were significantly more depressed than persons whose self-talk was affirmative and hopeful. The conclusion is that negative self-talk is clearly related to low self-esteem.

60. The Journal of Personality and Social Psychology, November 1988, Vol. 55(5), "Affect and memory: Effects of pleasant and unpleasant odors on retrieval of happy and unhappy memories," by Howard Ehrlichman & Jack Halpern.

61. Molloy, John T. The Woman's Dress For Success Book, Warner Books.

62. Brody, Jane, The New York Times Guide to Personal Health. Times Books.

63. In several experiments elderly rats — comparable to humans in their 80s or 90s — who lived in a stimulating environment showed improved problem solving ability. Later autopsies revealed thickening of the cerebral cortex, with signs of increased neural connections!

65. Of the University of California Medical School at Irvine.

66. Professor of physiology and anatomy at the University of California at Berkeley.

67. Brain Research, August 1986, Vol. 380(1), "Environmental conditions modulate degeneration and new dendrite growth in the cerebellum of senescent rats," by William Greenough, John McDonald, Robert Parnisari & James Camel. One of the many studies showing that a complex environment which stimulates sensory-motor activity in aging rats slows down the loss of brain cells and encourages the growth of new brain cells.

68. Of the University of Illinois at Urbana-Champaign.

69. Only about 20% of the thousands of patients Dr. Beck has treated at his Philadelphia clinic needed longer-term psychotherapy. These patients suffered from deep-seated personality disorders. Other studies have also shown significant improvement with the application of cognitive therapy. Also see the Journal of Abnormal Psychology, February 1988, Vol. 97(1), "Explanatory style change during cognitive therapy for unipolar depression," by Martin Seligman, Camilio Castellon, John Cacciola & Peter Schulman, et. al.

70. The New York Times Magazine, 8/30/87.

CHAPTER 4: How Well Do You Know Yourself?

71. MONEY, June 1986, "Living the Good Life on $40,000 a Year," by Eric Schurenberg.

72. Business Week, 4/21/86, "Executive Secretary: A New Rung On The Corporate Ladder."

73. The New York Times, 10/6/84, "New York Day by Day," by Susan H. Anderson & Maurice Carroll.

74. The New York Times, 1988, "For Rectors and Churches It Is Match-Making Time," by Ari L. Goldman.

75. The New York Times, 12/7/87, "Fewer Applicants to Law Schools," Stephen Labaton.

76. The New York Times, 9/5/87, "Selecting a Career Counselor," by Deborah Blumenthal.

CHAPTER 5: Facts You Will Need

77. U.S. News & World Report, 4/14/86, "What Makes Top Executives Run?"

78. Business Week, 4/7/86, "Annual Reports: The Good, The Bad, and The Ridiculous."

79. The New York Times, ?/?/??, "What's New in Annual Reports," by Stephen Labaton.

80. The New York Times, 2/9/86, "The Promise in Profit-Sharing," by Jeffrey A. Leib.

81. Business Week, 6/6/88, "Motorola Sends Its Work Force Back to School."

82. Although small companies in general have more openings, in high-tech companies there are more frequent layoffs when the market softens. However, rehiring increases when the market rebounds, reports FORTUNE magazine, op. cit., 4/11/88.

83. The study was sponsored and reported by The New York Times, 5/1/88, "The Little Englines That Could... And Do," by William Glaberson.

84. Although many small businesses fail in the first few years, those that thrive do so because of special skills or tailored products.

85. The New York Times, 9/9/86, "Placing the Older Manager," by Elizabeth M. Fowler.

86. INC, November 1987, "The Joy of Working."

87. Ibid.

88. The New York Times, op. cit., 5/1/88.

89. Levering, R., M. Moskowitz & M. Katz. The 100 Best Companies To Work For in America. Addison-Wesley.

90. The New York Times special section The Business World, 6/12/88, "An M.B.A. Runs The Gantlet," by Victoria P. Brown.

91. According to Professor Peter Davis, University of Pennsylvania's Wharton School, as reported in The New York Times, 6/12/86, "The Family Business: Wrestling With Vulnerability," by Steven Prokesch.

92. According to David Harbert, president of Sweeney Shepherd Company, as reported in Business Week, 7/11/88, "Personal Business. Braving a Family-Run Business."

93. Business Week, op. cit., 4/4/88.

94. Modern Maturity, June-July 1984.

95. AARP News Bulletin, February 1986. "Older Workers Find They're Still Needed in the Corporate World," by Bill Crawford.

Business Week, 4/3/89, "U.S. Companies Go For the Gray."

96. The New York Times, 4/13/88, "Reports Thrive in a Frugal Age," by Eric N. Berg.

97. An acquisition or a spurt in earnings may not mean more job openings. The latter could come from a sale of a division instead of from profits. Conversely, a sudden drop in earnings may be due to measures taken to improve the company's profitability. AM International's 1986 annual report showed a drop from $25.5 million to $5.7 million which was mainly due to its massive reorganization. The same thing happened when Lee Iaccocca became head of the critically ill Chrysler Corporation.

Look at income statement items — Net Sales, Gross Profit, Net Income. Compare the figures for the past five or more years, if tables are included. In the case of Essex Corporation, these showed a steady profit increase in all but one of ten years. Yet the company was taken over in 1988.

98.   Business Week, 4/7/86, "Annual Reports: The Good, The Bad, and The Ridiculous."

99.   Kennedy, Marilyn Moats, Office Warfare. Macmillan Publishing Company, 1985 edition.

CHAPTER 6: How to find a good job

100.   Speaking at a Midlife Conference sponsored by Marymount Manhattan College.

101.   The New York Times, 6/6/89, "Helping Older Workers Get Jobs," by Elizabeth M. Fowler.

102.   Business Week, 1/23/89, "You Got the Ax. Now What Should You Do?"

103.   If you are transferring to another industry or your previous employer has been the subject of a publicized problem or scandal it will probably take even more time, as reported in U.S. News & World Report magazine, 4/18/88.

104.   Business Week, 5/21/84, "Women in the Sciences: The Gains Look Solid."

105.   A recent survey of insurance company executives and agency owners found that most used networking when seeking outside candidates for sales and management positions. Advertising was used mainly for support staff positions. As Reported in Broker World, Vol. 8(10), October 1988, "Hiring Practices and Pitfalls," by Sherry L. Wileman.

        In a survey of members of the Administrative Management Society, 70% said a referral by another employee in the organization is the best method for getting a job interview with their firms. The second most popular method is to send a resume and cover letter. About 25% of the managers found their present job through referrals by friends, relatives and other contacts. As reported in Management World, September/October 1986, Vol. 15(7), "Managers Talk About Careers," by Joseph McKendrick.

106.   Business Week, 4/6/87.

107.   The New York Times, 1/2/85, "Capitol Hill's Job Market," by James F. Clarity.

108.   Modern Maturity, June/July 1983, "Engineering: A Dream Retirement," by Eleanor A. Baxel.

109.   Business Week, 1/23/89, "You Got The Ax. Now What Should You Do?" by Bill Symonds.

110   A 1983 comparison of Job Service listings over three consecutive months in Orlando, FL and listings in newspaper want ads during the same period found that many jobs listed by the Job Service were characterized by irregular employment and wages, low prestige and high turnover. The results suggest that employers prefer newspaper want ads, particularly when looking for professionals and managers. See Growth & Change, Winter 1987, Vol. 18(1), "Assessing the Labor Market Intermediary Role of the Job Service: Note," by Clyde Haulman, Frederick Raffa & Brian Rungeling.

111.   **Some Examples of Private Industry Council Programs:**
The Private Industry Council and the Employment and Training
Administration of Broward County, Florida operate a Senior Jobs
Project which has received national acclaim. First they did a survey to
learn which industries had job openings suitable for older workers.
Then they designed a training program to teach the needed skills. They
also developed a program of support services such as pre-employment
counseling, career update workshops and job placement.

The Wayne County and Southeastern Michigan Private Industry
Corporation retrained dismissed automotive and steel industry workers
for current job needs in the County. These included airline reservations
agents, machinists, mechanics, word processors, culinary arts specialists,
clerical and secretarial workers, health aides, horticulturalists, food
management personnel and many others. An on-the-job training
program enabled the trainees to earn money while they were learning
new skills. Classroom training was provided by local colleges and
training institutes.

112.   Modern Maturity, October-November 1983, "Program Boosts Older
Workers."

113.   Funding comes from Florida's Health & Rehabilitative Services
Program, marriage license and divorce filing fees and vocational
education funds. To be eligible, persons must be 35 or older — one
of the participants was a 78-year old woman — and deprived of their
main means of support through widowhood, abandonment, divorce or
separation. Persons with pending separations, whose spouses are
disabled or have been taken away for some reason, as well as men
whose wives had been their main providers are also eligible. They must
all be able to read and write English.

114.   Recommendations from the nearby Disney Studio and Universal Studio
led to the creation of more film-making courses at Valencia than at any
institution in the nation.

115.   It involves the media, speaking before groups, mailings to small
businesses and a newsletter for employers. State agencies are also
contacted.

116.   R. Levering, M. Moskowitz & M. Katz, The 100 Best Companies To
Work For in America. Addison-Wesley.

117.   The New York Times, op. cit., 5/9/86.

118.   The New York Times advertises over 100,000 job vacancies monthly.
On Sundays there is a Help Wanted supplement which lists vacancies
ranging from entry-level to top management and professional levels, in
every industry and every occupation. There are also jobs listed under
the Situations Wanted, Household Employment, and Career Training
sections. More vacancies at the professional, executive, management and
technical levels can be found in the Business supplement. Vacancies in
education, library and health services are in the Week in Review
supplement. Weekday job listings are found in the following sections:
On Monday through Saturday they appear in the Classified pages. The
Sports section carries additional vacancies in the sports, car, boating and
other specialty classified sections. Tuesday's Science supplement lists
openings in education, health, library services and high technology. Ads
for technical experts in engineering, law, marketing, finance and other

fields also appear. Tuesday's classified pages include jobs listed under "Office Technology." Wednesday's Business has a "Career Marketplace" for executive, managerial and professional openings. The Classified has a bannered feature for secretaries.

The National Business Employment Weekly lists high-level, high-paying job vacancies. It also has useful articles on resumes and letter writing, networking, interviewing, on-the-job strategies, weighing offers and entrepreneurism. There are also listings of franchises and distributorship. A monthly feature, "Business Offerings," lists opportunities for starting your own business. Articles in a recent issue included "How to Work With Executive Recruiters," "The Hiring Outlook for 1990," and "Job Search Tools." For $68 you can place a job-wanted ad in the "Talent for Hire" section which is read by personnel directors. To place an ad call 800/JOB-HUNT for details. A single newsstand issue costs $3.50. For information on a subscription call 800/562-4868 (New Yorkers call 212/808-6792) or write to The Wall Street Journal, 420 Lexington Avenue, New York, NY 10170.

Other well known newspaper sources include The Washington Post, Christian Science Monitor, Boston Globe and Chicago Tribune.

119. The New York Times, 5/28/89, "Working the Floor at a Job Fair," by N.R. Kleinfield.

CHAPTER 7: Find a Job Through Volunteer Work

120. The New York Times, 10/28/83, "Among Volunteers, Change in the Suburbs," by Andree Brooks.

121. U.S. News & World Report, 4/24/89, "Volunteer Jobs with Solid Payoffs."

122. Occupational Outlook Quarterly, Fall 1988, Vol. 32(3), "Careers in the Field of Aging," by Anne Kahl.

123. The New York Times, 9/20/84, "Day by Day."

124. U.S. News & World Report, op. cit., 4/24/89.

125. These include the following:

- Sierra Club: 530 Bush Street, San Francisco, CA 94108
- National Audubon Society: 950 Third Avenue, New York, NY 10022
- Friends of the Earth: 1412 16th Street NW, Washington, DC 20036
- Environmental Action: 1346 Connecticut Avenue NW, Washington, DC 20036
- National Parks and Conservation Association: 1701 18th Street NW, Washington, DC 20009
- Nature Conservancy: 800 N. Kent Street, Ste. 1800, Arlington, VA 22209
- Wilderness Society: 1901 Pennsylvania Avenue NW, Washington, CA 20006

CHAPTER 8: So Long, 9-to-5!

126. Some temporary agencies have a policy which prevents their recruits from accepting a permanent job offer in the companies they are sent to.

127. The New York Times, 8/14/84, "More 'Temps' Are Staying On."

128. AccounTemps has about 130 offices in the U.S., Canada, Britain and Israel. Manpower has about 1,075 offices in 32 countries. Kelly has offices throughout the U.S., Canada, Puerto Rico, England, Ireland, Scotland and France. Norrel Temporary Services has over 350 offices in the U.S.

129. In 1989 the median hourly wage for part-time clerical workers was only 65% of similar full-time workers. Nearly 80% of full-time permanent workers receive paid health insurance compared with less than 30% of part-timers. As reported in Business Week, 7/24/89.

130. A new law was expected to go into effect at the time this book was published that would extend company-paid health and life insurance benefits to part-time workers who put in more than 17 ½ hours a week. This would only apply to companies with many part-time employees, i.e., those in retail trade or service businesses. Small companies that employ few part-timers might be exempt.

131. Industry Week, 3/21/88, Vol. 236(6), "Rent-a-Boss," by Brian Moskal.

132. Cash Flow, December 1986, Vol. 7(12), "Part-Time CFOs Bring Results to Young, Fast-Track Companies," by Jay Pridmore.

133. The Retiree Job Bank of Travelers Companies hires people for a variety of positions. Most are clerical and secretarial. Retirees also write job descriptions, act as executive receptionists, coordinate special events, do research, work as accountants and underwriters, etc. Many of the job descriptions call for computer skills. Retirees can also enroll in company paid computer training. The Job Bank also has positions with flexible hours and job share positions. Two retirees, one age 70 and other age 79, have shared the job of running the company's Older Americans Program.

Corning Glass Works in Corning, NY also has a program to hire retirees for short-term projects.

134. Companies which have benefited from the skills of retirees include American Express, Burpee Seed, Chase Manhattan Bank, Continental Illinois Bank & Trust, Deer & Company, General Electric, Levi-Strauss, MacDonalds, Polaroid, Standard Oil, Travelers Insurance, Grumman Aerospace, Woodward & Lothrop (a Washington, DC-based retail chain), Yankelovitch, Skelley & White (a market research firm with offices in major cities. It employs retired executives, managers and professionals as permanent, part-time interviewers.)

135. Upjohn Healthcare Services, for example, places nurses, nurse assistants, home health aides, elder care workers, child care workers and other health professionals in jobs throughout the U.S. and Canada. INTERSEC recruits bilingual temporary workers for international organizations which have headquarters in Washington, DC. Science Temps of Cranford, NJ and Lab Support of Woodland Hills, CA specialize in placing chemists. Powerforce, a unit of IDC Services Inc., provides part-time sales merchandisers and sales personnel to the

packaged goods industry. RENT-A-CONSULTANT, Washington, DC, places temporary financial analysts, economists, engineers and other types of consultants. United Engineers, of Holyoke, MA, specializes in draftspersons, engineers and technicians. Corporate Staff Inc., based in San Francisco, places managers and executives in temporary jobs. Financial Managers Trust, Cambridge MA, has part-time financial management jobs. Richard Ward & Associates, Chicago, IL, has part-time sales management jobs.

136.   According to "9-t-5, National Association of Working Women."

137.   The New York Times, 9/23/84, "The Pros and Cons of Computer 'Commuting'," by James Brooke.

CHAPTER 9: Why Not Be Your Own Boss?

138.   Working Woman, November 1986.

139.   The New York Times, 1/3/88, "A Burst of Rural Enterprise," by John Lofflin.

140.   The New York Times, 8/18/86, "Female Entrepreneurs Thrive," by Eric Schmitt.

141.   Business Week, 10/6/86.

142.   Few of the many retired professionals and managers who started a consulting business made more than $10,000 a year in the 1985-86 period, reports Business Week, 8/4/86.

143.   Working Woman, January 1987, "The Eighth Annual Working Woman Salary Survey," by Hanna McCrum and Hanna Rubin.

144.   Time, 7/4/88, "She Calls All The Shots."

145.   Business Week, 12/22/86, "What Do Women Want? A Company They Can Call Their Own."

146.   The study was done by the National Federation of Independent Business, Washington, DC.

147.   The New York Times, 5/30/85, "A Small Baker Moves Into The Big Time," by Fred R. Bleakley.

148.   The New York Times, 3/5/87, "A Family Goes From Rugs to Riches," by Leslie Bennetts.

149.   Her 60-minute "Office Chatter" cassette is $14.95 and can be ordered from Laura Newman's company, Zable's Business Services, Kingston, NY.

150.   U.S. News & World Report, 1/13/86, "Ordinary Millionaires."

151.   Business Week, 3/23/87, "A Crusader Who Helps Offices Go Smoke-Free."

152.   Business Week, 6/8/87, "The Couple With The Hippest Greeting Cards in Town."

153.   FORTUNE, 4/25/88, "Filler's The Name, Odor's The Game," by Penny W. Moser.

154.   U.S. News & World Report, 10/21/85, "Hitting It Big By Going Out On Your Own."

155.   The New York Times, 9/28/86.

156.   The New York Times, 11/5/85, "Ventures Plan Now To Outlast Comet."

157.   The New York Times, op. cit., 1/3/88.

158. A study of <u>INC</u> 500 chief executive officers, as reported in <u>INC</u>, June 1986, "Main Street, Inc.," by Chris Hartman. Also see <u>INC Magazine's Guide to Small Business Success</u>, 1987, "Why Partnerships Break Up," by Stephen G. Thomas.

159. <u>INC</u>, February 1988, "Hands On."

160. <u>New Woman</u>, November 1985, "Making Real Money at Home," by Valerie Bohigian.

161. <u>Working Woman</u>, July 1985, "New Help for Start-Ups," by David Gumpert.

162. <u>New Woman</u>, July 1985, "Your Own Business: Ready-Made Offices You Can Afford," by Jan Alexander.

163. <u>Changing Times</u>, June 1987, "Start-Up Help For Your Business." Also see <u>U.S. News & World Report</u>, 12/21/87, "Starting Up a Business in 1988: A Postcrash Course."

164. You don't have to set up a complete office or store at the start. Many naive business owners have gone broke because they bought expensive equipment in the flush of early sales. It's hard to resist the temptation to buy expensive items, especially after you've been used to a steady paycheck, but you must steel yourself. Much of what you assume is needed now can be purchased later on.

165. <u>Business Week</u>, 11/3/86, "It Will Get a Bit Easier To Find Startup Cash."

166. A bill was passed in December 1987 by Congress to help unemployed persons start their own business. It authorizes the Labor Department to start three 3-year pilot programs which allow unemployment insurance benefits to be used for this purpose. Persons who are eligible can collect up to $5,000 over a 6-month period while trying to get their business going. The plan is for each state to enroll up to 3% of its unemployment insurance recipients in the program. For current information contact your congressman, the U.S. Department of Labor, or the nearest Small Business Administration office.

167. <u>The New York Times</u>, <u>op. cit.</u>, 1/3/88.

168. <u>INC</u>, February 1987, "The Hottest Entrepreneur in America," by Tom Richman.

169. <u>Changing Times</u>, November 1987, "Making It in Mail Order."

170. <u>Nation's Business</u>, February 1989, Vol. 76(2), "Finding The Right Franchise," by Nancy L. Croft and Meg Whittemore.

171. <u>Nation's Business</u>, February 1989, Vol. 76(2), "Franchising's Pathfinders," by Nancy C. Baker and Meg Whittemore.

172. <u>Success</u>, October 1989, Vol. 36(8), "The New Heavyweights," by Richard Poe.

173. <u>INC</u>, October 1987, "Franchising America (and the World!)."

174. <u>Venture</u>, January 1989, Vol. 11(1), "Wrapped Up With a Bow," by Sheryl Jean.

175. <u>Success</u>, January/February 1989, Vol. 35(1), "The Frontiers of Capitalism: Franchising is the Hottest Form of Entrepreneurship," by Echo M. Garrett.

176. <u>Business Week</u>, 5/23/88, "Want to Buy a Franchise? Look Before You Leap."

RESOURCES ON PSYCHOLOGICAL READINESS

I. *Resources to Build Self-confidence and Overcome Depression*

Publications

Beck, Aaron T. Anxiety Disorders and Phobias: A Cognitive Perspective. Basic Books.

Beck, Aaron T. Cognitive Therapy & The Emotional Disorders. New American Library.

Beck, Aaron T. Cognitive Therapy of Depression. Guilford Press.

Benson, Herbert and Miriam Klipper. The Relaxation Response. Avon.

Carrington, Patricia. Releasing: The New Behavioral Science Method For Dealing With Pressure Situations. W. Morrow.

Ellis, Albert, et al. Handbook of Rational-Emotive Therapy. Springer Publishing Co.

Lewisohn, Peter, et al. Control Your Depression. Prentice Hall Press. Includes relaxation techniques and activities that improve mood.

Viscott, David S. Risking: How to Take Chances and Win. Simon and Schuster.

Tapes

The following may be in your local library. Many of them can also be ordered from **Psychology Today Tapes**, Box 059061, Brooklyn, NY 11205-9061.

Beck, Aaron T. Rational Thinking.

Beck, Aaron T. Understanding Anxiety. How to identify and change distorted thinking that impedes performance and interferes with happiness and emotional well-being.

Ellis, Albert. Effective Self-Assertion Sound Recording.

Ellis, Albert. Rational Emotive Therapy. How to replace irrational ideas with rational thinking to increase effectiveness and build self-esteem.

Flack, Frederic. Coping With Change. Discusses emotional impact of change. Explains how to turn potentially damaging situations into opportunities for personal growth.

Friedman, Martha. Overcoming the Fear of Success.

Garfield, Charles. Peak Performance. Describes characteristics, attitudes, beliefs and behavior of successful people. Includes strategies for improving performance at home, at work and in other areas of life.

Goleman, Daniel. Deep Relaxation.

Lehrer, Paul M. Progressive relaxation training.

Pelletier, Kenneth. Visualization: Accessing the Higher Self.

Procter, Judith. Relaxation Procedures Sound Recording: Meditative Techniques, Breathing Techniques.

Rappaport, Alan R. Relaxation Procedures.

II. *Career Assessment Resources*

Publications

You can find the following publications in bookstores, public libraries and school career counseling offices. Many can also be ordered from JIST **Works, Inc.**, 720 North Park Avenue, Indianapolis, IN 46202, (phone: 800-648-JIST; in Indiana, Canada call 317-637-6643).

Bolles, Richard. The Quick Job Hunting Map. Ten Speed Press. Helps answer questions such as "What skills do I possess? Which do I enjoy using most? In what settings would I like to apply these skills?"

Career Compatibility Profile. Order from Women's Center for Executive Development, 111 East Wacker, Suite 2210, Chicago, IL 60601.

Dictionary of Holland Occupational Codes. Relates all occupational titles in the Dictionary of Occupational Titles with Holland's categories. See Holland, below.

Eckstrom, Ruth. Women's Workbook. For homemakers and others with little paid work experience. Identify skills from homemaking and other life experiences and match them to entry level jobs that have upward mobility. Detailed list of job descriptions.

Exploring Career Options. This multiple-choice inventory helps assess your interests, values, personality traits, and verbal and numerical abilities. After you mail in your answers, a computer grades them and matches the results against a variety of occupations. You then receive a report which describes your interests and abilities and lists about 10 to 15 matching occupations. This — and other self-assessment vehicles — is not a replacement for career counseling from a qualified professional. Order from National Computer Systems Inc., PO Box 1416, Minnetonka, MN 55440.

Farr, Michael J. Job Finding Fast. Identify skills from leisure activities, family responsibilities, education, etc. Identify your ideal job in terms of earnings, level of responsibility, location, special training or knowledge required, work environment, and other aspects. Data on 16 occupational clusters and about 200 jobs. Also covers how to find a job, make telephone contacts, write resumes and cover letters, and more.

Figler, Howard. The Complete Job Search Handbook. Exercises to assess your skills, values and needs, explore careers and develop a job objective. Tips on interviews and more.

Guide For Occupational Exploration. Originally published by the U.S. Department of Labor's Employment and Training Administration. A complete career exploration system, nearly 1,000 pages. Self-assessment forms and instructions. Over 12,000 jobs categorized by 12 occupational clusters. Helps you find related jobs in various industries that require similar skills to those you used in previous jobs. Identify jobs that match your values, leisure/home activities, school subjects and the military. Especially helpful for returning homemakers. Order from JIST Works.

Holland, John L. The Self Directed Search. Widely used by career counselors. Includes over 1100 occupations listed in a separate Occupations Finder which cross-references to the Dictionary of Occupational Titles and other sources.

Moore, Donna J. Matching Your Skills To The Marketplace. Explore government careers via a complete version of Holland's The Self Directed Search. Relates to Federal job titles.

Wisconsin Career Information System (WICS). On a list of job characteristics, you indicate those which apply to jobs you've had and those you would like to have in your next job. A computer then matches your responses with compatible occupations. These computer-generated occupations are added to a list which you have already checked on a written list. Then you narrow the list of occupations down to those which interest you most. Wisconsin Career Information System, Vocational Studies Center, University of Wisconsin, 1025 West Johnson Street, Madison, WI 59709.

Computerized Guides: A sample

Managing For Success Series: Career Planning. Helps assess your work experiences, job skills, ideal work environments, personal needs, interests, expectations and values. CBS Software, One Fawcett Pl., Greenwich, CT 06830.

DISCOVER, American College Testing Service and SIGI-PLUS, Educational Testing Service. Both are available in many libraries and college counseling centers. Easy to operate. A specially trained librarian or a career counselor is available if you need help.

"Our great advantage over all other social animals is that we possess the kind of brain that permits us to change our minds. We are not obliged, as the ants are, to follow genetic blueprints for every last detail of our behavior."
— Dr. Lewis Thomas

ℬ
RESOURCES ON JOBS, OCCUPATIONS & SALARIES

I. Resources on Occupations and New Careers

Many of the following publications are in the public library and in school career counseling offices. The U.S. Government publications can also be ordered from the U.S. Government Printing Office, Washington, DC 20402. Some can be ordered from JIST   Works, Inc., 720 North Park Avenue, Indianapolis, IN 46202; Phone: 1-800-648-JIST; 317-637-6643 for residents of Indiana and Canada.

Dictionary of Occupational Titles. U.S. Department of Labor, Bureau of Labor Statistics. Guide to over 20,000 job titles, organized by major job categories and cross-referenced by industry and title.

Emerging Careers: New Occupations for the Year 2000 & Beyond. U.S. Department of Labor, Bureau of Labor Statistics.

Occupational Outlook Handbook. U.S. Department of Labor, Bureau of Labor Statistics. Indispensable resource for career assessment. Full descriptions of nearly 200 jobs in 19 occupational clusters — requirements (skills, interests, aptitudes, personality, training and educational), work conditions, employment and advancement opportunities, earnings, related occupations. Sources of additional information; addendum with brief data for additional occupations; job prospects to the year 2000; overview of future jobs; etc.

Occupational Outlook Quarterly. U.S. Department of Labor, Bureau of Labor Statistics. Articles cover a wide array of career and work-related topics — e.g., effects of new technologies, work responsibilities in specific occupations, job outlook, changing career opportunities, emerging occupations. See Kahl in Appendix F, below.

II. Resources on Salaries and Benefits

You should know the market value of the job you want, the salary range you are willing to accept, and the frequency of salary reviews. The latter can compensate for a lower starting salary. So, too, can health insurance, pension plan, training and education benefits, incentives, and secondary financial aspects such as the costs of commuting.

Most salary surveys cover broad categories such as occupational groups and national, regional and/or metropolitan areas. These should be used only as general guides. More specific salary surveys are made by the U.S. Bureau of Labor Statistics and professional and trade associations. The National Society of Professional Engineers, for example, has data on salaries according to job type, level of experience, industry, and geographic location.

Another point to consider is that most are surveys of major companies and only a few are relevant to smaller companies (which typically pay less).

• Look at the salaries listed for your occupation in the local newspaper's help-wanted ads.

• Call the personnel department of companies in your community and ask what they are paying for the type of job you want.

• Read surveys of salaries for various industries and occupations. You'll find these in professional and trade journals, in the public library, the Job Service office and job placement offices of colleges.

• The U.S. Bureau of Labor Statistics periodically issues the following salary surveys. These are available from the U.S. Government Printing Office, Washington, DC 20402. The public library probably has these on file.

Area Wage Surveys for dozens of common occupations such as office, technical and maintenance jobs. Surveys are made in local job markets such as Canton, OH and Newark, NJ. The pay for each occupation is broken down further by skill and responsibility levels. Ten pay levels are given for the secretary/typist occupation, for example — Class E secretaries who work for lower-level supervisors and have the least responsibilities; Class A secretaries who work for heads of large companies and have broader responsibilities. Survey results are also broken down according to company size, location, and industry.

National Survey of Professional, Administrative, Technical, and Clerical Pay, which is issued annually, gives nationwide salary averages for 21 occupations which are broken down into 91 work levels; e.g., auditors, attorneys, computer operators, personnel directors, secretaries.

To make the best use of these surveys you need to define the requirements of the job you're interested in carefully. For example, the data for "personnel manager" is broken down into those who manage "operations level" personnel programs and those who operate "development level" personnel programs. The survey also takes into account the difficulty of the work and whether the company is based in an urban area.

Since salary levels often depend on economic conditions in a particular industry, the Bureau also issues a series of surveys that refine the salary data even further. The Directory of Occupational Wage Surveys lists studies of 32 manufacturing and 17 non-manufacturing industries ranging from refuse hauling to hotel and motel management. Also Look through the following publications.

Annual Compensation Survey by INC magazine, comes out in a summer issue. It gives the results of a national survey of salary levels for key positions in smaller companies.

Cohen, Theodore and Roy A. Lindberg. <u>Compensating Key Executives in The Smaller Company</u>. The American Management Association, 135 W. 50th St., New York, NY 10020.

<u>Dartnell's 13th Biennial Survey of Executive Compensation</u>. Dartnell, 4660 Ravenswood Ave., Chicago, IL 60640. It covers 67 executive and middle management positions for seven different sizes of companies.

Wright, John W. <u>The American Almanac of Jobs and Salaries</u>. Contains loads of information on jobs in government, business and other industries.

III. *Resources on How To Protect Your Job Rights*

Publications

<u>The Age Discrimination in Employment Act Guidebook</u>. Order from the American Association of Retired Persons, Worker Equity Division, 1909 K Street, N.W., Washington, D.C. 20049

Outten, Wayne N. <u>The Rights of Employees.</u> Bantam Books. Much valuable information. One suggestion is to get references — or approval to use the person's name as a reference — from people in the company whose evaluation of your job performance and behavior is more flattering than your manager's. Another is to keep a record of your achievements while you are employed. About a week before your performance evaluation, make copies of the documents in your file and give them to your employer as a reminder.

Gould, Richard. <u>Sacked: Why Good People Get Fired and How to Avoid It.</u> Wiley.

Government Agencies

Equal Employment Opportunity Commission, Washington, D.C. 20507. Has free pamphlets which describe the various discrimination laws. Specialists will answer specific questions on job discrimination. The toll-free telephone number is 800-USA-EEOC.

Civil Rights Division, U.S. Department of Health and Human Services, Washington, D,C. 20201.

Women's Bureau, Office of the Secretary, U.S. Department of Labor, Washington, D.C. 20201.

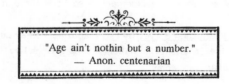

"Age ain't nothin but a number."
— Anon. centenarian

RESOURCES ON JOB TRAINING AND EDUCATION

I. *Publications*

Chronical Four-year College Databook. Chronical Guidance Publications Inc. Moravia, NY 13118.

Chronicle Two-year College Databook. Chronical Guidance Publications.

The College Handbook. The College Board. Descriptions of over 3,000 two- and four-year colleges and universities. Financial aid and how to apply for it, major fields of study, annual expenses, how to select a college and pay for it, and more.

Fact Book on Higher Education. Macmillan Publishing Co. A wide range of information on such matters as: Where will jobs for Ph.D.s be? Which fields of study will grow the most and which face the biggest decline? Also describes degrees, faculty, students, enrollments, institutions, and more.

Harris, Sherry S. Accredited Institutions of Postsecondary Education. Macmillan Publishing. Includes the accreditation status of two- and four-year institutions in the U.S. and certificate/degree programs accredited by professional agencies.

Index of Majors. The College Board. Lists 500 major fields of study and colleges that offer them. Contains separate sections for major programs leading to bachelor's, master's, doctor's, as well as professional and associate degree programs. Describes colleges that have special academic programs.

Kaye, Kim R., ed. Guide to Two-year Colleges. Peterson's Guides. Covers over 1,450 accredited schools that grant associate degrees.

National Guide to Educational Credit For Training Programs. Macmillan Publishing Co. Describes about 2,000 courses offered by more than 180 business, professional, labor, government and voluntary organizations, from AT&T to the Young Women's Christian Association. Describes course content, materials used, sites, and dates offered for each course as well as credit granted in semester hours on four levels — vocational certification, lower division baccalaureate/associate degree, upper division baccalaureate, and graduate.

NUCEA Guide to Independent Study Through Correspondence Instruction. Peterson's Guides.

Peterson's The Independent Study Catalog. Peterson's Guides.

Simosko, Susan. How to Earn College Credit For What You Know. Acropolis. How to get credit for knowledge gained outside the classroom. How to prepare a portfolio used by colleges and universities to assess such learning. Includes addresses of national testing organizations, examples of items to include in a portfolio, and accredited schools that grant such credit.

Sullivan, Eugene, ed. Guide To External Degree Programs in The United States. Macmillan Publishing. Describes over 100 undergraduate and graduate programs in accredited colleges, universities and professional schools that do not require regular classroom attendance.

II. *Learning by Computer*

The following software programs are described in order to give you an idea of what's available. The number and variety of software programs that help you learn job-related skills and know-how is increasing rapidly. You can get this information from the public library.

ACUMEN is a management training program whose major components include "Learning About Yourself," "Learning About Others," and "Improving Working Relations." The latter component, for example, discusses how to set limits and establish discipline, how to provide more effective leadership and improve communications. There is a questionnaire on personal management style which rates you on traits such as "achieving," "builds self up," "friendly." It shows your percentile ranking on twelve "thinking-style" scales — e.g., conventional, dependence, apprehension, oppositional, power, competition, perfectionism, achievement, self-actualization. You can compare your style to that of effective managers, poor managers, winning teams, losing teams and salespeople. Shows areas that need improvement. Includes exercises for personal development and recommendations for behavioral changes. Used by many companies. Contact Human Factors Advanced Technology Group, 4340 Redwood Highway, Ste. 26, San Rafael, CA 95903; Phone: 415-492-9190.

Business Simulator is an executive training program developed at the Wharton Business School, University of Pennsylvania. It is used by executives at major corporations. It teaches skills needed to move up the management ladder or to become a successful entrepreneur. Applies the flight simulator technique used to train pilots. It simulates running a business by putting you at the helm of a start-up company and giving you all the controls needed to guide it to $1 billion in sales and multi-national corporate status. You enter the high-level world of finance, strategic market planning, competition, operations issues and decision making. In the process, you also learn hundreds of business terms and concepts. Contact Reality Development Corp., 3624 Market Street, Philadelphia, PA 19104; Phone: 800-346-2024.

III. *Financial Aid Resources*

Organizations

American Professional Women's Foundation, 2012 Massachusetts Avenue, N.W., Washington, D.C. 20036. Awards scholarships and grants to mature women and loans for women in engineering and graduate business programs.

Ethnic and religious organizations also provide financial aid for their members. The following are some examples.

The American Institute For Polish Culture and the Kosciuszko Foundation each offer annual scholarships to Polish-Americans. The Pan-Dodecanesian Association of America gives scholarships to persons whose origins are the Dodecanese region of Greece. The Society Farsarotul (Romanian), the American Scandinavian Foundation, and other ethnic organizations also provide financial help for their members. Look in Gale's Encyclopedia of Associations for information on ethnic and religious associations that provide education awards.

Publications

Directory of Financial Aids for Minorities.

Directory of Financial Aids for Women.

Financial Aid for Veterams, Military Personnel and Their Dependents.

Hawes, Gene. College Board Guide to Going to College While Working. The College Board.

Paying For Your Education: A Guide For Adult Learners. The College Board. A description of financial aid and who qualifies for it. Discusses credit by examination and external and non-traditional degrees, financial aid for part-time study, available loans to adult learners, etc. Also covers how to apply to a college, how to cut time and costs, non-traditional paths to financial aid and how to organize a financial aid plan.

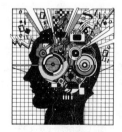

D

RESOURCES ON THE JOB MARKET

I. Occupations With The Best Hiring Outlook in The 1990s

The following occupations are expected to have the largest percentage increase in openings, according to the U.S. Bureau of Labor Statistics.

75% — Paralegal
70% — Medical assistant
68% — Home health aide
66% — Radiology technician
61% — Computer technician
60% — Medical records technician
58% — Medical secretary
57% — Physical therapist
56% — Operating room aide
55% — Operations analyst
55% — Securities and financial services broker
54% — Travel agent
53% — Computer analyst
53% — Physical therapist assistant
52% — Welfare aide
49% — Occupational therapist
48% — Computer programmer
45% — Human services worker
41% — Respiratory therapist
41% — Corrections officer

II. Resources on The Job Market

Publications

→   Emerging Occupations & Projections For Growth in Old Ones. U.S. Department of Labor, Bureau of Labor Statistics. Six reports covering the futures of over 250 jobs.

→   Kahl, Anne. "Careers in the Field of Aging," in Occupational Outlook Quarterly. U.S. Department of Labor. Fall 1988. Detailed discussion of job opportunities resulting from the rapid increase in the 65-plus population.

→   Job Projections and Training Data. U.S. Department of Labor, Bureau of Labor Statistics. Ranks occupations by employment growth, earnings, susceptibility to unemployment, part-time work and other characteristics.

→ Monthly Labor Review. U.S. Department of Labor, Bureau of Labor Statistics. Articles on economic, labor force and employment projections by state, industry, and occupation to the year 2000. Also has special articles like women's work expectations and worker training programs. See Silvestri below.

→ Occupational Projections and Training Data. U.S. Department of Labor, Bureau of Labor Statistics. Data on 700 jobs not found in the Occupational Outlook Handbook.

→ Projections 2000. U.S. Department of Labor, Bureau of Labor Statistics. Detailed analyses of economic and industrial outlook, the labor force, and occupational employment up to the 21st century.

→ **Silvestri, George and John Lukasiewicz.** "A Look at Occupational Employment Trends to The Year 2000," in Monthly Labor Review. U.S. Department of Labor, Bureau of Labor Statistics. September 1987. Brief summary:

Employment for each of the three groups with the most highly educated workers — executive, administrative and managerial, professional, technicians and related support — is expected to grow faster than average and account for almost 40% of the total job growth between 1986-2000. Many factors — which include automation, changes in consumer demand, and imports — are expected to slow growth or lead to a decline for occupational groups which require less education — clerical and other administrative support workers; farming, forestry and fishery workers; operators, fabricators and laborers. An exception to the general trend is the service workers group (with the exception of private household) which will account for more of the total growth in employment than any other broad group.

III. *Companies*

How to Get Information on Small Companies

• Information on small companies that are not listed in the above publications can be found in specialized directories. These are in the business section of the public library and the business school library of a local college or university.

• Telephone the business editors or reporters of local newspapers for information.

• Public libraries and university libraries keep files on local industries and companies.

• The Chamber of Commerce and the Board of Trade have information about companies that are preparing to locate in your area. They also have information on local industries and companies.

A Sample of Family-run Companies

Business Week reported on a study which found that about 175 of the largest 500 industrial companies in the U.S. were either owned or controlled by a single family in 1988.[1] Some are listed in The 100 Best Companies To Work For in America (see below). Here is a sample.

Anheuser-Busch	Marriott
Bain & Co.	Mars
Bechtel Group	McDonnell Douglas
Carlson Companies	Microsoft
Compaq Computer	Milliken & Co.
Corning Glass Works	Mrs. Fields Cookies
Digital Equipment	Occidental Petroleum
Federal Express	Publix Supermarkets
Ford Motor	S.C. Johnson & Son
H Group Holdings	Steelcase
Humana	W.R.Grace
Koch Industries	Wal-Mart Stores
Levi Strauss	Wang Laboratories
Loews	Weyerhaeuser
Malone & Hyde	

A Sample of Companies With Policies Favorable to Older Workers

• The Grumman Corporation, on Long Island, NY, keeps resumes of retired or laid-off workers on file, and hires them on a contractual basis through a temporary placement agency. Highly skilled people such as engineers, mechanics and other technologists find jobs there.

• Digital Equipment's job bank includes outsiders as well as its own retirees.

• Other companies that are noted for their concern about older workers include AT&T, Atlantic Richfield Company, Bell & Howell, Consumer's Union, Harris Bank, Honeywell, IBM, Kinder-Care Inc., Naugles, Inc., Northern Natural Gas Company of Nebraska, Oklahoma Gas & Electric, Prudential Insurance, SRI International. See Endnotes 133-34 for more.

"I don't believe in specially gifted people. The only thing I believe in is work. What I call a gift is doing something you like so much that when you work at it ten hours a day it seems like only two hours. "
— Michel Petrucciani, pianist.

E

HOW TO FIND THE FACTS YOU NEED

I. Employers & Industries
Indexes

Business Periodicals Index. H.W. Wilson Co. Good for locating articles on all business topics that have appeared in the most important business journals.

Predicasts F&S Index United States. Predicasts. Sources of articles about U.S. companies and industries that have appeared in over 750 financial publications, newspapers, trade magazines and special reports.

Wall Street Journal Index. Dow Jones & Co. Sources of articles on corporate and general news about publicly held American companies.

Directories

America's Corporate Families: The Billion Dollar Directory. Dun's Marketing Services. Information on companies with $50 million or more annual sales. Also lists their subsidiaries and divisions.

American Bank Directory. Lists about 18,000 banks. Has names of executives, addresses and phone numbers.

American Export Register. Thomas International Publishing. Lists names, addresses and telephone numbers of American companies doing business internationally.

Business Organizations, Agencies and Publications Directory. Has over 22,000 listings which cover business, trade, commercial and labor associations; government agencies; U.S. and foreign diplomatic offices; regional planning and development agencies; convention, fair and trade organizations; franchise companies; banks and savings and loans; computer information services; information centers and much more. Gale Research.

Capital Source. Has names, addresses and phone numbers of the three branches of the Federal government and its agencies as well as local governments, major corporations, unions, trade associations, law firms, advertising agencies, public relations firms, foreign embassies, and news media that deal with Washington, DC events.

Directory of American Firms Operating in Foreign Countries. World Trade Academy Press. Information on U.S. corporations controlling subsidiaries and affiliates in 122 foreign countries. Includes company address, name of CEO, officer in charge of foreign operations, personnel director, products/services, and number of employees.

Dun and Bradstreet. Facts on businesses which have a net worth between $500,000 and $1 million.

Encyclopedia of Associations. Gale Research. Information on thousands of American associations — addresses and phone numbers, key persons to contact, services provided, publications, meetings, etc. Arranged in three volumes: 1) business, finance, industry and trade, 2) science, medicine and technology, 3) social sciences, education and the humanities.

Guide To American Directories. B. Klein Publications. Includes nearly 8,000 trade, professional and industrial directories of American companies and organizations and a few foreign companies.

Macmillan Directory of Leading Private Companies. National Register Publishing Co. Lists about 6,500 private U.S. parent companies and their subsidiaries. Includes address, description of business, sales, assets, liabilities, net worth, number of employees, names of officers, number of manufacturing plants and offices.

The Market Guide. Market Service Corp. Two-page reports on smaller companies registered with the OTC.

Million Dollar Directory. Dun's Marketing Services. Brief descriptions of U.S. companies — address, phone number, officers and directors, type of business, approximate sales, number of employees, divisions, activities.

Moody's Manuals. Moody's Investors Service. Eight separate manuals — Bank and Financial, Industrial, International, Municipal & Government, OTC Industrial, Public Utilities and Transportation. Data on capital structure, corporate history, business/products, subsidiaries, officers, and chief executive's letter to stockholders. Includes an independent public accountant's report, 7-year income and balance sheet accounts, financial and operating data, long-term debt, financial review of management, number of employees.

National Trade and Professional Associations of the United States and Canada. Columbia Books. Includes date and location of meetings.

Reference Book of Corporate Management. Dun's Marketing Services. Brief biographical data on executives of top corporations.

Standard & Poor's Register of Corporations, Directors and Executives. Standard & Poor's Corp. Volume 1 has facts on about 45,000 corporations — name, address and telephone number, officers and directors, products/services, annual sales, number of employees. Volume 2 lists alphabetically directors and executives, place of birth, colleges attended, business affiliations and other information. Volume 3 lists new companies, new executives and names of recently deceased executives.

Standard & Poor's Stock Reports. Standard & Poor's Corp. These 2-page reports on U.S. companies usually include information on 10-year income, balance sheet, per share data, business summary, new developments, current outlook, capitalization, officers and directors, and dividends.

Thomas Register of American Manufacturers and Thomas Register Catalog File. Thomas Publishing Co. Over 135,000 companies are listed alphabetically and by product/service. Includes address and telephone, product, assets, and company trade catalogs.

Trade Directories of The World. CRONER Publications. Directories for countries, foreign trades, and professions. Contains indexes to industries, trades, professions and countries.

Value Line Investment Surveys. Reports on 1,700 stocks in 95 industries. Has a 1-page analysis of each company, arranged by industry — 5-year quarterly sales, financial strength, earnings predictability, brief description of the business, new developments, outlook.

Washington Information Directory. A guide to Congress, the Executive branch and private associations based in Washington, DC.

Wall Street Transcript. Wall Street Transcript Corp. A weekly compilation from brokerage house reports on companies; security analysts' views on industries and companies; company officials' speeches to financial analyst groups; data from annual reports, and more.

Who's Who in America is where to look if you want an off-beat job — research assistant, secretary, gardener, cook, butler — with a noted personality. It lists thousands of well-known persons in the theater, arts, science, education fields, and in government and community service. There are several volumes such as Who's Who in Finance and Industry, Who's Who in the East, Who's Who in the Midwest, Who's Who in the South and Southwest.

Other Helpful Publications

How To Find Information About Companies. Washington Researchers Publishing, 2612 P Street, NW, Wash, DC 20007; Phone: 202-333-3533. Valuable tips on how to get information on just about anything you need to know about companies.

Levering, R., M. Moskowitz & M. Katz. The 100 Best Companies To Work For in America. Addison-Wesley.

Telephone Directories — Most libraries have directories for the major U.S. cities and smaller cities and towns. Look in the White Pages for the addresses and phone numbers of companies located in the directory's area. Look in the Yellow Pages for a specific business or industry located there.

Trade Directories — Just about every industry has a trade directory; e.g., advertising, electronics, management consulting, department stores.

Whyte, William F. The Organization Man. Simon and Schuster.

Computer Databases

If you do not have a computer, there are private companies which will search through computerized data bases and other sources to find what you need. Information-on-Demand, for example, is a private company in California which accesses over 200 data-bases that offer information on a broad range of subjects.

Public libraries are also entering this field. Many subscribe to the major commercial databases. The service is free or costs little. You can use the library's own computers to access the databases or, if you own a computer, you can connect into them. The librarian can help you.

For information on these services see one of the following reference guides in the public library: DataPro Directory of On-line Services, Directory of On-line Information Resources, Directory of On-line Databases. The following is a sample of what's available.

CompuServe Information Services, PO Box 20212, 5000 Arlington Centre Blvd., Columbus, OH 43220, Phone: 800-848-8199. Has many databases. It has the latest news from AP News Wire, Washington Post, St. Louis Post-Dispatch, specialized business and trade publications, and more. The Tell Electronic News Service "clips" and files news for you. Another database, Supersite, gives demographic and sales potential information by state, county and zip code for the entire nation. CompuServe also continuously updates news and press releases on hundreds of companies worldwide. It also has specialized information for entrepreneurs, engineers, businessmen and others.

Compustat PC Plus Corporate Text has filings of the Securities and Exchange Commission — annual reports, 10K summaries, proxies, company profiles, basic facts and statistics.

Dow Jones News-Information covers over 6,000 publicly traded companies and 170 industry and government categories.

Dow Jones Text-Search Services has complete Wall Street Journal issues from January 1984 to 6:00 a.m. today. Articles can be quickly accessed by codes.

Economic Statistics gives the employment hours and earnings of industries and government services, broken down to the finest detail; e.g., dairy products, legal services, book publishing.

Newsearch: Daily Index is a daily indexing of over 400 periodicals, 5 newspapers, and 500 journals.

Standard & Poor's News Online has news on the latest developments on publicly held corporations. News items and financial data are from company reports, press releases, news wires, newspapers and other sources.

Wall Street Transcript covers the full text which includes reports by security analysts on various industries, interviews with corporate officers on products and service plans, speeches by chief executive officers to security analyst groups and brokerage research reports and recommendations.

Other Sources of Information

The Business Library of the local college or university may be open to community residents for free or for a small charge.

Labor unions have information on unionized companies and those they hope to organize — e.g., wage rates, work conditions, company finances, developments that may affect how many and what types of new workers are needed. Local labor unions are a good source of information on local wage rates, anticipated layoffs or hirings.

Professional and trade associations have general information about the industry and specific information on a particular company in the industry. Their publications have help-wanted ads and information about specific companies.

Local governments are a good source of information on local companies and new businesses coming into the community. You can learn about a plant closing, employee layoffs, plans for expansion, etc. They can also direct you to other sources of information.

Journalists who write about the local economy for local newspapers are a valuable source of information. You may be able to get answers to your questions by telephoning that person at the newspaper's office.

F

RESOURCES TO HELP YOU FIND A JOB

I. *Associations*

Association of Part-Time Professionals, Flow General Bldg., 7655 Old Springhouse Road, McLean, VA 22102; Phone: 703-734-7975. Promotes part-time employment on the professional level. Advocates fair compensation and benefits for part-time employees.

To become a member send $45 plus $5.50 if you want to take part in its Job Referral Service. (It's deductible as a business expense.) Among the benefits you'll receive are The Part-Time Professional newsletter, career counseling services, and information on current employment trends. Career9 counseling includes the administration of aptitude tests and interest inventories and private counseling.

While many job leads are listed in the newsletter, many are obtainable only through the Job Referral Service. Some of the part-time positions are project assignments of limited duration. Others involve a regular work week of 16-32 hours, either several full days a week or a few hours a day. Some involve working from home via telecommuting or telephone. In addition to openings listed in the monthly newsletter, others are mailed to members between publications.

Recent newsletters listed the following job openings with the Federal and State governments — public affairs specialist, environmental protection specialist, community planner, highway engineer, program director, research analyst, college instructor, clinical psychologist, social worker, management analyst, computer instructor. The following are some of the part-time jobs in the private sector — housing specialist, pharmaceutical sales representative, junior accountant, social worker in hospice home care, job description analyst, advertising sales assistant, bilingual counselor, staff accountant, activities assistant/program planner, public relations manager, family outreach counselor, marketing representative, statistical assistant, contract negotiator, editor, conference planner, trainer, proofreader, manager, director of maintenance, administrative assistant, patent investigator, office manager, staff administrator to a vice-president, fundraiser, recruiter.

New Ways To Work, 149 Ninth Street, San Francisco, CA 94103, is dedicated to increasing flexible and reduced work schedules. Provides information to the general public. For a free list of publications on job sharing, include a legal-sized, self-addressed stamped envelope.

The Office of Personnel Management. For information on jobs with the Federal government and a job application, contact the nearest local branch or write to: Job Information Center, Office of Personnel Management, 1900 E Street NW, Washington, DC 20415.

II. *Career Counseling and Employment Services For Mature Job Seekers*

State and City Commissions/Departments on Aging exist all over the U.S. They will direct you to local agencies which provide these and other services. Look in your phone book for the address.

There are also private, non-profit services to help persons age forty and over. The following programs are briefly described to show you the sort of help that is available in or near your community. Some, like Forty Plus and AARP Works, exist in many communities. Others, like GROW, only exist locally.

AARP Works. Career-development and job-search skills for midlife and older persons. It is not a placement service. For information on the nearest one, contact Work Force Education Section, AARP Worker Equity Initiative, 1909 K Street, NW, Washington, DC 20049.

GROW (Gaining Resources for Older Workers). An employment program of the Regional Council on Aging in Rochester, NY. It also serves younger, displaced homemakers (who are in their late 30's and early 40's). Low fees are charged for job placement, resume assistance, workshops and career counseling.

Over 60 Counseling and Employment Service, Chevy Chase, MD 20015; Phone: 301-652-8072. Many job listings are part-time. The service is free. Counseling includes skills assessment and job readiness training.

Forty Plus Clubs are located at the following addresses.
CALIFORNIA:
    7440 Lockheed Street, Oakland, CA 94603, (415-430-2400).
    3450 Wilshire Blvd., Los Angeles, CA 90010, (213-388-2301).
    23151 Verduga Drive #114, Laguna Hills, CA 92653, (714-581-7990).
COLORADO
    1330 Fox Street, Denver, CO 80204, (303-893-4040).
    3840 South Mason Street, Fort Collins, CO 80525, (303-223-2470).
    17 Spruce Street, Colorado Springs, CO 80905, (303-473-6220).
HAWAII
    126 Queen Street #227, Honolulu, HI 96813, (808-531-2168).

ILLINOIS
> 53 West Jackson Blvd., Chicago, IL 60604, (312-922-0285).

NEW YORK
> 701 Seneca Street, Buffalo, NY 14210, (716-856-0491).
>
> 15 Park Row, New York, NY, (212-233-6086).

OHIO
> 1700 Arlingate Lane, Columbus, OH 43228, (614-275-0040).

PENNSYLVANIA
> 1218 Chestnut Street, Philadelphia, PA 19107 (215-923-2074).

TEXAS
> 13601 Preston Road #402, Dallas, TX 75240, (214-991-9917).
>
> 3935 Westheimer #205, Houston, TX 77027, (713-850-7830).

UTAH
> 1234 Main Street, Salt Lake City, UT 84117, (801-533-2191).

WASHINGTON
> Forty Plus of Puget Sound, Seattle, expected to be in operation by 1990.

WASHINGTON, D.C.
> 1718 P Street, NW, Washington, D.C. 20036, (202-387-1562).

Note: Some Forty Plus groups also serve members from other states who can commute to the metropolitan area office — e.g., New York City's Forty Plus Clubs also serve New Jersey and Connecticut residents; Philadelphia's Club serves New Jersey and Delaware; Chicago's serves Illinois, Indiana, Iowa and Wisconsin

Operation ABLE

In 1988 the following cities had an ABLE program.

→ Operation ABLE of Greater Boston: World Trade Center, Commonwealth Pier, Boston, MA 02210-2004, (617-439-4580.

→ California ABLE: 870 Market Street, San Francisco, CA 94102, (415-391-5030).

→ Arkansas ABLE: 519 East Capitol Avenue, Little Rock, AK 72202-2419, (501-374-1318).

→ Project ABLE: United Community Services of Metropolitan Detroit, 51 West Warren, Detroit, MI 48201, (313-833-0622.

→ Southeastern Vermont Community Action, Inc., Box 396, Bellows Falls, VT 05101, (802-463-9957).

III. *Job Hunting by Computer*

The Career Network, Computer Search International, 1500 Fulgrave Avenue, Baltimore, MD 21201; Phone: 301-664-1000. Processed via <u>The Source.</u> Executive search firms pay an annual fee to place their applicants' resumes, job descriptions, and employment requirements onto the network where it is available to employers nationwide. Job seekers who join The Source pay a connect fee to look through the job listings. When they find something that interests them, they send a resume by conventional or electronic mail to the nearest executive search firm listed on the network or directly to CSI. Most of the job listings are in engineering, data processing and finance. Also represented are accounting, hotels, the arts, travel, and sports.

Career Placement Registry (CPR), 302 Swann Avenue, Alexandria, Va. 22301; Phone: 703-683-1085; toll-free 800-331-4955. Job seekers include recent graduates, experienced alumni, executives and others. Lists technical and professional job openings with employers in the U.S. and other nations. Subscribing employers include advertising agencies, engineering and high-tech, public relations, educational institutions, nonprofit organizations, federal and state government agencies, management consulting firms, retailers, food industry and restaurants, accounting firms, TV and radio, newspapers and magazines, scientific laboratories and others. Experienced workers seeking junior-level to senior-level positions pay a fee of $25 to $45 (based on salary requirements) to have their resumes put online. Resumes remain in the CPR database for six months and are available to employers 24 hours a day, 7 days a week.

CareerSystem, 1675 Palm Beach Lakes Blvd., West Palm Beach, FL 33401; Phone: 305-689-3337. For highly skilled job hunters in every profession. Employers include retail, insurance, data-processing, chemical, hotel, manufacturing, finance, and communications companies. They include big names like American Express, Coopers and Lybnrand, Data General, Marriott Corporation, Pratt & Whitney and Prudential. Free to qualified job seekers.

Computer Assisted Recruitment International (CARI), Crystal Gateway 11, 1225 Jefferson Davis Hwy., Ste. 600, Arlington, VA 22202; Phone: 312-490-7140. Free to job applicants. Most openings are for highly skilled specialists in high-tech firms — e.g., EDP, engineering, data processing, programmers, analysts. There are also administrative and management openings in sales and marketing, accounting and finance and personnel.

The Direct Connection, PO Box 3497, Honolulu, HI 96811; Phone: 808-595-2365. An electronic newsletter for computer and communications professionals. Job openings stay on-line for 6 weeks and are accessible 24 hours-a-day. Also includes The Computer Wire which provides career planning information and Industry Standard Data Bases.

JobNet Inc., 10 DeAngelo Dr., Bedford, MA 01701; Phone: 617-275-3010. Jobs listed are generally high-tech — chemical engineers, computer scientists, hardware/software specialists, systems analysts, data processors and scientific, technical and marketing professionals. Information is provided by employers on their job openings, company profile, employee benefit program, etc. Free to job seekers. Employer clients include Lockheed, Pacific Bell and Bank of Boston.

National On-Line Classified, Inc. (ADNET), 1465 Andrews Lane, East Meadow, NY 11554; Phone: 516-481-9222. For use by entry-level and experienced job seekers, personnel recruiters and technical consulting firms. Permanent and temporary jobs are available. Information on employers include benefits offered, work environment and technical information.

Washington Research Associates, 2103 N. Lincoln St. Arlington, VA 22207; Phone: 703-276-8260. Information on professional job opportunities in the banking, finance and computer industries, advertising, public relations and the federal government. Forecasts trends and developments affecting job opportunities. Company listings of current openings also available in print.

In addition to these private databases there are several school systems which have computerized job banks for students, graduates and, in some cases, local residents.

PRONET, Stanford University Alumni Association; Phone: 415-725-0696. Finds corporate jobs for Stanford alumni free of charge. Assists undergraduate and graduate alumni from all departments of the University.

IV. *Publications on Job Vacancies*

Community Jobs, is a monthly listing of job vacancies in community-oriented nonprofit organizations. Contact Community Careers Resource Center, 1516 P Street NW, Washington, DC 20005; Phone: 202-667-0661.

Federal Career Opportunities is a biweekly publication which lists Federal government jobs in the U.S. and throughout the world. Many openings are at the management and professional level. For a subscription contact Federal Research Service, P.O. Box 1059, Dept. D1, Vienna, VA 22180-1059 or phone 703-281-0200.

The Federal Jobs Digest also lists openings in every occupation, from entry to senior executive level. Job description and salary for each opening are given. Also lists overseas jobs with the Federal government. A subscription costs $29 and also includes application forms and individual consultation by phone. Contact them at 325 Pennsylvania Avenue SE, Washington, DC 20003 or call 1-800-824-5000.

Kranich. Ronald L.Complete Guide to Public Employment. Impact, 1986. Guide to Federal, state, local and international jobs.

Lewis, William and Carol Milano. Profitable Careers in Nonprofit Wiley. Professional & Trade Association Job Finder. Over 1,000 sources of information, referrals, and more.

Zehring, John W. Careers in Local and State Government. Garrett Park. Where to find them, how to apply, take tests, internships, and more.

These reference guides have the names and addresses of state and municipal departments you can contact for information on job openings — Book of the States, Directory of Recognized Local Governments, Municipal Year Book, Braddocks Federal, State, Local Government Directory, National Directory of State Agencies. The public library probably has these as well as other resources not listed here.

V. *Publications on Job Finding Skills*

Many of the following publications are in bookstores and libraries. They can also be ordered from JIST Works, Inc., 720 North Park Avenue, Indianapolis, IN 46202; Phone: 800-648-JIST; residents of Indiana & Canada call 317-637--6643.

Block, Deborah P. How to Write a Winning Resume . Helpful for older job seekers. Many resume samples of people with college degrees and substantial work experience.

Bolles, Richard. What Color is Your Parachute? Ten Speed Press. A classic. Revised annually.

Danna, Jo Winning The Job Interview Game: Tips For The High-Tech Era, Palomino Press. Loaded with valuable information.

Half, Robert. Robert Half on Hiring. Written for employers, it gives an inside look into how employers make hiring decisions.

Liebers, Arthur. How to Pass Employment Tests.

Kaplan, Robbie M. Resumes: The Write Stuff. Includes resume samples, critiques and final revisions to illustrate what you should/should not include and how to make your work experience stand out. For people moving up or changing jobs. $8.95 plus $2.00 postage/handling. Order from The Association of Part-Time Professionals, Flow General Bldg., 7655 Old Springhouse Road, McLean, VA 22102.

McDaniels, Carl. Developing a Professional Vita or Resume. Garrett Park. For professionals with advanced education or experience.

McLaughlin and Merman. Writing a Job Winning Resume . Considered to be one of the best.

Truitt, John. <u>Telesearch: Direct Dial The Best Job of Your Life</u>. Facts on File. How to get past secretaries and personnel, conquer phone phobia, and more.

VI. *Resources on Flexible Work Styles*
Publications

<u>APTP Employer Handbook</u>. A directory of employers — 480 firms and government agencies — of part-time professionals in the Washington metropolitan area. Gives name, address, phone, number of employees, number of part-time professionals and the types of positions they fill. Order from The Association of Part-Time Professionals, Flow General Bldg., 7655 Old Springhouse Road, McLean, VA 22102.

Lee, Patricia. <u>The Complete Guide to Job Sharing</u> Walker and Company.

Gillis-Zetterberg, Carol. <u>Working at Home</u>. Available from the Center for Flexible Employment, P.O. Box 1054, Langhorne, PA 19047.

Olmsted, Barney and Suzanne Smith. <u>The Job Sharing Handbook</u>. Covers personal and professional assessment, creating a team, presenting the idea to the employer, managing in the first three months. Includes sample joint-resumes and work proposals. Order from the Association of Part-Time Professionals, Flow General Bldg., 7655 Old Springhouse Road, McLean, VA 22102.

Rothberg, Diane S. and Barbara E. Cook. <u>Part-time Professional</u>. How to find a part-time professional job and avoid/solve problems on the job. Lists employers who use part-time professionals. Order from The Association of Part-Time Professionals, (See address above).

KARAT & DIAL,
CLOCK AND WATCHMAKERS.

AGENTS FOR

Ladies' Year-Delaying Time-Keepers.

G

RESOURCES FOR STARTING
A SMALL BUSINESS

Until recently only city residents had access to services like small business networks, women business owner networks, consulting services and community and academic business libraries. Today residents of rural areas can connect electronically with most of these services. When Mrs. W. lost her farm during the recent farm crisis, she started Sweeter Measures, a now successful mail order clothing firm for larger-size women. At the start, no one in her Nebraska home town (population 400) had answers to her marketing and pricing questions. She found the toll-free number of the American Women's Economic Development Corporation which is based in New York City. After a half-hour phone consultation she had the answers.[2]

I. *Business and Professional Associations*

Business networks are for-profit enterprises. Members pay a fee to attend meetings and exchange tips on how to start and run a business. For example, in New York's **Metropolitan Business Network** the members are from noncompeting fields such as law, accounting, engineering and fashion consulting. Membership is kept small so people can get to know one another and exchange leads. The **Entrepreneur Network**, based in Minnesota, expanding to other cities. For information about similar networks in or near your community contact the Chamber of Commerce or the Small Business Administration.[3]

Employer alumni groups; e.g., Proctor & Gamble, IBM, Xerox and Time-Life. Members include former executives who have become entrepreneurs. At gatherings they make deals, find suppliers, customers, and get valuable advice. Some meetings have a trade fair, where members promote their business, and seminars for those who plan to start one.

Trade associations are listed in the <u>Encyclopedia of Associations</u> and <u>National Trade & Professional Associations of the United States</u>. Here are some examples:

Direct Marketing Association, 6 East 43rd Street, New York, NY 10017, sponsors programs on a variety of topics. Write for a free program calendar and information on how to start and run a mail-order business.

International Association for Home Business, P.O. Box 14850, Chicago, IL 60614, publishes a monthly newsletter, <u>Mind YOur Own Business at Home</u>.

International Franchise Association and the Small Business Administration jointly offer seminars on how to buy a franchise. The seminars are held in various cities. They also sponsor franchising expositions.

National Association of Small Business Investment Companies, based in Washington, DC, is a trade group of investors in small businesses. Call (202) 833-8230.

National Association of Home-Based Businesses, PO Box 30220, Baltimore, MD 21270, (301) 363-3698. Offers business opportunities, mail order services, joint mailer services, seminars, conventions, newsletter and more.

Computer SIGS (Special Interest Groups): A subscription to The Source or to CompuServe brings a universe of valuable business information. CompuServe, for example, has business forums on specialized fields. One of these is the Working From Home Forum where self-employed computer buffs exchange tips and advice on how to solve problems. Another is the Public Relations Forum. Most of these special interest groups also maintain data libraries. The data library of the International Entrepreneurs Forum, for example, has a business plan which was donated by Price Waterhouse and other documents on topics like how to get financial assistance.

II. *Government and Community Programs*

Each state has an economic development office which gives information and the names of community organizations where residents can go for help and training in business ownership. You can find the exact name and address in your phone book. For example, The Council of Smaller Enterprises, a division of The Greater Cleveland Growth Association, has thousands of member companies and offers many programs to help local small businesses.

U.S. Department of Commerce has a Roadmap service which tells where to get help on taxes, financial aid, trade, business licenses, and other government services. Contact the Office of Business Liaison, U.S. Department of Commerce, Rm 6411, Washington, DC 20230 or phone 202-377-3176.

Small Business Administration (SBA) is another government agency which helps small businesses and gives advice to people who hope to start a business. It offers a variety of services including many helpful publications which are free or cost very little. Private counseling and training are also free. The SBA can help you get government contracts, put together a loan package, set business goals and find ways to do market research on your product or service, competitors and customers.

The Management Assistance Program offers courses, conferences, workshops and clinics which are often co-sponsored with local Chambers of Commerce, lending institutions, and academic institutions. Many training sessions are for neophyte business owners. The pre-business workshops, for example, give tips on how to apply for a loan. If you want to discuss the advisability of starting a business or if you need help in choosing a business location or making a business plan, the Management Assistance people are the ones to see.

The Small Business Institute (SBI) Program offers long-term counseling to new and troubled small businesses which are located in or near colleges or universities. The students and faculty of the business administration departments do the counseling.

Financial assistance in the form of various loan programs is also available. To be eligible, you must show proof of having been turned down by a commercial bank or two savings banks. There are special loan programs for the physically handicapped, for people who are considered socially and/or economically disadvantaged, and for businesses suffering from the effects of Federal renewal or other construction programs.

Send for a free starter packet which includes a list of SBA courses and workshops in your area and a list of SBA publications. The address is 1441 L Street, NW, Wash, DC 20416. For the phone number of the nearest SBA office, call 1-800-368-5855; in Washington, DC call 202-653-7561.

Small Business Development Centers (SDBCs) are found in most states including the District of Columbia, Puerto Rico and the Virgin Islands. They offer private counseling, seminars and courses, and planning assistance. The counseling is free but small fees may be charged for other programs. They are often run by state university systems with local branches operating in university extensions and community colleges. The **Association of Small Business Development Centers** — 1050 17th Street NW, Suite 810, Washington, DC 20036 — can direct you to a program operating in your state. You can also call the SBA Answer Desk, 800-368-5855; in Washington, DC, call 202-653-7561.

III. *Programs and Services For Veterans, Women and Minority Group Members*

There are many programs and associations which help these and other business owners who are labeled disadvantaged. Women are also in this category. A 1987 report by the U.S. House of Representatives' Small Business Committee stated that the increase in the number of companies owned and managed by women is one of the "most significant economic developments of recent years." Yet, women business owners still face many difficulties especially in getting commercial credit and government contracts. Women also need better technical and managerial training. The Committee recommended that the Government take steps to help women entrepreneurs, from giving them more loans to making it easier to get federal contracts. If passed, the legislation can help women win a bigger slice of the Government procurement pie.[4] The following is a small sample of services that are currently available.

Each state has a program to help such persons start and operate a successful business; e.g., The New York State Department of Commerce has a minority and women's business division which offers the following services:
• Conferences, workshops and seminars on pricing, marketing, selling, financing, advertising, public relations and other essentials.
• Help in developing a business plan.
• Direct loans or help in getting loans.
• Sponsored trade shows that bring business owners into contact with procurement officers from state agencies, municipalities and corporations.

American Home Business Association, 397 Post Road, Darien, CT 06820, (203) 655-4380. Offers health insurance group plan, assistance, counseling, information and a monthly newsletter.

AWED (American Women's Economic Development Corporation offers training, counseling, and courses in business basics. It also has a telephone hot line that gives advice to women throughout the U.S. at a low hourly fee. Call 800-222-AWED or 212-692-9100 if you live in New York City. Similar bootstrap programs for women have also emerged in Illinois, Pennsylvania, Minnesota and other states. Example: **The Small Business Association** has a Women's Business Enterprises unit to help women start their own business.

IV. *Consultants and Professionals*

To start off on the right track, you can also hire an accountant, lawyer and/or banker. There are also business services which will set up a record-keeping system for you. Some also prepare personal and business tax returns, loan packages, and help with business and budget planning. The fees vary according to the size of a business. To find good consultants, ask owners of small businesses in your community. You can also find consultants through your business contacts, professional organizations, trade associations and the chamber of commerce.

SCORE (Service Corps of Retired Executives) and ACE (Active Corps of Executives) give free advice. ACE volunteers are still active in business whereas SCORE volunteers are retired. Contact your local SBA office.

V. *Publications and Tapes*

The U.S. Department of Commerce offers a series of pamphlets, Ask US: U.S. Department of Commerce Programs to Aid Women Business Owners. Among the valuable data these contain are the following:

• A list of Department of Commerce offices that assist women business owners and purchase supplies and services from them.

• Information on the Patent and Trademark Office.

• The address of the Office of Small and Disadvantaged Business Utilization which gives procurement officers information on women-owned businesses.

• Tips on how to sell to the federal government.

For a free copy write: Director of Office of Small and Disadvantaged Business Utilization, U.S. Department of Commerce, Rm 6411, Washington, DC 20230.

It also publishes the Directory of Women Business Owners: MegaMarketplace East/West which helps women locate new markets and suppliers. It lists names and addresses of women-owned businesses, major corporations, and federal, state and local agencies interested in doing more business with female-owned companies. It costs $50 to be included. To order send $12 for the title, stock No. 003-000-00651-4, to Superintendent of Documents, Department 36-zb, Washington, DC 20402.

Other recommended publications include these:

Business Information Guide. Order from the American Institute of Certified Public Accountants, Order Dept., 1211 Avenue of the Americas, New York, NY 10036. Explains and illustrates business records.

Free Money for Small Businesses and Entrepreneurs by Laurie Blum (John Wiley & Sons) lists sources of funding.

"How to Really Start Your Own Business," INC Magazine videotape, 38 Commercial Wharf, Boston, MA 02110, (617) 227-4700.

How to Set Up Your Own Small Business. American Institute of Small Business, 7515 Wayzata Blvd., Suite 201, Dept. CT, Minneapolis, MN 55426. This 2-volume reference covers every aspect of starting and running a small business, from setting up the books to customer relations.

Price Waterhouse publishes six guides on planning your business, financing, getting government help, marketing and other topics. Contact National Director of Smaller Business Services, Price Waterhouse, 1251 Avenue of the Americas, New York, NY 10020.

250

Periodicals: Magazines that specialize in articles for the entrepreneur include INC, Entrepreneur, Inc, Venture.

Direct Marketing

Cohen, William A. Building a Mail Order Business. John Wiley & Sons. Step-by-step guide with instructions for a marketing plan.

The Direct Marketing newsletter, 224 Seventh St., Garden City, NY 11530. $45 per year. This is the bible of the industry.

Muldoon, Katie. Catalog Marketing. R.R. Bowker. Details all aspects of selling by catalog.

Shopping by Mail. Leaflet that describes legal obligations of the seller. Free from Public Reference Branch, Federal Trade Commission, Room 130, Washington, DC 20580.

Franchising

Directory of Franchising Organizations. Pilot Books. Lists franchise opportunities. Concise descriptions, addresses and cost of investment.

Franchise Opportunities Handbook. U.S. Department of Commerce. Lists most of the major franchisors. Call 202-783-3238 or write to the U.S. Government Printing Office, Washington, DC 20402.

Kushell, Robert E. How To Be a Franchisor. Written from an operational and legal perspective.

Source Book of Franchise Opportunities. Dow Jones-Irwin. Costs and rules of running your own outlet in any of 3,200 chains, including Hilton Inns, Century 21 Real Estate and Catfish Stations of America.

International Franchise Association Directory. Lists over 700 members. Has information on franchise expositions held in the U.S. Order from 1350 New York Avenue, Ste. 900, Washington, D.C. 20005; Phone: 202-628-8000. The following publications are also obtainable from IFA.
- Answers To The 21 Most Commonly Asked Questions About Franchising.
- Fels, Jerome L. and Lewis B. Rudnick. Investigate Before Investing.
- McIntosh, Robert K. How to select a franchise.
- What You Need to Know When You Buy A Franchise. Principles, practices, federal regulations, state laws, sources of information and assistance, complete listing of member franchising companies.

Money Matters

Business Planning Guide. Upstart Publishing. Guide to writing a business plan and financial proposals. An underground best seller.

Cohen, William A. Entrepreneur and Small Business Problem Solver. John Wiley & Sons.

Gladstone, David. <u>Venture Capital Handbook</u>. Prentice-Hall. Includes an excellent guide to writing a business plan.

Rich, Stanley and David Gumpert. <u>Business Plans That Win $$$: Lessons From The MIT Enterprise Forum</u>. Rich (founder of the MIT Enterprise Forum) and Gumpert (associate editor, Harvard Business Review) are the founders of Venture Resources, a company that provides planning and other services for growing businesses.

<u>Small Business Reporter Series.</u> Small Business Reporter, Bank of America, Dept. 3120, Box 37000, San FRancisco, CA 94317. It includes "Financial records for small business," "Avoiding management pitfalls" and "Cash flow/cash management."

Home business

Behr, Marion and Wendy Lazar. <u>Women Working Home: The Home-Based Business Guide and Directory</u>. WWH Press, PO Box 237, Norwood, NJ 07648.

Bohigian, Valerie. <u>Real Money From Home: How To Start, Manage and Profit From A Home-Based Service Business</u>. NAL/PLUME. Focuses on service businesses.

Brabec, Barbara. <u>Homemade Money</u>. The author is the publisher of a quarterly newsletter on home businesses.

<u>Business Use of Your Home</u>. Free Internal Revenue Service publication # 587. Call 800-424-3676. Official rules on deductible expenses.

<u>How To Succeed In A Home Business</u>. An <u>INC</u> magazine videotape. 38 Commercial Wharf, Boston, MA 02110, (617) 227-4700.

VII. *Courses On How To Start And Run A Business*

There are numerous short-term courses you can take through classroom attendance, home study, or by electronic media such as computer, radio, and television.

- The Small Business Administration offers programs in many communities, as noted above.
- City and state economic development programs offer workshops, conferences and other educational materials.
- Adult education centers and continuing education departments of colleges and universities offer a wide range of courses.
- Trade associations and minority business associations also sponsor workshops and seminars on various business topics.

H

RESOURCES FOR WOMEN

Organizations

OWL (Older Women's League) — 1325 G Street, NW, Lower Level; Phone: 202-783-6686.

Women's Initiative and Worker Equity Program, American Association of Retired Persons — 1909 K Street NW, Washington, D202C 20049; Phone: 202-872-4700.

Displaced Homemakers Network — 1411 K Street, NW, Ste 930, Washington, DC 20005; Phone: 202-628-6767.

The following local programs are described here at some length in order to give you an idea of what's available elsewhere.

Resources For Midlife and Older Women, Inc. — 226 East 25th Street, Ste 1D, New York, NY 10010; Phone: 212-696-5501. The services include individual consulting, support groups, phone information and referral, workshops, seminars, conferences, crisis intervention, and networking.

Connections is a 10-week career seminar for management, administrative and other top level women who are unemployed or under-employed. Guest speakers include experts in career management, stress reduction, assertiveness training and image development. The groups are small so each member can get individual attention. The fee for the entire program is $55.00.

The support groups help women who face important life decisions and have low self-esteem. The fee is $5.00 per session. There are also workshops on topics like creating your own job, making a financial plan, career and life changes, interviewing strategies, widowhood, and writing a resume. The fee per workshop is $5.

YWCAs are found in most communities. They offer a variety of services. The Lexington Avenue Y in New York City has one of the most comprehensive programs in the nation. Its programs reflect the more limited offerings in smaller communities. Men as well as women of all ages can participate.

A career development program for working women includes professional career counseling in small groups. The participants also undergo assertiveness training which helps them in decision making, resolving feelings toward authority figures and overcoming the fear of disapproval and rejection.

One-day career seminars are held on topics like running an import/export business, how to start a free-lance secretarial business, and legal careers. There is an annual career awareness night at which executives from different fields talk informally with the participants to increase their knowledge of different career areas.

The business school offers a variety of courses on basic business and computer skills. They include typing, word processing and spreadsheet software. A real estate salesperson's course qualifies those who pass the final examination for a license to sell. Other departments offer courses in personal development (i.e., "Reversing the Aging Process," "The Awakened Mind") as well as the usual recreational, sports and social activities. One of these courses prepares women for college study.

Scholarship aid is available for those who meet income and other eligibility guidelines.

Publications

Career Compatibility Profile. Order from Women's Center for Executive Development, 111 East Wacker, Suite 2210, Chicago, IL 60601.

Directory of Special Opportunities For Women. Over 1000 resources for women entering and re-entering the work force.

Loden, Marilyn. Feminine Leadership: How to Succeed in Business Without Being One of the Boys. Times Books.

Osborn, Ruth H. Developing New Horizons for Women. How to improve self-esteem, identify strengths and develop long range life and career plans.

Scholz, P. and Miller. How to Decide: a Guide For Women. The College Board. A workbook to help women set goals and develop a plan of action to reach their goals.

FINIS

INDEX

A

Ability Is Ageless 127
Active Corps of Executives 249
Achievement 210, 211
& cognitive style 32
tests 32
see career assessment 50,
53, 60
Adaptability 11, 13, 14
Aging
& Diet 35, 211
& Exercise 35, 211
& Intelligence 41, 210, 212
American Association for Counseling & Development 77
American Association of Retired Persons 128
AARP Works 239
Volunteer Talent Bank 145
American Professional Women's Foundation 229
Annual Reports 99, 213
family-run company 92
job vacancies, clues to 100
work culture, clues to 83
Apprenticeship Information Centers 73
Aptitudes 55
tests 68
& occupations 47
& personality 47
see career-assessment 50, 63
Area Agencies on Aging 129
Association of Part-Time Professionals 238
American Women's Economic Development Corporation 248

B

Beck, Aaron T. 43, 221
Better Business Bureau 77
Bolles, Richard 110, 222, 243
Bureau of Labor Statistics 93, 103, 209
Business & Professional Associations 245
Business Ownership
American Home Business Association 248

consulting 218
consultants 248
costs 219
direct marketing, resources 250
failure rate 167, 213
financing 189, 255
franchise 250, 254
government & community programs 246, 250
home business, resources on 184, 251
International Franchise Association 246
National Association of Home-Based Businesses 246
National Association of Small Business Investment Companies 246
programs for veterans, women, minorities 247, for the unemployed 219
Service Corps of Retired Executives 248
Small Business Administration 246
small business development centers 247

C

Career Assessment
computerized guides 223
publications 222
Career Change 15
& volunteer work 143
& education 71
employer attitudes 81
see Career Assessment 47, 49
Career counseling 73
Career guidance & placement offices 75, 122
for older persons 239
college career guidance center 117
Cassell, Frank H. 116
Catalyst 74, 130
Change 208-212, 214, 216, 221
benefits of 27
& brain development 27
fear of 14, 15
resistance to 11, 13, 81

& self-confidence 14
& stress 14, 27, 42
Chief Executive Officer 219
  clue to job outlook 87
  clue to work culture 83
Civil Service 124, 141
Cognitive Behavior Therapy 42, 211
  effectiveness 212
  job/career problems 209
  see Mental Health
Cognitive Style 13, 210
  & achievement 32, 210, 211
  depression 14, 210
  & intelligence 33
  pessimism/optimism 14, 109, 210
  & success 32, 33
Colleges & Universities 122, 132, 214
  career counseling 62, 74
  financial aid 73
  programs for adults 17, 71, Valencia Community College 132, 144, 215
Commuting 94
Companies 207-209, 213, 214, 217
  advancement opportunities 88
  company alumni Associations 112, 245
  employee turnover 87
  job training & education 9, 20
  family-run 91, 232
  foreign 6
  growth 87
  information on 231 – 236
  job vacancies 80
  older job applicant 92
  overseas branches 6
  profits as clues to jobs 88
  relocation 4, 87
  technology companies 116
  dismissed workers 85
Company Size &
  job opportunities 89, 110, 213
  job satisfaction 90
  job security 90

job training & advancement 80, 90
  pay, benefits 91
Computer Sigs (special interest groups) 246
Conferences, Conventions, Trade Shows 103
Consumer Protection Agency 77

Depression 39
  & job loss 28, 126
  optimism/pessimism 32
  & diet 34
  emotional support, need 38
  & exercise 34
  harmful effects 32
  & mental alertness 41
  normal 31
  & appearance 41
  self-help for 39
  severe, symptoms 32, 38
Dictionary of Occupational Titles 116, 224
Directory of Counseling Services 76
Discrimination 5, 207, 226
  Age Discrimination in Employment Act Guidebook 226
  Civil Rights Division 226
  employer stereotypes 81
  Equal Employment Opportunity Commission 226
Dismissed Older Managers, job opportunities 89
Displaced Homemakers 62, 123, 131, 133, 252
Displaced Worker 74, 123, 132

Education and Job Information Centers 96
Ellis, Albert T. 44, 221
Employee Manual 9
  work culture, clues to 84
Employment Agencies 89, 117
Employment Services, non-profit 121

National Directory of Employment Programs For Women 131
Operation ABLE 127, 240
Senior Employment Services 127
Senior Community Service Employment Program 128
State, Municipal Services 123
U.S. Office of Personnel Management 124, 239
Employment and Training Administration 133
Employment Tests 243
Employment Trends 136

F

Fired, warning signals 22
Flexible work styles 4, 147
  & career advancement 151
  executives 153
  government jobs 153
  high-skill jobs 217
  information on 244, 248
  New Ways to Work 238, 242
  pay/benefits 217
  see Employment Agencies, Flextime, Job Sharing, Part-Time, Telecommuting, Work-at-Home
Flextime Jobs 155-157
Forty Plus Club 125, 239

H

Handicapped 5, 123, 148, 158
  business ownership 166
Health & career change 71, 209--212, 215, 217
Hiring Criteria, changes in 7 – 12
Holland, John 223

I

industries 138, 223, 225, 226, 231-233, 235-237, 242
  changing 25
  clues to work culture 84
  find a job in another 25, 209
  declining 20, 87
  insurance 3
  transfer skills 110, 209
  thriving 86
Information Interview 110
Interest Inventories 68 – 70
International Association of Counseling Services 77

J

Job 208, 209, 211, 213-217
  advancement 109
  create your own 114
  dissatisfaction 18, 53
  loss 15, 20, 24
  second job 20
Job Fairs 137
Job Hunt 79, 105, 222, 238, 240
  best time 106
  computer, by 120, 240 – 242
  direct contact with employer 114
  expenses 16
  homemakers, retirees 108
  job vacancies, newsletters 96, 242
  key persons to contact 107
  job finding skills 122
  telephone, by 107
  time it takes to find another 16, 105, 208, 214
Job Interview 1, 30, 48, 79, 82, 86, 103, 110, 214
  clues to work culture 84
  resources 243
Job Loss 28
Job Market 17, 24, 80
  changes 3
  international work 144
  job market & salaries 103
  rural residents 207
  resources on 230
Job Offer 110
Job Relocation 207
Job Service 122
  career counseling 74
  job listings 214
Job Sharing 154
Job Skills 208, 213, 215, 217
  changes in 9, 207

computer skills 11, 207
homemaker 58
obsolete/need updating 2, 8,
71 – 73
professional 73
see Career Assessment 51
Job Stress 14, 80
Job Titles 115
Job Training & Education 8, 17,
54, 73, 122, 227, 228, 229, 237
Job Training Partnership 125, 215

Manager's Guide, clues to work
culture 82
Mental Health
& diet 34
& exercise 36
professional therapy 42
resources 42, 221
& social activities 36
unemployment 28
Monthly Labor Review 98, 115,
231

National Council of Senior Citizens 129
National Executive Service Corps
130, 146
Networking 102, 111, 214, 216
by computer 113
Newspaper, Help-Wanted Ads
134, 215
job trends 116
The New York Times 115, 215
Non-profit Organizations
older applicants 91
pay, benefits 91

O

Occupational Outlook Handbook
62, 224
Occupational Outlook Quarterly
115, 224, 230
Occupational Projections and
Training Data 231
Occupations 6

accountants 11
administrative assistant 59
aptitudes needed 47, 63, 68
bank tellers 3
best hiring outlook 230
business administration 3
changing 3, 8, 79
clerical 3
compatibility with 21, 47, 62,
65
emerging 3
Emerging Occupations & Projections for Growth in Old
Ones 115, 224, 230
engineering 3, 48
information on 97, 224
& interests 55
legal aide 55
managers 3, 4, 8, 11, 59, 80
obsolete 3, 115
ominous signs 87
secretaries 3, 11, 59
& skills 60, 61
Occupational Clusters 64
Occupational Outlook Quarterly
63, 98
Occupational Outlook Handbook
97
Older Workers 108, 123, 213-215
negative stereotypes 208
retiree job bank 217
younger bosses 207
Organization Chart, clues to work
culture 82

Part-Time & Temporary Jobs 4,
147
Association of Part-Time Professionals 151, 242
executives 149
high-skill, professional 150-152
pay, benefits 150, 152
job security 151
medium, lower-skill 151
Pay, Benefits 91, 93, 103, 110,
254
Directory of Occupational Wage
Surveys 225

The American Almanac of Jobs
and Salaries 226
Personality 210-212, 222, 224, 235
& occupations 65
inventory 70
see career-assessment 66
Personnel Department 107
Private Industry Councils 133
Professional 207, 209, 215, 216
Professional and Trade Associations 102, 237
Public Library 95, 106

R

Recruitment Firms 121
References 23
Rejection, how to deal with 105, 139
Resume 1, 60, 103, 106, 134, 141, 214, 243

S

Senior citizens, help for 74
State Department of Labor 131
Stock Market, clues to jobs 102

T

Technology 207, 215, 216
adult education courses 72
impact on work culture 8
innovations 1
occupations 79
see Job Skills
Trade and Business Journals 98
Travelers Companies 92
retiree job bank 217

U

Unemployment 209, 219
harmful effects 27
help from colleges 16
Unemployment Insurance Office 125
U.S. Department of commerce 246, 249

V

Veterans 74, 123
Vocational rehabilitation office
career counseling 74
Volunteer Work 141
see Career Assessment 54
& job advancement 105
unemployed, helps the 216

W

Women 252
assertiveness training 132
homemakers, job training 25, 55
job hunt 108
job training 132
management style 5
O.W.L. (Older Women's League) 252
Resources for Midlife and Older Women 252
Women's Bureau 132, 226
women's centers 42
Women's Initiative and Worker Equity Program 252
W.O.W. 131
YWCA 130, 133, 252
Work Culture 6-10, 12, 82
teamwork is in 4, 11, 207
Work-at-home jobs 147
schemes, beware of 161
see Telecommuting
Workers
women, non-European, immigrants 5
older 2, 5, 11, 32, 81, 92
negative employer stereotypes 2, 6
Workplace
changes in 4
high technology 1
international 6
stress 27, 80
work conditions 80

YW/MCAs, YW/MHAs 252